Ignite! Enrichment Through Exercise

ISBN# 9781475295856

Dedicated to the memory of

JR Thomas.

Love. Respect. Always.

ENRICHMENT THROUGH EXERCISE

Cooper and Belanger, 2011

Introduction

Settling under the bar, Kris didn't appear nervous at all. I sure was; it was his third attempt at bench press in his first Powerlifting meet. He was lifting a weight he'd never attempted before. I could see him working through a mental checklist: heels set. Scapulae pinched. Chest up. Unrack with elbows locked. Big breath, and down. Heels drive...*explode!* The bar rose, unevenly, slowly....but it kept moving. His elbows locked. His spotter yelled, "rack!" and Kris racked the weight, sat up, and grinned. The crowd of 20 or so, silent until they saw his grin, exploded. They pounded him on the back. They jumped up and down and high-fived him. Everyone in the room was excited...but not for the weight. It was hardly a world record, after all. They were excited to see his pride.

Kris is autistic.

Five years ago, I was walking through a park with one of my clients, and we were talking about a third client, who was close with both of us. The absent exerciser, on that morning,

was Kris' dad. He's spent every waking moment (and hundreds of thousands of dollars) working toward a cure. He's been in court for years; he's fought school boards, lawyers, other parents, and too many bureaucracies to mention. He's the reason we started to get interested in autism – and ADHD, Asperger's, and the brain in general – way back then.

When he started, Kris' therapist would drive him to the gym. His first goal: change his shoes while his Therapist slipped me a little plastic baggie, out of his line of sight. In the bag were small faces on green and red paper, each about the size of a dollar coin. The green faces smiled; the red frowned. I split the faces between my two pockets. When Kris rose after tying his own shoes, he saw a smiling green face in my hand. Score one in the positive column.

Through the hour of Therapy, Kris would score more happy faces for listening to instructions and performing the correct action. We didn't assign a number of repetitions to his exercises; instructions were simple and single-task. For example, he'd be told to sit down OR stand up, but never, "sit down and then stand up." Occasionally, he'd drift to the large window, and the resulting 'red face' would cancel out a 'green face' that he'd already earned.

As time went on, Kris would earn more and more happy faces, and fewer sad ones. Eventually, the day came when I called his mother at work to tell her that he'd gone 13-0: perfect adherence to my instructions. It was a big deal: over six months of hard work, and Kris was performing simple instructions to the letter. Next step: linking tasks together.

Climb on the box; jump off the other side. Do three squats, and then run to the statue and back. To us, it seems remarkably unremarkable. To Kris, at first, it was a quadratic equation: variables everywhere. That was 2006.

Today, Kris goes to high school. He still prefers to answer questions than to initiate conversation on his own, but he CAN if he has to. He's not shy. Where he was once terrified of a tennis ball, he now asks to throw a football around to warm up before his workouts.

Most important of all: Kris cares. He cares how quickly his workout finishes. He cares if he's done it right, cares if girls are watching. He cares if the weight is a personal best.

Last week, Kris got his first summer job.

Kris is still autistic, and his case isn't typical. He's got a lot of things going for him. For one – and maybe most important – he's got parents who just won't lie down on the issue. They've never accepted the 'sentence' of autism. They accept that, while he perhaps 'can't,' it doesn't mean he 'won't.' They've pushed, and pushed...just like any other teenager.

Second, Kris genuinely likes some things, and dislikes others. He's had trouble expressing these in the past, but his preferences are still there.

Third, Kris has access to world-class coaching, and the resources to pay for it. We, like many people reading this book, would love to be able to provide this service for free. But like you, we have to eat; we like sleeping under a good roof; we like our kids to wear clothes. That means there's a cost associated with the service to the parent, and Kris' parents have never balked.

Change isn't easy, but it IS simple. Throughout this book, you're going to be given powerful ways to affect permanent, meaningful change in yourself, and help affect those changes in others. You'll have all the tools to do things that some people will view as 'miraculous.' But first, you have to learn how to apply those tools. You have to know how and why people change; the best environment and exercises for brain stimulation; and the right procedure for applying your knowledge.

On its own, *Ignite!* is a powerful program: it can help anyone *move* better. Through movement, it can help anyone *learn* better. And through the combination of movement and learning, it can help anyone focus and remember better.

When used before lessons or at times when focus and attention is hard to attain, it has a huge amplifying effect. As we've seen firsthand, kids appear to suddenly make huge strides at tasks which have caused anxiety for years. In fact, some of the transformations have been so rapid that teachers have asked, *"How'd you do that?"*

In school, the ability to focus, concentrate, and retain more information is critical to earning higher test scores, as demonstrated in the Dr. John Ratey's famous Naperville study[1]. Early research suggests a 30% improvement in overall grades when physical exercise is combined with academic work.

In life, while the affects may be more difficult to measure, the benefits are far more

rewarding. The social stigma attached to learning difficulties or movement challenges can be overcome. This is very exciting news for kids and adults who struggle to 'fit in,' and for the parents of kids whose disabilities make them 'stand out' for the wrong reasons.

Change, Risk, and Environment: The *Ignite!* Story

In 2009, Tyler and I were working together at Catalyst Fitness. Tyler was quickly becoming our go-to sports-specific coach, having played nearly every sport imaginable at a competitive level.

---

[1] Viadero, Debra. 2008. Exercise seen as priming the pump for students' academic success. Education Week 27:14–15

A teacher in the daytime, Tyler excelled at helping kids learn new ways to think about simple things. For instance, a football pass means something different to the quarterback than it does to the receiver. Though the play may be the same, and the ball flies only once, the experience is greatly different depending on which end of the catch you find yourself. Turning the situation around can add perspective that is invaluable to the learner.

Ten years ago, a hockey goaltender may have been told by his coach never to play any position other than goalie, because the skillset is so different that the athlete may develop the wrong reflexes. However, we now appreciate that the value of the perspective gained by spending some time in the shooter's shoes – skates, in this case – far outweighs the minute amount of shift in skills. Plus, it's fun to change roles; that's why we call it 'role-playing' when we take on the persona of a new character in a skit, video game, or sport.

This idea of shape-shifting came intuitively to Tyler. In one instance, a young teen with Asperger's was brought in to learn to catch a football. Asperger's sufferers shy away from touch, and seem to carry an aversion to fear that's not in context with the source of the fear. For instance, they can be deathly afraid of being startled, or in this case, of being hurt by a flying ball.

Tyler started in the logical way – with wiffleballs, then tennis balls, and then soft foam balls... but the final transition to the hard, pointy football wasn't as easy as the other steps. Finally, Tyler asked the student to throw the ball to HIM; then he'd roll the ball back. The young would-be athlete threw the ball to Tyler, harder and harder; Tyler, with quick hands a years of football catches behind him, caught every single ball. Even when the thrower TRIED to make a pass that Tyler would bobble, Ty would just smack it to the ground if he couldn't make the catch.

When they switched roles, the teen practised catching; when he got nervous, he would smack the ball to the ground. It took a few more sessions, and a little challenge from Tyler to catch more balls, but the fear was gone, replaced with the knowledge that the athlete was in control of himself, even if he couldn't control the ball.

Tyler was born to teach. His parents gave him a wide scope of life experience as a child, and he was confident and charismatic; well-seasoned; accomplished in sport. His students loved him, and he was eager to be in the classroom.

Unfortunately, the education system in Ontario is very tough to crack. In simple terms, a teaching job is very attractive, mostly for all the right reasons, and the waiting list for positions is immense, with hundreds of qualified young teachers ready to go. These soon-to-be teachers survive by taking 'supply' jobs – on any given morning, you could be called to any school, at virtually any level, to fill in for virtually any teacher – and try to get by on two or three days' work per week. Some great teachers sit on the 'supply' list for years, hoping for at least a short-term contract position that may never come.

At the same time, we'd been doing research at Catalyst on exercise adherence: specifically, what makes people LIKE exercise, and choose to keep exercising? This was largely self-indulgent (we wanted to keep more clients around, of course!) but opened our eyes to the need to change the way we coached people.

In college, and the media at large, we're often told that we must set small, reasonable goals; stick to them steadfastly; find a workout buddy when we get 'lazy.' The notion that success depends on the willpower to stick with the drudgery is hardwired into most college grads; as a professor of kinesiology, "But how do I help them LIKE it?!?" and most won't know the answer. Our best guess, at the time, was to create a fun atmosphere AROUND the exercise, in the hope that we could cloak the hard work necessary for success in layers of colourful fantasy.

The truth, though, is that low-challenge exercise is NOT more motivating. People are NOT more likely to drive to the gym, change their clothes, wreck their hairdo and possibly their soft palms, and repeat five times every week if it's easy. In fact, they're less likely to continue for more than a month when this is the case.

Even among the chronically injured – people who have to complete a series of stretches every day – adherence rate is less than 50% after a single month. Even if you're in too much pain to go to work, it's not enough reason to do 10 minutes' stretching every day. Even if stretching will solve the problem; even if you need the money.

The above paragraph is a summary of all that's ever been studied in the name of exercise adherence and retention. Starting in 2006, we struck out to figure out how to get people to like exercise; to enjoy the challenge itself, rather than the carnival surrounding the sweat.

We started by recruiting two groups of non-exercisers from the community. One group was given a nice booklet with a list of exercises, including pictures, and a 30-day workout plan to follow.

The other group was given the same booklet, without the workout plan. Instead, we would email them their workout every day, first thing in the morning. They'd read their workout of the day (WOD) and then check their technique in the booklet. We called this, "Morning Catalyst," and the original text-based website is still available for view somewhere on the internet.

We didn't know what to expect. When the two groups met at the end of the month, we noticed a curious phenomenon, even before we had the final tally: they talked to each other about the workouts. Strangers, for the most part, would start conversations with, "How did you do on number eleven? Man, that was brutal!" They'd commiserate, "What about Twenty-three? Wow! That was so fast, but so painful!" and laugh. The implication went right over our heads at the time, but over the last five years, the 'community' aspect of a great exercise program has become obvious to us. Had we realized, at the time, that the level of bonding that was happening at that end-of-study meeting was encouraging future participation from ALL exercisers in the study, we'd have dropped the website delivery and started group classes. From follow-up studies we've done since, it's clear that those who were part of the discussion but HADN'T completed Workout Number Eleven started to *wish they had*. Thus is the power of social connection and comparison: realizing they'd missed out on an opportunity to bond with the group, they regretted their decision to not exercise on the eleventh day of the month.

What we DID know, after a month, was that a person was far more likely to complete a workout when they didn't know what to expect in advance. Novelty made a huge difference, in other words.

The next month, we continued the study but put everyone into the "daily delivery" group. They'd receive their WOD via email every morning, and respond via email with a score each evening.

A word about 'scoring': we frequently use objective criteria to measure progress within workouts. For example, we may ask you to do exercises X, Y and Z for 20 reps x 3 sets each...for time. On the clock. That way, we're not asking just one question (did you perform the workout, or not?) but several: did you finish? How hard was it? Did you push yourself as hard as possible? Was it easier than last time? Etc. Then, if we repeat the workout in the future, we can compare results on a more reliable scale than, "did it feel easier than last time?" This has the added benefit of making the workouts feel like a game. More on this to come...

Our adherence rate slowly climbed. Over the months, we'd change different variables; what would happen, we'd ask, if we moved the harder workouts to Mondays, and the easier ones to Fridays? Would more people be likely to perform the workouts? As it turns out, the inverse is true: when people are tired, they NEED something challenging to motivate them to exercise. If the threshold for success is too low, people won't make the attempt at all, believing the workout to be less important than other priorities (like watching television.) This flies in the face of modern "healthy habits" recommendations made by various government and non-government bureaucracies.

After a year, we introduced the variable that we believed would make or break our theory: we started charging for the program. Still more interested in science than in a novel way to make money, we wondered if paying for the program would increase adherence. Right away, several people dropped out (they were paying for personal training in our facility, after all, and preferred that contact to an email.) Of the remainder, though....adherence went up. We hypothesized that the perceived value – and therefore relevance – of the program increased due to people's fear of wasting money. To rephrase: people aren't scared to SPEND money, but they're petrified of

WASTING money.

And, slowly, new people started to sign up for the program. By 2008, we were boasting an adherence rate of 83% - if you started the month, you would complete 83% of the workouts, on average. This was nearly DOUBLE the adherence rate of physiotherapists, the only other group who thought it important to keep track of their clients' visits...and we still hadn't considered the 'community' link.

At this point, we realized we were on to something. We also realized that our program was beginning to closely resemble CrossFit in its delivery, challenge, and workout format. We decided to give the CrossFit program a shot; first one Trainer, and then two, tried the program on for size. Tyler was that first Trainer, and he blogged about his month on CrossFit on something we called the Shotgun Wedding project.

We didn't set out to prove that CrossFit is helpful for building adherence; after all, it belonged to someone else. After his first month, though, Tyler was hooked. Another trainer switched, and then another. Soon, our conversations in the hallways were dominated by, "what did you score on that WOD today?" and, "I'm going to hit 'Angie' (the name of a popular CrossFit workout) at 4pm today. I'm already fired up!"

Three months later, we offered CrossFit-style groups – for free – to participants in our Morning Catalyst email-based workout program. The program was successful in that it showed us how to create workouts that our clients would love...but very time-consuming. Workouts were frequently created in the wee hours, during valuable sleep time, and scored late at night. Sundays were devoted to spreadsheets for tracking and comparing exercisers for nearly two years. Frankly, it had run its eye-opening course.

Some participants from Morning Catalyst switched to Personal Training; some fell off the map. Seven, though, took up the gauntlet in person, showing up at 6am every weekday for a month. They went live. After a month, we tried another free group...and then we became a full-time CrossFit Affiliate.

The emphasis on continuing education, and the new knowledge that we were much further down the learning curve than we'd imagined in 2006, was very attractive. Our Trainers began to study like never before: exercise technique, metabolism, food combinations....what was old became new again. We learned how to better motivate people; how to eat for real performance, and not just "health"; what hard work and intensity REALLY meant. For the first time in years, we began to look forward to our OWN workouts, and our excitement for our clients' workouts *doubled*. I mean, when have you ever CLAPPED for someone? We were now doing it ten times per day. That changes you.

There was, of course, some cognitive dissonance to overcome. Don't eat grains? Go sprinting? 100 pullups in one workout? NO rest???

At around that time, we were lucky to have a talk about Beginner's Mind with a local martial arts coach. Collectively, we decided that it would be irresponsible of us to NOT practise what we preached. Individually, though, we all knew that we were already addicted to CrossFit, and that anything new that we learned from different resources would be brought back to CrossFit and applied there.We sent our data to the CrossFit Journal; they published a summary entitled, "The

Science of Sticking With It."

A few months later, CrossFit Kids (www.crossfitkids.com) made its internet debut. While the "no grains, high variety of movement, short-but-tough" mentality made a few waves, the CrossFit Kids program stirred up a tsunami. It had been held, unchallenged for years, that kids should never lift weights for fear of "stunting their growth." CrossFit Kids faced down that firestorm, and has been the main force for turning the tide of misinformation surrounding youth exercise in North America. Though it's always been popular in European cultures, weightlifting in children has been shunned in North America for decades; ironically, gymnastics, which features far more impact to the growth plates, has been embraced as a "safer" alternative by the majority of parents.

The original notion of 'lifting weights stunts your growth' came from the late 1800s, when British expeditioners visited child-labour mines in India. Young children would routinely work 18-hour days, carrying heavy loads on their backs, from deep in the mine shaft to the surface. They would survive on one meal – primarily carbohydrate – per day, seven days per week, until they died around age 20. The visitors attributed the childrens' small stature to the loads they were carrying, not the lack of sleep or the malnourishment.

The idea of Long-Term Athletic Development has been around for awhile in Canada. Linear periodization came for our Olympic athletes when Tudor Bompa immigrated, and produced our first wave of Olympic success in the Summer Games. Though that first wave of Elites (Ben Johnson included) became tarnished, the long-term planning for athletic success stuck around and became part of the school curriculum. At least, that's what happened in the better schools...

Canadian Sport For Life promotes exercise as "training stages" throughout life, beginning with such phases as "Active Start" - movement for babies and toddlers, and proceeding to "FUNdamentals" - physical play for small children. The federally-supported program then recommends a "learn to train" phase – at about age eight, which correlates well with CrossFit Kids and the age at which children begin learning weightlifting techniques in many Scandinavian countries. The next phases, "Train to Compete" and "Train To Win," will appeal to an ever-narrowing segment of the national community; however, the exercises and skills recommended for the broader, noncompetitive community are still the same.

To a coach interested in the betterment of athletes, these ideas make so much sense that they may seem obvious. To the public at large, however....it's not the case. To the bureaucrats whose mandate is to balance the public health with the promotion of a higher GDP, it's much more attractive to promote "whole grains" and a carbohydrate-based food pyramid than the radical notion that a person should "eat what grandma ate."

Sadly, the mandate passed down from Ministers and Department Heads and Senators is this: toe the line. Toe the same line we've held for decades, and toe it stricter. Want to lose weight? Do the same thing we've been telling you for thirty years; if it doesn't work, it's your fault.

We beg to differ. More coaches and Personal Trainers and Nutritionists and other health professionals are now decrying the public healthcare policies than ever before. Parents, even, realize that government recommendations don't meet the reality of 21st-century USA; that "limiting screen time" is not going to help save their kids from diabetes, and that gardening is not going to help them drop a pants size by the summertime.

With these things in mind, then, Tyler faced a conundrum: continue to teach Physical Education (his specialty) part-time, on an as-needed basis, until...? Teach the Canada Food Pyramid – largely grain-based, to match our principal national export – or teach what he knew to work? Extol the virtues of running long distances as the way to lose weight, or teach kids to commit that penultimate sin: lift weights? Teach teenagers the rules of handball, or show them what it took to ENJOY exercise for life? Finally, go with the regular volleyball/basketball/floor hockey rotation...or bring a CrossFit WOD into a high school?

In other classes, should he continue to punish students who couldn't sit still during a lecture on cellular division...or let them collaborate to try and find some personal context? Should he hand out burpees as punishment in math class...or use them to stimulate the brain chemically, as John Ratey was doing in Naperville, IL?

His resolution came in September 2010. He'd had enough of the old system. He resigned his spot on the 'supply' list, and took on the task of developing a better system for learning.

Right away, we started studying, and enlisted the willing help of a local school Board. We ran programs in elementary schools; we brought at-risk youth to our gym. We showed them how to squat. We showed them how to focus. We read, and studied, and travelled to learn. Through our contacts, we gained first a contract to conduct research (and publish the results) on 10th-grade math classes; then we gained referrals to clients with ABI (Acute Brain Injury.) From there, our web of therapy and education spiralled outward, and after months with little sleep, we published our first textbook. A month later, we found ourselves lecturing to a group of local teachers and CrossFit coaches at our first Certification, and working with patent attorneys. The learning curve is immense, and as the internet continues to bring new information to the masses quickly, we find ourselves swimming hard to stay on top of the wave (or fight the current, as the case may warrant.)

Currently, we maintain a growing roster of clients undergoing NeuroMotive Therapy after head injury and stroke; we operate the Ignite! Academy to provide Enrichment services to school-aged children AND adults; we're working with our local Hospital to open a post-chemotherapy clinic; we operate programs in schools several times per week; and we still find time to work out both our bodies and brains. The ongoing development of the Ignite! Program has been our Enrichment course, and though we don't ask that you put out as much material as we have in the last few years, we hope that you're as well rewarded.

First and Foremost: How To Change.

Chances are, your goals aren't out of reach forever. However, most people don't know how to set realistic goals, or draw maps; they're just good at looking at the top of the mountain. If you're familiar with the fitness world (our stomping grounds!) you've seen it before:

New Year's Resolution – lose 30lbs.

Step One: uh.....eat fewer calories? Eat less fat? Follow the Food Pyramid? Do Step Aerobics? Jog?

We've all been taught, since we were very young, that we need to change. Stop running in the halls! Quit picking your nose! Get better at studying! Go on more dates! Get to bed on time! Lose weight! Strengthen your bones!.....it's a never-ending list, because none of us are perfect.

The problem is, we're never taught HOW to change habits. No one has ever told you the steps necessary to develop long-term change, have they? It's critical that we start out the right way.

First off, figure out what you're already doing right. NO ONE is ever missing the mark by 100%. There's some little thing you're already doing well; some way in which you're already succeeding.

We call that a '**Bright Spot**.' Cling to that.

When Kris started with us, his parents' goal was for Kris to behave more 'normally' in social situations. We didn't take Kris to a speed-dating event on the first day (or ever, for the record.) But Kris WAS already involved in therapy; he was used to listening to a therapist. He was already used to the system of emotional reward (happy faces) and following simple instructions. He had a solid therapist; he had parents who supported the ideas we put before them. No, Kris wasn't very verbally inclined. But if you consider all the Bright Spots we began with, you'll see that the environment was already primed for Kris to succeed. The deck was already stacked in our favour.

To use the example of fat loss: over the last sixteen years as a Personal Trainer, I've been lucky enough to meet a lot – hundreds – of people who want to lose weight. These people come from all backgrounds – social, genetic, geographic, economic – but many of them share a depressing trait: they perceive that they're not doing anything right.

If your goal is to lose weight, there's a good chance you're already doing something well: perhaps you like to go for walks. Maybe you have a dog, and he needs to be walked. Maybe your mailbox is a quarter mile from your house; maybe – as a worst case – you stand up to iron your clothes. None of these things, taken alone, are enough to help you lose fat. However, they're habits that you've already adopted, and it's much easier to help you modify a positive habit than to start a new one, or drop a negative one.

Next, duplicate (clone) the Bright Spot if possible.

In Kris' case, he could follow single commands properly. Linking commands together was simply a matter of issuing separate commands with decreasing periods of time in between. His pace determined the time before the next command.

Next, we began issuing two commands before he could start the first task. Since his therapist was working with reading at the same time, we decided it would be beneficial to write the commands, in order, on our whiteboard. A workout was born!

In our weight loss example: while walking your dog, I want you to stop and do 5 squats every time your dog stops. Next week, I want you to cover the course in 10% less time. The next week, I want you to do half your walk, and then come inside, do 30 squats, and then resume the walk. When the time necessary (or the task itself) is already firmly imprinted – blocked off – in your mind, it's easy to modify. The key is to maintaining a constant challenge, rather than to start a flurry of new activity.

Next, try on success. If you woke up tomorrow and your

problems were solved, what would be the first thing you'd notice that would tell you that things are different? THAT is your first goal. Example: if you wake up and your pajamas feel looser, you're losing weight. Future Bright Spot #1: pajamas feel looser.

With Kris, this was a different process, because even if he COULD imagine himself catching the football, he found it difficult to iterate how he'd feel if successful. By this point, Kris' training had been shifted to Tyler. Slowly, Kris began to take on sport-specific drills as part of his training – including catching a ball.

Over the next two years, Kris moved from the fear of catching a tennis ball thrown from three feet to practising football passing patterns. The change is remarkable – his new goal is a drivers' license, and he's an accomplished sculptor and painter – but it didn't happen by accident. The high school student is light years ahead of the eight-year-old whose parents were told he would never speak, and many of the tools we'll outline in this book are testament to that success. However, each taken individually wouldn't have had nearly the profound effect that all – together with the correct environment for success, and room for slow change – has had.

The North American Educational Culture, 2011: A Review.

Unhealthy is the new 'normal.' Though our access to information is now completely unlimited by time or resources, our actual knowledge and practice of healthy lifestyles is on the decrease. Environmental changes, work habits, increased leisure time, increased access to foods built around marketing (and not sustenance) have contrived against our species. For the first time EVER, the life expectancy of our children will be less than that of our own generation.

While the physiological pitfalls of less movement and easy access to food are well recorded, and alarm bells are sounding everywhere, the cognitive decline is less well realized. For learning, movement is absolutely CRITICAL, not just beneficial. As you'll learn from this book, the same cultural habits that are killing us off too early are also dumbing us down too far.

If there existed a society-wide measure of intellect; if we could predict our relative brainpower in the same way that we predict life expectancy, we believe that our society stands at an inflection point. Looking forward into the fog, will we see the slow uphill trend continue...or will we see a drop-off, as in the case of our physical state?

Ask your family doctor how to lose weight, and you'll likely be advised to reduce your caloric intake and walk more often. Follow the food pyramid, and eat more whole grains At face value, weight loss appears to be a simple matter of mathematics: burn more calories than you take in.

Ask an expert on weight loss whose income depends on the success of his clients, however, and you'll likely hear something very different. The growing trend in our field revolves more around food QUALITY, blood glucose buffering through insulin control, and intense, regular exercise across a broad spectrum. In-the-trenches experts – including Personal Trainers, coaches, nutritionists, and other private-sector fitness personalities, whose paycheck depends on results – frequently decry the recommendations of governmental organizations, bureaucrats, and even many well-meaning charitable organizations. Sadly, it is a rare case that a member of the overweight majority can achieve lasting change by following RDI (Recommended Daily Intake) guidelines; the Food Pyramid; and the minimum daily exercise guidelines of various government agencies.

At *Ignite!*, we believe that our system of educating our students is weighed down by much of the same baggage as our healthcare system: it's simply too big to change. Weighed down by bureaucracy, opinion, and outdated science, there simply isn't room within the system to accommodate learners who don't conform to the 'average.' Students who struggle – perhaps at the top end of the learning curve, perhaps toward the bottom – become marginalized, and parents are forced to seek external help for their children.

In the physical world, if you can't lose weight, you get a Personal Trainer or join a gym. In the more cerebral realm, though....what options exist? This is the void *Ignite!* aims to fill, in a variety of ways, including:

- ⅄ Enrichment service for students who excel in school;
- ⅄ Multi-step services for students who struggle in a single or multiple subjects;
- ⅄ In-class 'interventions' to trigger better learning and memory in students;
- ⅄ Education and Certification for teachers who seek to implement the most efficient strategies for movement and learning in the classroom;
- ⅄ Education, research, and Certification for Therapists who seek to incorporate brain-based modalities in their practices;
- ⅄ One-on-one therapies for students with ADHD, Asperger's Syndrome, and autism
- ⅄ Rehabilitation combining movement and executive brain function for victims of head trauma, including injury, stroke, post-chemotherapy "brain fog," or aneurism.

We believe in a Good-Better-Best approach.

Good: incorporate movements into a student's school day. This is the bare minimum required for the brain to store and process information. Likewise, introduce more movement into the typical workday for adults.
Better: Use specific movements to enhance learning in different skills.
Best: Do one-on-one training with a NeuroMotive Coach to enhance cognition and retention.

A note about Knowledge vs. Intelligence:
While most methods of teaching revolve around the storage and recall of data (facts, figures, dates, personalities...) we prioritize the ability to think critically; to analyze; to impart; to apply.

It's undeniably useful to be able to recall things on demand. On a school exam, memorization of the Pythagorean Theorem could mean the difference between an entire letter grade. Twenty years on, however, will the former student understand how to calculate the board length needed for the roof of his dog's new house?

To this end, we eschew the model of rote memorization. We DO spend time teaching *Ignite!* clients how to remember facts and data more efficiently, but the goal is the ultimate application of those facts, not the ability to recall them out of context in a high-stress situation.

As educators, we should be creating safety nets for failure. Like rituals in sports, they allow us to feel safe when we feel pressure. If we approach learning as 'practice,' we're allowing our students to focus on the work instead of the outcome, and feel safe and confident. We're permitting them – and giving them the space to – switch on both sides of their brains. What are these 'safety nets?' Preparatory drills. Technique practice. Warm-ups, both mental and physical. Things that are routine and basic, but ultimately the foundation of a skill. It is our role to uncover these exercises for students, and that requires understanding multiple intelligence iterations; personalities; motivation.

Learning is a natural process, sparked by interactions with people, places and things. We internalize – learn - through our sensory-motor experiences.

Learning is rooted in our movement. Our entire cognitive, sensory and motor development is dependent on our movement. Exploring, receiving and then reacting to stimuli IS the process by which we learn. It is no coincidence that when we map our cognitive, sensory and motor development from conception, they follow a similar path: from very simple to very complex. However, our brain development does not run parallel to our physiological progress, but along the same road, at the same speed.

Gross motor proficiency allows the mind to develop memory, social skills, language, emotional elaboration. "High-order" centres, like the Prefrontal Cortex, are not fully developed until young adulthood, and are influenced more heavily by the environment than by heredity. The environment is responsible for enhancing the higher order thinking. In the circumstance where there is exposure to exploring, use of right and left brain activities, positivity, exercise, practice, and a growth mindset, you will find a person that is well on their way to becoming an optimal user of the brain: a Learner.

According to Jean Piaget[2], every organism strives for

---

2 Lavatelli, C. (1973). *Piaget's Theory Applied to an Early Childhood Curriculum*. Boston: American Science and Engineering, Inc.

equilibrium: a balance of organized structures (sensory, motor, and cognitive.) When structures are in equilibrium, they provide effective ways of interacting with the environment. Adaptation, assimilation, and accommodation are all ways in which we respond to stimuli, and everyone responds to each stimulus in a different way.

In the next section, we'll go into greater detail about how the brain works, both physically and chemically; how it's evolved from a very basic responder to pain to the complex system that now carries us to the moon and back. We provide this information as background. You will NOT be tested on this knowledge later, but it will make some concepts easier to understand if you have a basic grasp of the anatomy and actions involved.

What we believe – the *Ignite!* Manifesto

⅄ We believe in constant intervention. The body is built to move not only one hour per day, or four times a week, but to remain in constant action and reaction.

⅄ We believe in mass practice. Success and mastery are determinable, not predetermined.

⅄ We believe in the Growth Mindset: that there's no limit to the learning curve.

⅄ We believe in creating a positive environment. For many, it will be their only positive experience all day.

⅄ We believe in taking the benefits of sports and spreading them out over the course of a lifetime of learning.

⅄ We believe in neuronal plasticity. Learning is a lifelong endeavour.

⅄ We believe in creating our own circumstances, and teaching others to create theirs.

⅄ We believe that skill comes from adapting to challenges, and that novelty is as important as intensity.

⅄ We believe in creating Bright Spots and teaching people to celebrate small victories daily.

⅄ We believe in the gross warmup, the skill-specific warmup, and the rampup as preparation for learning. As in sport, so in the classroom.

Section I – Anatomy or Better Living Through Chemistry.

"'Evolution is a tinkerer, not an engineer." - Francois Jacob

The *mind* is beautiful.

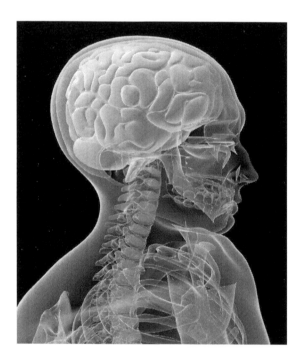

It's an electrical symphony. It's a chemical ballet. It's the home of our ego, our identity; the seat of the Self.

However, "..the *brain* is an inelegant and inefficient agglomeration of stuff, which nonetheless works surprisingly well." This was the observation of David Linden in his excellent book, *"The Accidental Mind: How Brain Evolution Has Given Us Love, Memory, Dreams and God."*[3]

Linden makes another terrific analogy: "The brain is built like an ice cream cone (and you are the top scoop): through evolutionary time, as higher functions were added, a new scoop was placed on top, but the lower scoops were left largely unchanged."

All that potential for art, memory, creativity, calculation and discovery...contained in a soft, slippery grey mush. And protected only by 1/3 of an inch of bone, all the way around. Put that much delicate potential inside the barest of protection, and things sometimes don't work perfectly. Bogged down with yesterday's technology, our brain is one of our least efficient organs.

Imagine being instructed to create a computer that would perform calculations to control a satellite. After you accepted the contract, you found out that you had a few conditions:

1) you had to include all previous technology – from cloud computing and the Internet, down through the abacus

2) all of these technologies had to be turned on, all the time, and interact with one another.

Exciting new research is offering a glimpse of how the brain works from the inside out. Anyone, at any age, can learn; and everyone can learn to learn better. The core of the *Ignite!* program is the improvement in efficiency,

3   Linden, David J. The Accidental Mind: How Brain Evolution Has Given Us Love, Memory, Dreams, and God. Belknap Press, 2008.

coordination, and recruitment within the inefficient brain.

Why learning is difficult at times

Chemical imbalances; neurological disconnects; physiological impairments; altered arousal states; poor coordination between hemispheres; fatigue; blood sugar level....these all have the effect of altering your brain's ability to learn and operate the body.

Chemical imbalances will control not only your brain's potential to learn, but also your response to stimuli. While one person sees a nonthreatening joke in the raised eyebrow of a stranger, another will see a sarcastic challenge, depending on the hormone levels present at that particular moment. Without the right chemicals (which we'll review later,) your brain is incapable of storing some information, and retrieving other information.

Neurological disconnects are literally electrical misfirings. Even with a new string of lights, a tiny short anywhere between bulbs will leave you with an unlit room. Imagine a house that must operate all its rooms at once, but doesn't have enough wire; a little electrician is constantly pulling wiring from one room to rewire another, leaving only the most important wiring in the walls. Back and forth from room to room, depending on which is needed at that moment. Now imagine what happens when a door sticks, or the electrician can't connect two rooms. NOW imagine a house with a thousand rooms; and now, a thousand houses with a thousand rooms, all sharing the same electrician.

Brain injury, of course, can alter the function of the brain by interrupting the delivery systems for these electrical and chemical pulses. The brain can also be incompletely formed; connections can never have been made; or a tragedy, like a stroke, can interrupt blood flow to one region while choking another.

On a more day-to-day occurrence, blood sugar levels can rise and fall to a dramatic extent, depending on the nutritional intake and timing of the body. Maintaining a steady blood sugar level is ideal.

Interhemispheric coordination means that the two hemispheres of the brain, left and right (which we sometimes refer t o as the 'right brain' and 'left brain,' tend to specialize based on function. Teachers frequently refer to 'right-brain learners' or 'left-dominant learners' when they're talking about students who are better at maths and logic than art, or vise versa. In truth, though, both hemispheres are working together all the time, and they can become more efficient at cooperating to complete tasks. We refer to this as 'whole-brain functioning.'

There are many factors that can interfere with learning. However, turning on whole-brain functioning is the first step to eliminating these factors from interrupting the learning process.

When one side of the brain is on virtual 'standby' while the other side is 'trying' to make a connection, we tend to make tasks more difficult than they actually are. One side of the brain is not meant to work by itself, and doesn't have the ability to make long-lasting connections. Through cross-pattern movements, motions that require the body to break the invisible midline of the body, and specific cognitive-development movements, we can start making the brain function as a whole. Whole-brain functioning means more available connections. Two brains are better than one!

Why *Ignite!* will work....and work faster

The program literally 'ignites' the learning process through three vital steps:

> 1) Increasing production of neuron-growing hormones through heart-pumping exercise.
> 2) Performing cross-pattern movements that trigger specific cognitive functions, and whole-brain functioning.
> 3) Reinforcing the learning goal that challenges the brain to use both sides together in an environment that is focused, positive and self-motivating.

When a student uses *Ignite!* methods before they tackle a reading assignment, listen to a lecture or solve a math problem, they absorb new information with the whole brain turned on! Now that's an optimal learning environment.

Working With Limitations

Learning is different for everyone, but every brain has the potential for learning. Because of the large amount of neurons (100 billion), the number of connections possible on each neuron (around 5,000) and the ability to grow more, there are an unlimited number of pathways available to make long lasting connections. It also means we can be flexible and creative in how we retrain the brain.

Students with outstanding attention needs will require more one-on-one attention, which is beyond the scope of this book, and is available through our NeuroMotive Therapist Certification Course. While they'll benefit even more than other students, their best progress will be made through individual, personalized programming.

Physiology Of The Brain

Think of your brain as a muscle. The more you use it, the stronger it gets. Just like the muscles in our body that perform different functions, our brain is also responsible for different functions.

But that's not all the mind and body have in common.

This 3-dimensional, 3-pound beauty is directly influenced by our movements. Movements grow the brain and, what's more, specific movements can *enhance* specific cognitive function.

Before you start growing your brain we need to understand the different parts and how they work. This is a very small overview, with the goal of giving a person a macro view to provide context for the discussion to come.

The Three Dimensions of the Brain

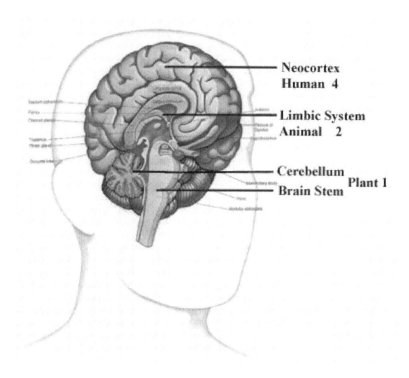

Neocortex
Human 4

Limbic System
Animal 2

Cerebellum
Brain Stem
Plant 1

1) The *Cerebrum* or *NeoCortex* is the largest part of the human brain, responsible for higher brain functions such as cognition and behaviour. The effect of movement on this part of the brain is extremely positive: the increase in blood flow, the introductions of hormones (IGF-1, BDNF, etc.) not only enhance the function of the cerebrum, but are critical for its full development.

Cognition: includes functions such as intellectual function, memory, speech and language, complex perception, orientation, attention, judgement, planning and decision making.

Behaviour: the organization of these cognitive functions listed above, and also the processing and regulation of emotions.

The cerebral cortex is divided into four sections, called "lobes": the frontal lobe, parietal lobe, occipital lobe, and temporal lobe.

What do each of these lobes do?

- ⚓ Role of the Frontal Lobe in *Cognition*- reasoning, planning, language, emotions, impulse control, social and sexual behaviour, and problem solving
- ⚓ Role of the Frontal Lobe in *Movement* – fine motor movements and strength in the arms, hands and fingers. Also involved in long, complex movements requiring proper sequencing.

- ⚓ Role of the Parietal Lobe in *Cognition*- orientation in space, recognition, perception of stimuli, and writing.
- ⚓ Role of the Parietal Lobe in *Movement*- spatial awareness, proprioceptive stimuli, pain and touch receptors.

- ⚓ Role of the Occipital Lobe in *Cognition*- visual processing in the left and right brain, and colour reception.
- ⚓ Role of the Occipital Lobe in *Movement* – differentiation of visual stimuli based on balance, depth, peripheral sight and colour.
- ⚓ Role of the Temporal Lobe in *Cognition*- perception and recognition of auditory stimuli, memory, and speech. It also contains the Hippocampus, the part of the brain responsible for learning.

- ⚓ Role of the Temporal Lobe in *Movement* – aggression and arousal, 'fight or flight.'

2) The *Cerebellum* and *Brain stem* are the parts of the brain that hold all of our basic survival needs (bottom of the ice cream cone.) They're also

responsible for our sensory development: hearing, smell, taste, touch and sight. In the development of movement, their role is to respond to reflexes from core muscle activation, the neck muscles, and the arms and legs; the progressing to rolling over, belly crawling, sitting, creeping and walking. As we grow and gain the strength to perform more complex movements, this part of the brain grows along with our bodies.

3) The *Midbrain* or *Limbic System* is the smallest of the 3 dimensions, but controls a huge variety of functions. It's the conductor of our emotional expression; sleep; attention; imagination; temperature regulation; hormones; sexuality; smell; and the producer of most of the brain's chemicals. To keep this system functioning at its highest level, we have to control our stress; eat properly; get enough rest; and exercise to produce more brain-growing chemicals. When this system is 'firing on all cylinders', our gross motor skills (larger, more complex movements) are performed with more accuracy and efficiency.

More Brain Anatomy You Should Know

The Amygdala: Your 'Lizard Brain'

The A*mygdala* is largely responsible for the fight-or-flight response, and largely prefers 'flight.' It's the "duck and cover" stimulator. The amygdala is primarily concerned with the protection of the being, and so prefers to fit in with the crowd, or keep the body as unobtrusive as possible. To that end, the amygdala dislikes exposure to stress; it makes you want to avoid new situations or awkward social settings. The amygdala is to blame for passive-aggressivity; shyness; and fear of public speaking.

The amygdala is frequently believed to be the most primeval part of our brain stem; it represents our most animalian traits, and controls our most basic primordial behaviour. It's still necessary, but in our current culture, the behaviours it encourages are often discouraged.

The Nucleus Basalis

The Nucleus Basalis produces acetylcholine and dopamine to increase plasticity. Anything requiring highly focused attention – learning new physical activities that require concentration; solving challenging puzzles; making a career change; learning a new language, or mastering new skills and materials – triggers the action of the Nucleus Basalis.

As children, the Nucleus Basalis is switched on during our critical periods. We absorb everything we are exposed to and deem important. During that time, acetylcholine levels are high, as well as dopamine.

Its role: the expansion of a 'brain map' to allow for a new or improved skill. Obviously, plasticity is key for the Nucleus Basalis to function.

When researchers are able to artificially 'switch on' the Nucleus Basalis, learning becomes easier for the subject.

Known as neurogenesis and neuroplasticity, the brain's

ability to grow new cells and rewire neural structures, respectively, means that by exercising the brain in the right way we can improve cognitive processing ability. By stimulating the Nucleus Basalis with mental tasks that strengthen memory, processing speed, and problem-solving ability, we can maintain and even improve those key mental functions.

The Basal Ganglia

Brain structures that are involved in learning and motor control, the basal ganglia lie deep in the cerebral hemispheres. Dopamine, a substance used in the transmission of signals between neurons, is important for learning and the plasticity of the basal ganglia.

More on neuroplasticity to come. For now, rest easy: you not only have the ability to learn the rest of the contents of this book, but we'll give you the methods, too.

Wiring the Brain

"What makes us move, makes us think." Jean Blaydes Madigan, Neurokinesiologist, Murphy, TX

Your brain attempts to be as efficient as possible. It strives to make connections simple, so that information may be quickly retrieved. While this is a very positive – and necessary – trait, it also has a downside: it seeks patterns, and rigidly adheres to those patterns once found.

When you take in any information, your brain seeks first to match it with a pattern it recognizes. Take this example: I say, "Why did the chicken cross the road?" and you answer: "....to get to the other side." You're simply completing a memory pattern of a tired old joke.

Likewise, when a teenager performs a squat exercise, you'll typically see them allow their knees to drift forward over their toes and their heels rise from the ground. Though a functional movement screening doesn't show any flexibility issues, the child still doesn't squat properly because they've 'learned' a movement pattern that's incorrect. Rather than relearn the movement each time, the brain seeks the most efficient path to completion.

Even though you don't hear the words, your brain is following a checklist when you squat: "Shift the shoulders forward. Push the hips back. Check for balance feedback. Seek proprioceptive data on the knees' position in space...."

These patterns – or sequences of commands – are called Engrams, and are stored and transmitted through neurotransmitters, which 'deliver' the information in the correct order.

It's difficult to change a person's mind because you're literally changing their biology when you attempt to do so. They'll have to make new neural connections; remap the pathway for the delivery of the information; and eliminate the old information. The brain, which likes to make things MORE efficient, does NOT like to travel back over the same ground.

We, however, want information to embed more permanently, and that's why we want to 'rewire' the brain.

Crossing the midline of the body is when a person's hand moves from left to right, or right to left, across the middle of your skeleton. Think of a tennis racket moving from right to left: information and biofeedback is first delivered through one eye, and then the other as the racket moves across the body. When one crosses the midline, the brain begins to make new connections and the right and left hemispheres begin to work together. This communication process organizes the brain for better concentration and problem solving. Crossing the midline with a limb integrates brain hemispheres to enable the brain to organize itself as a whole unit, instead of different parts. The brain still strives for efficiency, but must do so across a broader spectrum.

When students perform cross-lateral activities, blood flow is increased in all parts of the brain, making it more alert and energized for stronger, more cohesive learning. Movements that cross the midline unify the cognitive and motor regions of the brain: the cerebellum, basal ganglia, and corpus callosum while stimulating the productions of neurotrophins that increase the number of synaptic connections. *(Dennison; Hannaford)*[4] [5]

Several complex motor tasks cross the midline and require coordination of body systems for mastery at any level. Daily quality physical education, then, becomes essential for optimum learning.

A simple example: eye-tracking exercises and peripheral vision development helps reading.

One of the reasons students have trouble with reading is because of a lack of eye fitness. When students watch screens, their eyes lock into a constant perception of a single distance, and the muscles that control eye movement atrophy. Physical education curriculum provides an opportunity for strengthening eye muscles, but isn't always utilized. Tracking exercises, manipulatives, navigation activities and target games exercise the eye muscles, making the eyes "fit to read."

The brain is attracted to novelty. The brain learns best when more of the senses are involved, and as we'll see later, would prefer to remember a picture than a number. Colour, sounds, music, smells, manipulatives and

4   Dennison, Paul E. Brain Gym.

5   Hannaford, Carla PhD.Smart Moves: Why Learning Is Not All In Your Head, Second Edition

navigating space are all reinforcing details that help your brain store information that's more readily accessible. Learning environments filled with enriched sensory input enhance cognition. Brain-compatible learning perceived as FUN increases success.

Balance and Coordination play a very important part of your brain functioning. fMRI and PET scans clearly show that movements which are novel require more brain activation than exercises with which the student is well familiar. Efficiency of recruitment is the cause: as movement pattern becomes more ingrained, the brain requires less thought (and less energy) to execute the movement.

Not every single movement requires the same brain activity. The more complicated the movement, the more brain activity is required. The newer the movement, the less efficient the neural pattern. As the movement or academic skill is practised, though, the pattern of recruitment becomes more ingrained, or *intrinsic*.

This is a two-sided coin: on the one-hand, hard-wiring the data sequence makes for fast, efficient recall. Remembering how to use a fire extinguisher in an emergency is critical, and practice certainly helps. Practising CPR on a dummy in a high-stress environment? Also great.

However, PROPER practice is important. While *Ignite!* advocates a practice environment that is nonjudgmental and focused on hard work, it's important that the practice be purposeful, with the end goal being proper technique. Like the brain, we strive for movement and cognitive EFFICIENCY...but we stress quality first.

Hard-wire good mechanics, and you're building an

athletic champion. Hard-wire good memory techniques, and you're propelling a student far beyond the classroom. However, reinforcing BAD habits also means that they'll become permanent.

The brain has no system for judgement of quality. It can't discern when your squat is perfect; it simply compares your current effort to previous efforts. It can't tell when you've finished a math problem as quickly as possible, just whether you've done it faster or slower than last time.

In traditional 'bodybuilding' training, in which isolation (single-joint) exercises are prioritized (ie, a single biceps curl,) there is one part of the brain activated which is responsible for voluntary movement. In a complex workout system that uses compound movements, a high technical demand, AND frequent change, the movements require proper balance, coordination and muscle timing. The net effects on the brain? These movements will activate not only the area of the brain responsible for voluntary movement but also the area responsible for balance and coordination: the cerebellum.

In addition, another part of the brain - the basal ganglia - is involved in motor-coordinated movements. Remember that constant changes in the physical program will trigger the hippocampus, which is responsible for memory and learning of new movements. This constant learning will promote the creation of new neural pathways, on which new information can later be stored for quick and efficient recall.

Brain Chemistry

Neurotropins

A neurotropin is a protein that promotes the development, maintenance and survival of neurons. Neurotrophic factors are a type of growth hormone that signal a cell to survive, differentiate, or grow. These proteins bear names such as *Vascular Endothelial Growth Factor (VEGF)* and the 'miracle-gro' protein gene which actually grows thicker, bushier neurons in the part of brain responsible for learning, *Brain-Derived Neurotrophic Factor (BDNF)*. There is one non-neural growth factor existing in the brain that has been shown to aid in the survival of neurons, *Insulin-like Growth Factor (IGF-1)*, which is found throughout the body and active in the development of ALL tissues.

Movement that increases heart rate also releases these very important growth hormones into the brain. Dr. John

Ratey's early research on brain development and exercise centred largely around the production of BDNF following aerobic activity (more about Dr. Ratey later.)

When we move, our muscles produce these proteins, which travel through the bloodstream and into the brain. VEGF stimulates the growth of new blood vessels, and the more blood is pumped to your brain, the more the vessels will grow. IGF-1 is also a growth hormone which, after being triggered by exercise, is pumped up the bloodstream and into the brain to aid in growth. BDNF is a gene that aids in the process of growing thicker, bushier neurons in the Hippocampus. This is the part of the brain that is vulnerable to degenerative diseases and also responsible for learning. Scientists have found that exercise causes BDNF to show up in this area. And like the other proteins, the more exercise you get, the higher the levels of BDNF. We call this a dose-specific response; more is better. After exercise, the brain is a fertile place, optimized to learn and prepared to make new, long lasting connections!

Neurotropins are found in areas of the brain such as the Basal Ganglia, Hippocampus, and Brain Stem .

BDNF and Intracellular Signalling

A child's brain produces large amounts of brain-derived neurotrophic factor (BDNF, discussed above.) This substance stimulates the brain's centre of attention and memory formation, the Nucleus Basalis. The copious production of BDNF means that the child's brain is constantly ready to take in new information and form new brain structures. Ironically, when we get frustrated that children aren't paying attention to us, it's because they're paying so much attention to everything else!

In our late teens our bodies produce a lot *more* BDNF,

until we reach a point in life where specialized knowledge becomes more important than a broad (but shallow) knowledge base. This triggers the Nucleus Basalis to shut off the process of effortless learning. From an evolutionary perspective this makes good sense. As adults we need to consolidate what we've learned and discriminate between important data and distractions.

On the other hand, the idea that the adult brain is hopelessly cut off from further growth and change, as we've heard in the past, is simply untrue. Recent studies have proven that when we engage in tasks or activities that require focus and attention, and provide novelty and relevance, we reactivate the Nucleus Basalis, prompting the brain to absorb and retain new information and even stimulating the growth of new brain cells.

BDNF is a neurotrophin that bears a lot of the responsibility for neuronal survival and repair; growth; and differentiation. It's been called, *"Miracle-Gro for the brain"* by John Ratey, Ph.D., and been labelled as the main molecule translating the ability of exercise to promote neurogenesis at the cellular level and enhance learning and memory at the behavioural level. In one study, BDNF mRNA levels were increased by more than 40% in exercising animals compared to their sedentary counterparts! In another, the gene coding for tyrosine kinase receptor (Trk) B, the cognate receptor for BDNF, was found to be up-regulated. This means that not only was there MORE BDNF to go around, but the receptor sites are more willing to absorb it. Great news for learning!

BDNF acts chemically through two pathways: via calcium/calmodulin-dependent protein kinase II (CaMKII) AND mitogen-activated protein kinase (MAPK)/extracellular signal-regulated kinase (ERK) . CaMKII and MAPK are both important in synaptic plasticity and memory formation. Both intracellular signaling pathways induce the expression of genes important in learning and memory, so the up-regulation of genes that contribute to either pathway would result in an enhanced ability to learn. This means that it doesn't matter HOW you stimulate the production of BDNF; you'll still get a cognitive benefit. This will be an important point later.

Synaptic Plasticity

Synaptic Plasticity is the ability of the connection, or synapse, between two neurons to become weaker or stronger, depending on how often it's reinforced. Your shoe colour in kindergarten? You probably don't use that information much, and so that synapse weakens over time. Your wife's favourite flower? Hopefully, this information is at the top of your mind. Plastic change also results from the alteration of the number of receptors located on a synapse. The more detailed the information stored on the synapse, the more receptor sites become available for use. This is why the brain can more easily remember a picture (multiple stimuli) than a number; or why adding a smell, texture, sound or taste to a memory strengthens the brain's ability to store it for the long term.

Wonder why your father insists on playing his Kenny Rogers albums, but you can't make yourself like the music? It's because he remembers the context differently. In the 1970s, your father may have had a beard; wore similar clothing to Kenny Rogers; parted his hair on the side. Perhaps your father has a fond memory of driving along a dirt road, arm out the window, your mother by his side...and *"The Gambler"* came on the radio. YOU hear a raspy story about knowing when to fold 'em; he sees a summer day, free and easy with the woman he loves. His synaptic connection is stronger, because he has more receptor sites (warm sun, emotional feelings, dusty smell of the road...) engaged in the memory.

Synaptic plasticity is influenced both by the quantity of neurotransmitters released into the synapse AND how effectively the cells respond to those neurotransmitters. A healthy, active brain with more neurotrophins means that cells respond better to the neurotransmitters. Exercise helps you secrete more neurotrophins; the cells become more plastic. This means that learning becomes easier THROUGHOUT life, not just at a very early age.

Synaptic plasticity is one of the most important neurochemical foundations of learning and memory. Memories are MADE from vastly interconnected networks of synapses in the brain, and exercise clearly helps the brain improve the density of those networks and, as you'll see, the recall efficiency.

Neurotrophic factors are released during intense exercise. When the heart rate is increased, levels of BDNF-1 and IGF-1 rise proportionally.

Whole-Brain Plasticity

Regions of the brain should be considered specialized and not localized. Certain areas of the brain are dedicated to a particular kind of memory activity, but only if the individual makes significant commitment during development via daily activities. Due to developmental tendencies and the brain's competitive nature, neurons in the centre of each brain area are more committed to the task than those on the border. These border neurons are actively recruited by adjacent brain areas regularly to aid in the processes THEY prioritize. It is the daily activities of the individual that determine which brain area wins the competition.

Jordan Grafman, PhD. has identified four kinds of plasticity:

1) Map expansion - which occurs largely at the boundaries between brain areas as a result of daily activity. These boundary areas can expand

quickly, within minutes, to respond to our moment-to-moment needs.

2) Sensory Reassignment - occurs when one sense is blocked, as in the blind. When the visual cortex is deprived of its normal inputs, it can receive new inputs from another sense, such as touch.

3) Compensatory Masquerage - which takes advantage of the fact that there's more than one way for your brain to approach a task. We will expand on this topic in a later book. One example is allowing kids to use audio books for reading assignments rather than teach them strategies on how to read. This is a good strategy *only* if it's used to practice different stimuli on the same topic for anchoring, not for substitution or learning modifications.

4) Mirror Region Takeover - when part of one hemisphere fails, the mirror region in the opposite hemisphere adapts, taking over its mental function as best it can.[6]

Ignite! creates the proper circumstances for these plastic changes to occur due to its variety of physical and academic skills practice.

Long-Term Potentiation

Earlier, we spoke of synaptic plasticity, which is the brain's ability to change its sensitivity to external signals. It's experience-dependent (you can't just read about being calm and magically become calmer; rather, it's the practice that develops the capacity.) We made the case that synaptic plasticity is greatly enhanced through physical activity, and thus primes the brain to better recognize, react, and respond to stress and new

6Handbook of Neuropsychology: Plasticity and Rehabilitation , Jordan Grafman PhD. Elsevier Health Sciences, 2002.

situations.

Long-Term Potentiation is the ability to keep these gains in synaptic plasticity over, of course, the long term. It's defined as an enduring increase (lasting longer than an hour) in synaptic efficacy that results from an intense stimulation of an input pathway.

To simplify, a short-term exposure to stress through exercise will encourage a long-term increase in your ability to handle stress. Long-term potentiation is a measure of how MUCH of the synaptic efficiency you can keep over a longer time frame.

This effect can be amplified and made to 'stick' better over the long term. Creating memorable experiences of fear (and then overcoming fear, of course,) accomplishment, adherence, perseverance....they all help the brain to 'keep' the gains in synaptic plasticity.

The brain would rather remember a story or picture than a number. For example, "I lost two pounds last week" is not a memory significant enough to store over the long haul. Asked again a year later, "How much weight did you lose last March?" the exerciser would likely have trouble recalling the precise number (two pounds.) However, if the coach can build a story AROUND the exercise, by using a workout that induces the senses of fear, accomplishment, and perseverance, it's more easily remembered.

"What was your fastest mile last spring?" is a vague statement, but usually answered accurately, because the exerciser can clearly recreate most of the picture in her mind, using multiple sensory memories. "It was 6 minutes, 30 seconds. I remember because it was hot and very dry that day, and I wanted to collapse with a glass of cold water right afterwards. I did the mile with Jill, and I thought she'd beat me, but I pulled ahead right at the end, and...."

This type of long-term potentiation, aided by memory cues, is:

- experience-dependent (you won't remember Jill's time in the mile if you weren't there yourself,)

- input-specific(you won't remember the OTHER things that happened on the day of your 1-mile time trial just because they were on the same day,)

- rapidly induced (it's stored right away,)

- characterized by long-lasting spikes can last from 24hours to 10 days up to 2 months (the more experience you have practising memory, even if not doing so consciously, the better you become at remembering details.)

The Effects of Stress On Learning

Dendrites in the brain (responsible for receiving information) are very susceptible to the stress hormone Cortisol. In a prolonged high-anxiety state, cortisol stays present, and can alter the size of dendrites in any area of the brain. Studies have shown that, when under stress, the brain shrinks dendrite size in the frontal lobe (responsible, again, for executive function) and increases dendrite size in the amygdala (fight or flight.)
When a child becomes frustrated, the automatic response to stress sends a signal to the brain that the body is in danger. The more often this occurs, the more

the brain will favour new dendrite formation in the amygdala over the frontal lobe, effectively programming the child to react to stress in a more physical way.

Knowing what we do about the amygdala, consider two sample cases:

1) a child who's been encouraged to practice skills through the growth paradigm, and encouraged based on his hard work;

2) a child living in a higher-stress environment at home, who is berated for failure and lives in fear of reprimand.

Now, between those two children, imagine a high-stress scenario: a teacher announces, "Class, today we'll be doing a pop quiz. I'd like you to stand in front of the class by yourself, and I'll ask you questions about math to solve. You have ten seconds to answer. The child with the most correct answers will win a prize."

Student #1, who views the challenge as an opportunity for fun practice, eagerly agrees. *Student #2,* who perceives the threat of social humiliation and retribution immediately (remember, his amygdala dominates his thought patterns,) immediately tries to avoid the stressful situation. He may ask to go to the washroom, or be the scorekeeper; or, in certain situations, may internalize the stress, successfully covering up his anxiety, but further programming his brain to react physically to stress.

Student #1, in a relaxed but excited (aroused) state, successfully answers the first question, and then the second. He misses the third, but recovers on the fourth and fifth. When his time expires, he's answered 8 out of 10 questions correctly.

Student #2, in an agitated state, is fighting the impulse to vomit. He doesn't like public speaking: too much risk of social failure. As a result, he's much more likely to do poorly. "Why can't I just relax?" he asks himself. He misses the first question, and things quickly spiral downhill.

In an extreme situation, the student may physically act out, or even give in to self-destructive behaviour. Unfortunately, this downward spiral continues unless recognized and halted. The dendrites in the frontal lobe shrink, giving more credence to the argument for physical action made by the dendrites in the amygdala.

In one case, we were working with an autistic teen who had a self-biting habit. When faced with stress, the amygdala immediately took over, and the youth would immediately become physical.

When he was young (age 7 or 8,) he had just such an episode. Under duress, he bit himself in the forearm; the teacher immediately attempted to restrain him. Unfortunately, the amygdala was fully in control, and the resulting physical struggle resulted in a 'violent' label for the child, which continues to plague his school file a decade later.

At the end of this section, we'll return to the idea that learning is state-dependent. For now, we'll set that notion aside while we consider childhood development more fully.

The Effects of Movement On Learning

As infants, we use all of the different senses available to us to learn about our body and the environment around us. We have to make decisions based on stimuli received from our senses to tell us whether we are safe and able to explore new things; or if we are in danger, and need to react for safety through crying or staying away from harm. It is through movement that we are able to learn these things; the more complex the movements become, the more we are able to learn. Scientists have now discovered a direct relationship between areas of the brain responsible for movement and areas of the brain used for learning. Movement is hardwired into our system to trigger cognitive action. If we skip over certain movements - such as crawling, moving straight to walking instead - we will have missed out on some important cognitive development. Later in life, this could re-emerge learning disability. This also means that we are able to develop these cognitive processes through movement at any age.

The Evolutionary Process

The first nerve cells appear on organisms that lived around 500,000,000 years ago. Organisms created this 'analog' system of stimulus/response to coordinate movement, which would allow the single-celled creature to move in search of food. Until that point, an organism would have to wait for very simple sources of food – amino acids, very simple carbon strings – to enter its cell on its own, through diffusion.

For example, jellyfish and sea anemone, which were the first animals to create nerve cells, had an evolutionary advantage over sea sponges, which are incapable of movement and thus must wait for the nutrients to arrive on their own, by chance.

The coordination and sophistication of the more complex nervous systems in modern animals took millions of generations to produce. Trial and error, eons of stagnation, and a few jumps forward gave preferential advantage to the animal who could use more complex series of movement, even though that movement was still largely reflexive and reactive.

Despite all those millions of years of development, the goal of the nervous system remains the same: to move the being. As we age, the function of the nervous system loses efficacy, and one of the greatest hallmarks of age is the inflexibility of body and mind, and decreased movement.

Development from these simple-celled fauna to the exceedingly complex system that we now enjoy was a very long process. Consider that we STILL don't have a computer that can reason; experience emotion; forecast accurately; or apply logic beyond the data given in a mathematical way.

Our modern Nervous System has developed both by addition AND subtraction of function. While it's adapted to perform a very wide variety of tasks, and now controls our metabolism, movement, hormonal response, and response to thought, it's also been required to shed some of its less-vital functionality along the way. Consider the difference between short-term and long-term memory; while it's important that we remember things that are important to our well-being, other extraneous occurrences aren't critical to our survival, and are quickly forgotten. If we remembered EVERYTHING, we'd have trouble accessing important information quickly, because the selection of available data would be too diverse.

In turn, these selection procedures enhanced the functional capabilities of our Nervous System. As our needs as a species changed, our Nervous System developed to allow for things like differentiation (not all food is edible, or beneficial), alertness (arousal states when in danger, hungry, or excited), metabolism of different nutrients, and even body anthropomorphism (changes in body type and functionality.)

The evolution of the human brain occurred in the same way: from simple to complex. The billions of cells in our brains have been present for some time, but the connections between each are relatively new in the great scheme, and are still being developed. Evolution is NOT over.

While less-complex organs like the heart or liver serve only one or two purposes, the brain is far more multifunctional. However, it has still followed Darwin's Theory of Evolution by ridding itself of unnecessary or redundant processes as part of its development. Certain mutations took place within the nervous system as the human body evolved. Just as the body changed to adapt to the new needs of humanity, so too did the brain grow and become more complex.

An interesting debate in the anthropological community is the chicken-and-egg scenario of skull size and brain size. While some argue that the skull is already as large as possible in relation to the neck's ability to support weight, the spine's curvature, and the shoulder girdle, others reason that the skull's size is determined by the size of the brain. Through the last decades, this debate has brought on skull measurement as a means of assessing intelligence (a theory thoroughly discredited); searching for 'bumps' on the head; and even the late-night 'B'-grade science-fiction movies, in which visiting aliens have giant foreheads to hold their giant brains.

Consider this, though: if our brains were permitted to grow unimpeded by the skull, would the connections between cells be as dense? Would individual areas work as well together? Would information be accessible as quickly? As the adage goes, small houses mean few arguments.

Our ancient, pre-hominid ancestors acquired 'new and improved' sensors to help them survive in a very hostile world. The brain had to adapt, then, to allow for the senses to develop, including sight; hearing; touch; smell; and, later, speech. Each of these new tools required a high level of new brain interactivity, which in turn made other processes possible.

Today, when we see a tiger approaching us, we automatically enter a 'fight or flight' mode that's been programmed into our systems by thousands of years of experience. This was not always the case. The Darwinian model explains each of these automatic responses by the theory of Natural Selection: those who could process the 'danger' signal best fled earliest, and survived to pass the ability on to their children. Those who thought, "nice kitty!" were eaten.

As the nervous system was forced to become more complex, it gained capacity. A single-cell organism doesn't have a working memory, because there are no connections upon which to store data. An organism with two cells, though, can store tiny pieces of data on the connection between the cells for very short periods, until that bond is broken and reformed to store NEW data. Evolution dictated more brain cells, and more connections, and that meant more 'hard-drive' space for storing and processing information.

It's critical to understand the evolutionary process of the

brain so that we may understand the mysteries of human behaviour, emotion, and cognition. In "*The Emotional Brain,*" Joseph LeDoux[7] breaks apart the origins of human emotions and links them to our complex reaction processes, which were developed to help us survive.

According to LeDoux, emotions – unconscious feelings – originate in a very old part of the brain (the amygdala.) These emotions override our conscious thoughts, making them irrelevant. For instance, there were many times in our development when 'Fight' was necessary; there were many times when 'Flight' was necessary; and there were other times when "Avoid Confrontation" was critical.

Survival of the Beta Wolf, the second-in-command in a wolf pack, depends not only on his dominance over Wolf #3, but also in his subjugation to the Alpha Wolf. If he confronts the Alpha Wolf in an aggressive manner, he's cast out or killed.

Drug dealers, too, learn to 'fit in with the pack' or be left on their own in the urban wild. Belonging to the group means subjugation to the leader, including the receipt of abuse. Challenges to the leader of the gang will mean death, physical abuse, and social dismemberment. In a less dramatic example, teenage girls have been shown to 'tone down' their intelligence when in a group of their peers, so as not to pose a 'threat' to the social Alphas.

We call this 'learned helplessness.' An extreme example is Stockholm syndrome, where a captive subjugates himself to his kidnapper or torturer to avoid abuse, and eventually rationalizes the behaviours of his tormentor. In time, even pretending to sympathize with the aggressor can lead to a REAL bond and shared viewpoints. Tell an

7   Ledoux, Joseph E. The Emotional Brain: The Mysterious Underpinnings of Emotional Life.Simon & Schuster, 1998.

abused child that she 'deserves' a beating, and many times they'll come to believe it's true. Tell a student that he's bad a math, and the logical outcome is the belief that math is beyond him. When a child starts to fall into the role of learned helplessness, it's a long road to recovery.

LeDoux also argues that our emotional responses are permanently wired through evolution, but our REACTIONS to those emotional triggers are learned through experience. Taking candy from a baby, for instance, will trigger a tantrum; taking candy from a coworker will trigger only masked irritation.

Phobias and post-traumatic stress are malfunctions in the processing of these emotions. These conditions are very real, exist on a broad spectrum (you can have a 'little' phobia or a 'large' one with paralyzing effects, depending on the situation) and should be further studied as a means of better understanding the reaction to emotion-triggering stimuli.

LeDoux claims that our emotional systems evolved as a way of coordinating physical reactions to meet external stimuli. Therefore, emotion could not exist "without a body attached to the brain that is trying to have the feeling." We have developed responses to a very wide variety of stimuli, but NEW stimuli would find us unprepared until we adapt.

Larger changes in our environment require a longer period of adaptation. For example, let's imagine that the air we breathe decreases in oxygen content overnight. To metabolize the oxygen from the air as efficiently as we do now, we'd need to improve our system. One way may be to increase the surface area of the alveoli in our lungs, which would mean either greater density of alveoli, or bigger lungs. If our lungs were required to grow, our chest cavity would necessarily have to expand, and our diaphragm would have to become more powerful to expand and contract the larger lungs. People who developed this larger chest cavity first would therefore have a genetic advantage over the rest of us; survive longer, and produce more offspring; and eventually become the genetic majority.

In an example from our own history, Jared Diamond[8] makes the case for skin colour on the basis of migration and the availability of vitamin "D" from the sun. Humans in the more southern climates had access to more sunlight (and thus, more vitamin 'D',) and therefore didn't need to create as much melatonin in their skin. Melatonin captures and synthesizes the vitamin 'D' from the sun, but also turns the skin pale; humans in more northerly climates, then, produced more melatonin and had paler skin through which to absorb the sunlight available.

There is an association between low levels of Vitamin 'D' and cognitive impairment, but inadequate levels of Vitamin D does not cause cognitive decline. Sufficient levels, - maintained through food or supplementation - will improve cognition through a number of mechanisms - by increasing acetylcholine concentration in the brain, which increases neurotrophin synthesis, which enhances neuroprotection against neurodegeneration and diseases such as Alzheimer's.

Throughout the brain are Vitamin D receptors, which affect proteins involved with learning and memory, motor

8   Diamond, Jared M. Guns, Germs and Steel: The Fates of Human Societies. W W Norton and Company, 1999.

control, and possibly social functions as well. Previous research has linked vitamin D deficiency to global cognitive impairment in elderly women. Researchers from France recently published the results of a community survey which has explored the association between vitamin d intake and cognitive performance in older adults.

Sources of Vitamin D include fatty fish, along with fortified milk. For vegans, mushrooms are the only natural source of Vitamin D aside from sunlight exposure.

The best source of Vitamin D? The sun! Our skins can synthesize Vitamin D from ultraviolet light. Increasing sun exposure carefully – by a few minutes without sunscreen, and then adding sunscreen to protect against sunburn – is a very simple way to increase Vitamin D in the brain.

Our modern-day Nervous System is built from over 100 billion neural cells; connections between the cells are estimated at around ten times that amount. This means that the total amount of connections made within the brain are virtually immeasurable, and that our capacity far exceeds our ability to fill it within a lifetime.

The growth cycle for both our brain and body is the same: when presented with a new stimulus, the brain responds. This stimulus comes from the external world, and our response can be either internal OR external. Both stimulus and response require movement, however.

Our basic cognitive processes such as perception, categorization, attention, memory, language, problem solving, decision making, comprehension, representation and imagery all rely on our ability to move. They were all created by– and continue to rely on - our primitive reflexes that keep us alive. Eye tracking; hand movements; reaching; putting hand to mouth, putting foot to mouth; kicking; asymmetrical tonic neck reflex; rolling over; lifting your head; crawling; standing; crawling; and eventually, walking and running....each cause a change in the brain. Those changes facilitate the development of the cognitive processes above; we couldn't have memory, for instance, if we had never learned to move our eyes, because we would not have developed enough neural connectivity. The response to the physical stimulus has created the ability to develop the cognitive capacity.

Movement, thus, affects the capacity of the brain through cell splitting and rewiring. But it also changes the chemistry of the brain, which determines WHICH information is stored, and with what priority.

Hebbian Theory and Engrams

Hebbian theory attempts to explain how neurons connect themselves to become engrams.

> "Let us assume that the persistence or repetition of a reverberatory activity (or "trace") tends to induce lasting cellular changes that add to its stability.... When an axon of cell A is near enough to excite a cell B and repeatedly or persistently takes part in firing it, some growth process or metabolic change

takes place in one or both cells such that A's efficiency, as one of the cells firing B, is increased."

A more simple explanation: Cells that fire together, wire together.

"The general idea is an old one, that any two cells or systems of cells that are repeatedly active at the same time will tend to become 'associated', so that activity in one facilitates activity in the other." (Hebb 1949)[9]

"When one cell repeatedly assists in firing another, the axon of the first cell develops synaptic knobs (or enlarges them if they already exist) in contact with the soma of the second cell." (Hebb 1949)

Engrams are memory traces stored as biophysical or biochemical changes in the brain (and other neural tissue) in response to external stimuli.

They are also sometimes referred to as a "neural network" or "memory fragment." Engrams are an all-encompassing phrase for the connections discussed earlier in this chapter. While no one disputes the existence of engrams, their exact mechanism and location has been the focus of persistent research for nearly a century. Research in the field of neuropsychology – even neurophysiology – is far from exhaustive – there's still a lot of turf to be uncovered.

Sequencing

Sequencing is the ability to recognize a process and carry out the steps in the right order to completion.

---

9   Hebb, D.O. *The organization of behavior*. New York: Wiley & Sons (1949).

Studies have clearly validated the idea that ADD is a reliable predictor of motor skill deficiencies. It's also been shown that children with motor skill deficiencies experience restricted reading abilities.

Since complex relationships with our environment can't be avoided, relying on both sensory data and appropriate translation of the data, it's important to improve the brains of students to meet these challenges. As children age, they're required to carry out more complex patterns requiring multiple steps both at school and at home – and, later, in the workplace.

The knowledge that there is significant interaction between neural networks involved in ADHD and motor recruitment gives us a tremendous tool: the ability to improve sequencing ability using exercise-based treatment.

A student's ability to improve motor skill ability impacts her ability to sequence movements or cognitive skills. It's critical to academic success to be able to correctly sequence data, events, or processes, and this capacity can be enhanced through physical practice. Exercises and combinations that have been designed to improve these neural connections for movement are also very beneficial to improve their use for logic, as we've shown earlier.

Working Memory

The ability to transfer information into a memory is essential to the learning process. It is a core Executive Function, and efficiency at storing and retrieving memories is what gives us the ability to multitask.

When reading, our ability to hold information allows us to

make inferences; keep meanings of a sentence while decoding an unfamiliar word; make connections and relationships with other information. In mathematics, we are able to compute multistep equations, apply formulae and solve multistep problems. In Language, the presence of a high functioning Working Memory is illustrated when ideas and words flow right off the tongue or pen without interruption.

We sometimes take for granted how our memories are formed. To recap, we receive information through our senses, attach an emotion to it and store it according to its perceived relevance. When we forget information like a date, name, or place, the blame is typically directed towards ourSELVES: "I'm having a senior moment." "I don't have a good memory." "I'm ADD." It's not our SELF that is to blame, though; we simply haven't created a bond to the memory in the form of a familiar picture, smell, sound, taste, colour, or feel. We haven't created context around the memory, and therefore our brain simply doesn't deem the information important enough to remember easily.

We all have the capacity to hold information in the brain; it would be impossible to survive without it an efficient memory, and efficient implicit reactions (also a form of memory.) We CAN increase the capacity to hold information through proper practice, even at old age, or when labelled as having a Learning Disability.

Ignite! has been making some very remarkable breakthroughs recently during working memory sessions. Clients are remembering personal schedules, 10-digit phone numbers, and adding together 6-digit numbers in their head. Tasks that were said to have been lost due to brain injury or lacking because of a learning disability are now both accessible and smoothly efficient. "I feel smart!" said one client, who scored 100% on his biology test on blood flow through the body - after two sessions.

"I wish that phone number I remembered was real!"

another client spouted, as she recalled the fake phone number she had used to practice this skill.

The *Ignite!* method for increasing working memory puts the responsibility into the hands of the individual. As you'll read later in the Delivery Section, rather than adapting the material to better suit the learner, we are adapting the learner to improve how they approach the material. By creating an emotional attachment to the information received, they can form a connection to the information. To strengthen the connection, proper and persistent practice is then applied. Over and over and over and over.......

In a very relevant recent study[10] prospective memory was tested using different methods of learning.

Researchers used children of different ages and tested their memories using tasks that were time-based, activity-based, and event-based. Children remembered event-based tasks significantly better, and IQ, working memory, and inhibition all improved when the children were exposed to more event-based learning.

From Results: "Results of the study highlight the importance of contextual cues, such as activities and events, for prospective remembering in children. In addition, they have provided a general picture of PM [Prospective Memory] development in school-age children and have implications for educators and parents."

This study examined the ability of children to recall details based on time. In a time-based environment, where children would be asked to remember details in the order that they occurred (for instance, in a normal classroom,) students had a low recall rate. They could recall details better from specific activities, but best when associated with a one-time event. It's interesting to note

10("The Development of Prospective Memory in Typically Developing Children." Yang, Chan, Shum. In American Psychological Association 2011)

that the data the children were asked to recall didn't relate to the actual event, but the heightened awareness and contextual associations around the event helped them recall their lessons from that date.

These three studies combine to underscore one of the main points of *Ignite!*, using the Good-Better-Best paradigm:

1. *Good* - any exercise before study.

2. *Better* - more exercise, and exercise breaks during study.

3. *Best* - Exercise 'interventions' during study that incorporates contextual learning (creating stories, pictures, or other context around the lesson.)

Another study that's relevant in this section is *"Enhancing visuospatial learning: The benefit of retrieval practice".*[11]

In this study, researchers attempted to teach students a foreign script (Chinese characters) through several different methods, and tested their retrieval (ability to recall the information.) It's been shown in several previous studies that information may be permanently stored in the brain, but not retrievable without extreme measures (hypnosis, various pharmaceuticals.) While no exact proportions have been estimated, it's safe to assume that even if we fail to recall 10% of the information we have stored in our brains, we're missing a massive piece. While our most popular system of rote memorization in schools focuses on how much information we're putting INTO the students' minds, it's now clear that we should also focus on helping them get the information back OUT again as well.

Researchers used several methods to aid recall, but they revolved around three central themes:

[11] Enhancing visuospatial learning: The benefit of retrieval practice." Kang, in Memory & Cognition. Dec 2010, Vol 38, Iss. 8: 1009-1018

1. repetition
2. associative pairings
3. contextual cues.

Repetition: the students simply repeated the Chinese characters and their matching English words over and over.

There are several small organs involved in vestibular sensation. From them we gather information about the head's position relative to the ground. These are the most sensitive of all the sensory organs, lying in the mastoid bone and part of the inner ear. They include the utricle, saccule, semicircular canals, and vestibular nuclei of the medulla and pons. The vestibular nuclei, a plexus of neurons lying in the medulla oblongata and pons, carries impulses from the semicircular canals and cerebellum to the Reticular Activating System (RAS) in the brain stem. The RAS is a nerve reticulum which extends from the hindbrain (medulla oblongata and pons) to midbrain and make contact with the forebrain. This system alerts the neocortex to novel or significant stimuli or changes in the state of the sensory information being processed. This is similar to the way in which novel experiences switch on Nucleus Basalis, which release Acetylcholine a neurostransmitter involved in memory and learning, RAS gets us ready to take in and respond to our environment and to learn.

Associative pairings: To cue you to remember that a symbol stands for "bread," I say, "toast." When I point to a Chinese symbol and say, "toast," you're expected to remember that the symbol represents the word, "bread."

Contextual cues: If I show you the Chinese word for 'table,' I note that it bears a resemblance to a table with two eggs falling off. I could also group symbols together - 'table,' 'chair,' 'meal,' 'fork' - to see if the picture created aids in memory.

From the conclusions: "the subjects who had practised retrieval [contextual cues] were more accurate at writing/drawing the Chinese characters than were those who had studied repeatedly [repetition cues.] The same result was replicated when learning condition was manipulated within subjects....however, the subjects seemed unaware that retrieval practice was more effective than repeated studying."

Contextual cues - creating a story, rephrasing the problem, building a picture in the mind - is better for creating memories that can be easily recalled. However, most teachers and students don't yet appreciate the difference.

Synaesthesia

Daniel Tammet knows that the number '9' isn't really out to hurt him.

Though large and towering, the number '9' isn't as bad as the number, "289," which Tammet describes as "particularly ugly."

Synaesthesia is a condition where one sense elicits others. Tammet, known for his 2006 book, *"Born On A Blue Day,"*[12] is well-known for his very vivid synesthesia.

Every integer, to Tammet, up to 10,000 has its own unique colour, texture, taste and feel. "25," for example, is very attractive: "The kind of number you would invite to a party." This is a helpful trait: Tammet holds the European record for remembering the most consecutive digits of Pi - 22,514 digits - and can 'see' results of calculations without conscious effort.

Tammet is also a hyperpolyglot - someone who is fluent in more than six languages - and once rose to the challenge of becoming conversational in Icelandic in a single week. He claims to have learned Spanish over a

---

12 Tammet, Daniel. Born on a Blue Day. Hodder (Feb 22 2007)

weekend.

While Tammet's sort of savanthood receives a lot of attention and praise - he's now written his second bestseller, and has been on 60 Minutes and David Letterman, synaesthesia can also be paralyzing. For instance, Tammet (who changed his last name from 'Corney,' because it didn't fit with the way he saw himself) hates brushing his teeth because of the scraping sound the toothbrush makes.

In more extreme cases, students shy away from negative associations with numbers and letters. Imagine if the number "three" evoked a putrid, rotting smell, which you experienced just as realistically as if an old, wet running shoe were pressed under your nose. Alternately, what if the colour blue triggered a loud hum - could you remain in a blue room for long without being distracted?

As with many other types of savant syndrome, synaesthesia appears, on first glance, to be an interesting trait with many advantages. However, it's a challenging syndrome to handle; is most often associated with Asperger's syndrome; and can appear in milder doses, too.

Consider the ramifications for contextual learning, however: synesthetes automatically link colour, sound, smell or other senses to memories. Some are positive, some are not; when we can CHOOSE the linked sense, we can overcome the potentially negative feedback associated with numbers, people, words, or places. It's a powerful tool.

Exercise and Pain

While the subject of exercise's pain-reducing benefits are not central to our theme of cognitive benefit, it's an important peripheral benefit. Frequently, brain injury or cognitive impairment go hand in hand with physical injury, and not just to the spinal cord.

While we can improve comprehension and memory with exercise, the inverse is also true: LACK of exercise can cause a dulling of the senses and deterioration of mental capacity. Since limited mobility and movement is a leading cause of musculoskeletal injury and chronic pain, parents, teachers and coaches are bound to come across cases in which they have to deal with both the brain issues and body issues together.

Exercise can treat depression - it's well documented to be more powerful than most antidepressant drugs. Exercise will improve memory, and cure a host of problems while preventing even more.

In particular, exercise leads to the release of certain neurotransmitters in the brain that alleviate pain, both physical and mental. It's also one of the very few stimulants that causes the brain to produce NEW neurons.

Much of the research done in this area has focused on running, but running – while beneficial – is not magical to the exclusion of all else. The key is elevated heart rate, which can be accomplished through a very wide variety of modalities.

The pain-reducing nature of exercise works in several ways: neurogenesis, mood enhancement, and endorphin release. These are powerful chemicals that effect the reward centres of the brain, just like highly addictive drugs like morphine. Exercise, though, is not typically habit-forming to the point of physical dependance for mood elevation. It can be used at will, avoided for a few days, and picked up again. It works immediately, and provides a long-term benefit.

Neurogenesis is the creation of new neurons in the hippocampus. The hippocampus is the very centre of learning and memory in the brain. While the exact sequence and stimuli for neurogenesis is still being uncovered, the prevailing theory among scientists is that the mild stress generated by exercise stimulates an influx of calcium, which activates transcription factors in existing hippocampus neurons.

The transcription factors kick off the secretion of the BDNF gene, which creates BDNF proteins that act to promote neurogenesis. BDNF also repairs the myelin sheath protecting the axon, which helps to reinforce the recruitment path of information AND prolong the destructive effects of axon-destroying diseases like Multiple Sclerosis. As the theory goes, generation of BDNF is a protective response to stress, and BDNF acts not only to generate new neurons, but also to protect existing neurons and to promote synaptic plasticity. Signals are transmitted across the synaptic cleft between neurons more efficiently, which means that recall comes more quickly and easily.

Interestingly, until the last decade, most physicians were warning their clients with Multiple Sclerosis to avoid exercise. Since BDNF was present during periods of physical regression, many assumed that the BDNF was causing the damage to the myelin sheath, rather than acting to protect the axon. As a result, many MS sufferers avoided exercise, which would likely have delayed onset of their worst symptoms. Science is ever-

As mentioned, BDNF's effects are more than protective, they are *reparative*. In a comparison between sedentary and active mice, scientists found that active mice regenerated more sciatic axons post-injury than sedentary mice. This effect was not observed when the active mice were injected with a neurotrophin-blocking agent, suggesting that exercise stimulates injured neurons to regenerate axons by secreting BDNF, and that this occurs through physical stress. In this case, physical stress is of a comparatively mild nature (exercise) rather than a traumatic or chronic nature (the injury ITSELF didn't trigger BDNF release.) That's significant to our theory.

Beginning around age 30, humans start to lose nerve tissue. Exercise that increases heart rate reinforces neural connections by increasing the number of dendrite connections between neurons, creating a denser network, which is then better able to process and store information.

In a more extreme example, diseases such as Alzheimer's and Parkinson's, which speed up the rate of neuron loss, could possibly see a reduction of symptoms and the slowing of the downward progression through exercise. Science has already demonstrated a strong correlation between healthier lifestyles and a reduction in the severity of Alzheimer's. In mice, exercise has been shown to decrease the rate of loss of dopamine-containing neurons for those infected with Parkinson's. BDNF may be starting to sound like a 'miracle drug,' and its benefits aren't fully uncovered yet. The favourite neurotrophic chemical of John Ratey (author of "Spark,") BDNF is frequently referred to as "miracle-Gro for the brain."

But wait...there's more! BDNF is also a trigger for serotonin release, and since exercise increases BDNF production directly, there is a reinforcement of the serotonin-BDNF loop, and the exercise acts as a mood-enhancer.

Exercise And The Brain Healing Process

Injured neurons – whether from traumatic injury, like a car crash, or disease like Alzheimer's, can be stimulated to regenerate their axons by exercise. Axons, you will recall, are the 'telephone lines' of the nervous system, and their repair will mean faster processing time for spatial awareness, recall, memory, and other high-level cognitive functions.

According to a study published in the Proceedings of the National Academy of Sciences,
"Our experiments show that the nervous system responds to injury in the same way that it responds to activity that creates or eliminates connections needed for brain cells to communicate with one another," said Jeffery L. Twiss, head of Nemours neuroscience research lab and corresponding author of the study, titled "Voluntary Exercise Increases Axonal Regeneration From Sensory Neurons."[13]

Synaptic plasticity is enhanced by neuronal activity, and stronger connections are formed between neural pathways that are used frequently. Synapse function is made more efficient this way. Twiss' team and a group of researchers from UCLA, under the leadership of

13 Twiss, Jeffrey L., et al. Voluntary exercise increases axonal regeneration from sensory neurons. Proc Natl Acad Sci U S A. June 2004.

Fernando Gómez-Pinilla, each found that this plasticity can affect the ability of nerves to regenerate.[14]

Gómez-Pinilla, professor of neurosurgery and physiological science, has done experiments whose results demonstrate that following exercise, neurotrophin levels increase in the brain and spinal cord. As discussed earlier in this section, neurotrophins promote more synaptic plasticity, which is the underlying basis of high-order neural processes such as learning and memory, and walking. This research proves that monitored exercise – at the right time, in the right amounts, and of the right type - can be a powerful therapy to promote functional recovery after brain and spinal cord injury.

In one study, Twiss and Gomez-Pinilla's teams recorded the growth of sensory neurons from rats that had access to running wheels for zero, three or seven days.

The researchers saw that animals that had exercised grew longer neurites, a type of neuronal extension, compared to sedentary animals. Neurite length correlated directly with the distance that animals ran. This is important, because it demonstrates that MORE exercise will help create MORE neuronal growth; there isn't a tapering-off point. Exercise is dose-specific; more IS better, as long as overtraining is avoided.

To take the study further, the researchers destroyed the sciatic nerve of animals that had exercised for seven days prior to the injury. The animals that had exercised regenerated significantly more sciatic nerve axons than the sedentary animals. If the scientists blocked neurotrophin receptor activity with a chemical inhibitor prior to exercise, the activity-induced axon growth wasn't observed.

According to researchers, these results indicate that physical activity may alter synaptic plasticity and

---

14 Fernando Gómez-Pinilla, Voluntary Exercise Induces a BDNF-Mediated Mechanism That Promotes Neuroplasticity

regenerative capacity through the signalling of neurotrophic production.

"There is much work to be done, but we hope to take advantage of the molecular changes seen after exercise to optimize repair or regeneration of the nervous system in the future," Twiss said.

The Cerebellum makes up only 10% of the brain's total volume, but it contains more than 50% of its neurons. It's the area of the brain primarily associated with movement, and Jensen (1998)[15] refers to the cerebellum as a "virtual switchboard of cognitive activity."

The cerebellum is the area of the brain responsible for voluntary (not reflexive) physical movement, and is connected to all parts of the neocortex by neurons. High-order thinking occurs in the cerebellum, and Jensen (1998) points to nearly 80 studies suggesting a strong link between the movement and memory, spatial perception, language, attention, emotion, non-verbal cues, and decision-making.

Myelenation

Myelenation thickening occurs through practice (rehearsal); application of skill (context,) sleep, and memorable experiences. Malnutrition can limit myelenation; some studies suggest that supplementation with fish oil can encourage better myelenation.

The more myelenation occurs, the faster processing speeds may occur between both hemispheres of the brain.

The Corpus Collossum is the white matter joining the two hemispheres in the brain. It's responsible for the 'reward' sensation and feelings of pleasure. It's made of white

15Jensen, E. 1998. Teaching with the brain in mind. Alexandria, VA: ASCD.

matter – connective motor and sensory axons – and allows for cross-activation of both sides of the brain.

The more often cross-brain activation occurs through use, the more dendritic connections extend across the Corpous Colossum, and the heavier their myelination.

Just as the 'time under tension' principle changes the physical properties of muscle, 'time under activation' changes the characteristics of both hemispheres of the brain in a positive way.

Unconscious Learning

Our learning systems, as humans, use areas of the brain that also exist in the most primitive vertebrates like fish, reptiles, and amphibians. In a study from the Swedish medical university Karolinska Institutet[16], researchers investigated the limbic striatum – one of the oldest parts of the modern brain – and its ability to learn movements through repetition.

The limbic striatum predates most parts of the brain, including the cortex, which provides us with consciousness. Impulses, actions and reactions originating in the limbic striatum are largely automatic (like breathing or digesting,) rapid (pulling your hand away from a hot stove element) and very basic (stimulus-response.)

[16]Anke Karabanov, Simon Cervenka, Örjan de Manzano, Hans Forssberg, Lars Farde & Fredrik Ullén Dopamine D2 receptor density in the limbic striatum is related to implicit but not explicit movement sequence learning *PNAS, online early edition 5 - 9 April 2010*

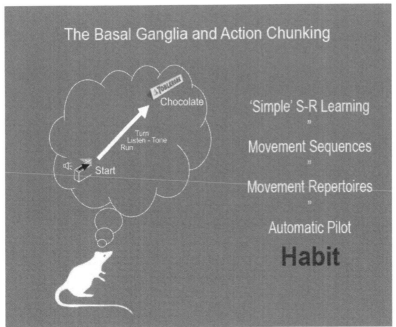

The Basal Ganglia and Action Chunking

'Simple' S-R Learning

Movement Sequences

Movement Repertoires

Automatic Pilot

Habit

"Our results strongly substantiate the theories that say that the implicit, by which I mean non-conscious, learning systems of the brain are simpler and evolutionarily older," says Associate Professor Fredrik Ullén from Karolinska Institutet and the Stockholm Brain Institute.

When we perform a movement that has become automatic to us – tying our shoes, typing – we're still relying on a sequence of tiny movements that must be carried out in the correct order. We learn these skills through one of two learning systems:

1) Implicit – we learn without the awareness that we're learning;

2) Explicit – we're aware of what we're doing, and consciously training ourselves through practice.

In Ullen's study, researchers examined both the implicit and explicit learning of motor sequences in relation to the number of dopamine D2 receptors in the basal ganglia. While they found a correlation between D2 receptor density and both forms of learning, they also noted that the oldest part, evolutionary-wise, of the basal ganglia -- the limbic striatum -- was only involved in implicit learning.

"In other words, we probably have certain fundamental learning systems in common not only with rats, mice and other mammals, but also with the most primitive vertebrates, which also have a limbic striatum," said Dr Ullén.

Recall that basal ganglia function is important to neuroplasticity. Disorders of the basal ganglia include Parkinson's and Huntington's, as well as several types of impaired motor skills.

Resistance Training and The Brain

To date, in most published literature regarding exercise and the brain, the discussion has centred around aerobic / anaerobic training: movement that increases the heart rate, flooding the brain with blood and stimulating the production of neurotrophins like BDNF and IGF-1. But resistance training – weightlifting, plyometrics, calisthenics, swimming, and bodyweight movement – also plays a huge role in the release of neurotrophins.

BDNF levels circulating in the brain increase after intense resistance training, says Joshua Yarrow, PhD[17], lead researcher and postdoctoral associate at the University of Florida in Gainesville. Exercise, he explains, is effective at protecting and improving brain function. Yarrow examined the effect of resistance training (including weightlifting) on levels of neuroprotective molecules like BDNF. Recall that BDNF serves the role

[17]Joshua F. Yarrow et al.Training augments resistance exercise induced elevation of circulating brain derived neurotrophic factor (BDNF) Neuroscience Letters Volume 479, Issue 2, 26 July 2010, Pages 161-165

of repairing the myelin sheath as well as aiding cognitive functions; the presence of BDNF, no matter what the trigger, will help with learning as well as protecting the neurobiology of the brain.

Yarrow's team put 20 college-aged men in a trial to determine whether repeated resistance exercise resulted in increased circulating BDNF at 1, 30, and 60 minutes after exercise. Serum BDNF was 23,304 ± 1,835 pg/mL at rest and increased 32% 1 minute after exercise ($P <$ .05). Serum BDNF levels returned to baseline within 30 minutes and was 41% below resting levels 60 minutes after exercise ($P < .01$).

The study shows that resistance exercise kickstarts a huge increase in circulating BDNF immediately after the workout. Previous studies have demonstrated the benefits of endurance exercise, and its potential to spur BDNF creation in the brain. However, BDNF is produced in many tissues, including muscles and endothelial tissue. Triggering the production of BDNF in other areas of the body with resistance training is relevant because we know that BDNF crosses the blood–brain barrier and can act within the brain.

Another study, presented at the ACSM General Meeting in 2010, demonstrates clearly that resistance exercise promotes the release of BDNF and other neurotrophic factors. This adds credence to the idea of using CrossFit-style programming to a student's educational day.

"The study reveals that resistance exercise induces a robust transient increase in circulating BDNF concentrations. It has been shown that during endurance training, BDNF is produced in the brain. But BDNF is produced in many tissues, including musculoskeletal tissue and endothelial tissue. The production of BDNF peripherally with resistance training, which might then affect the brain, is important because we know that BDNF crosses the blood–brain barrier and can act within

the brain," Dr. Yarrow said."[18]

Also important: BDNF levels returned to baseline 30 minutes postexercise, which means that for greatest effect, frequent interventions through the day (another *Ignite!* theory) are better than one long burst of exercise, which in turn is much better than nothing.

In short, it's not as important WHERE the BDNF is created, because it will eventually make its way into the brain with ease. Not every chemical can be produced in the body and cross the blood-brain barrier, but Yarrow asserts that this is possible with BDNF.

"Resistance exercise may essentially feed BDNF to the brain, which is why we see an increase in circulating levels immediately postexercise and then a decrease in protein within an hour," he states.

"This is important because we may be able to say that endurance exercise is not necessary for everyone who seeks the neuroprotective benefits of exercise. We may be able to tailor resistance training programs to optimize the exposure of neural tissue to neurotrophic factors like BDNF," Dr. Yarrow explained.

Increasing the presence of neurotrophins can have a positive effect on cognition, mood, emotions, and several other domains of brain function. J. Carson Smith, PhD, associate professor at the University of Wisconsin, Milwaukee, believes:

"In addition to the possibility that the BDNF circulates to the brain and crosses the blood–brain barrier to act in target tissues in the brain, it is possible that the BDNF is released peripherally and then is simply cleared from the circulation after a relatively short amount of time."

---

18 American College of Sports Medicine (ACSM) 57th Annual Meeting: Abstract 735. Presented June 2, 2010.

Neurogenesis – Other Considerations

It's clear that exercise alone is enough to increase neurogenesis in the hippocampus, and that this improves memory and learning. Newly-formed cells are activated much more than previously-existing cells. In addition, it's not a surprise that new cells with similar functions as the existing cells can lead to better performance on spatial memory tests like the Morris Water Maze, Y-Maze, T-Maze, and Radial Arm Maze tests. After all, many hands make light work, as the saying goes.

On the other hand, though, an environment with high stress or a lack of stimulation REDUCES neurogenesis and, thereby, intellectual capacity.

Physical activity is frequently prescribed for children as a means of experiencing "team building," an "ego-boost," a "confidence builder," or a "self-esteem enhancer." But these are not only empirical observations. In fact, fear conditioning (a biological response to stress in the hippocampus,) passive avoidance learning, and novel object recognition are ALL improved through physical activity, though they involve little movement themselves.

When you exercise, it's not just your physical fitness you're improving, but also your reaction to stressful situations and confrontation with new situations.

Summary

It should now be clear that exercise and physical movement play a critical role in developing the capacity to learn. Your brain REQUIRES movement to store information, grow larger, and form connections that help with language, recall, and other higher-level thinking.

The traditional 'benefits of exercise' – confidence, strength, heart health, weight control, self-esteem, etc – are typically touted as the best reason to include physical education in schools. Other advocates cite the need for children to "blow off steam" or "refocus" during the day, and those arguments are also very valid. As we've shown in this chapter, however, a lack of physical activity restricts the student's ability to absorb every other subject during the day.

Removing physical exercise from school is like entering a math contest with your mouth wired shut. Not only is it a handicap, but it makes the REST of the event more painful.

At *Ignite!*, we prefer to consider a situation from the perspective of "Good-Better-Best." Daily activity through active play during recess is good. Guided discovery and practice, including specific exercises to aid in focus, eye tracking, and information processing during a daily physical play time (ie, Phys. Ed.,) is better. Frequent 'interventions' – short, intense physical movement throughout the day – is best. As you'll see in subsequent chapters, *Ignite!* delivers the best-case scenario for improving learning both in the short- and long-term.

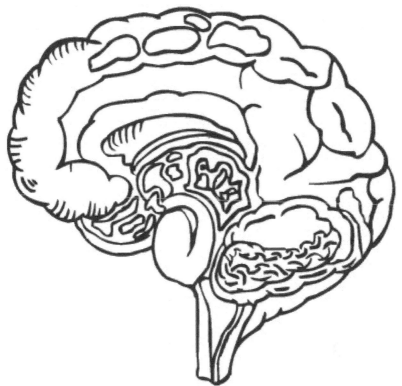

Activity: colour and label the parts of the brain, above.

Section II - Childhood development

When parents or support workers bring new students to

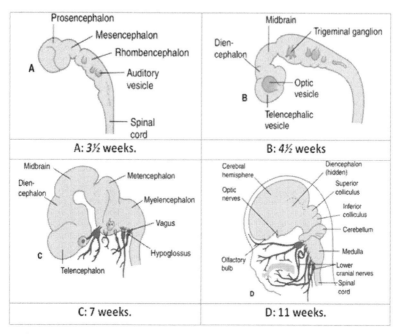

A: 3½ weeks.

B: 4½ weeks

C: 7 weeks.

D: 11 weeks.

Ignite! – or they find their way on their own – they're typically surprised by the questions they're asked. The first assessment includes the usual health history and chatting to build rapport; but soon, that gives way to pointed questions which often baffle the new student.

"Did you crawl much as an infant, or did you move straight to walking?"

"Did you have many ear infections when you were young?"

These questions are usually met with blank stares, but

as you'll see, they can greatly influence a human's development, from birth until death.

As Neuroscience and Neurobiology and the other areas of Brain Science develop and expand, scientists are slowly peeling back the layers of neural circuitry to understand how the brain develops over our lifetime. Considering the millions of precision engineering and sequencing calculations that go into one tiny movement – for example, breathing – it's beyond a miracle that ANYTHING works as well as we can.

Each neuron, measured in micrometers, links up with thousands of other neurons to form memories and series. If we measured the total length of these neurons, we'd wind up with around 62,000 miles *(Coveney & Highfield, 1995.)*[19]

Until very recently, researchers largely believed that the amount of 'wiring' available in our brains, and therefore our potential for higher-level thought, was predetermined by our genetic blueprints. However, we now know that only the main automated circuits – autonomic systems like breathing, digestion, and reflexes – are unalterable. Further, these 'original' circuits contain trillions of potential connections that remain to be 'programmed' or used.

Programming these connections is a result of experience, practice, stimulation and feedback from and in the environment. It is THIS stimulation and feedback that completes the brain's architecture.

Though the debate between 'nature' and 'nurture' is still a hot topic, the vast majority of psychological experts now

---

[19]Coveney, P., & Highfield, R. (1995). Frontiers of complexity: The search for order in a chaotic world. New York: Fawcett Columbine.

support a theory unifying the two. The precision required of the mature brain can only be achieved, we realize, by stimulation in the form of movement and sensory experiences during the early developing years *(Greenough and Black, 1992; Shatz, 1992.)*[20],[21]

As we saw earlier in Section 1, experience strengthens and bonds synapses, which are the connections made between neurons. Synapses which are NOT made by activity, or reinforced through experience, and shed quickly. The brain's overriding nature is to act efficiently, which means the discarding of 'waste' information that's unnecessary for survival. Information that isn't repeatedly used is deemed of less value; the bond is not strengthened, and is eventually discarded.

If the bond is reused, it becomes a more permanent part of the brain's circuitry. *Chugani (1998)*[22] demonstrated that, due to different experiences through life, not even identical twins share the same wiring.

Decades ago, when the 'nature/nurture' debate had its origins, scientists performed studies on the brain structures of animals. The animals were raised in various environments: normal, deprived, or enriched settings. 'Enriched' settings provided toys, treadmills, and challenges in the form of obstacle courses, climbable walls, or moving objects. These studies overwhelmingly showed that stimulation is a significant factor in long-term brain development *(Jones and Greenough, 1996;*

20 Greenough, W ., & Black, J. (1992).Induction of brain structure by experience: Substrate for cognitive development. In M. R. .Gunnar & C. A. Nelson (Eds.), *Minnesota symposia on child psychology*24: *Developmental behavioral neuroscience* (pp. .155-200). Hillsdale, NJ: Lawrence Erlbaum.

21 PENN, ANNA A.; SHATZ, CARLA J.Brain Waves and Brain Wiring: The Role of Endogenous and Sensory-Driven Neural Activity in Development Pediatric Research: April 1999 - Volume 45 - Issue 4, Part 1 of 2 - pp 447-458

22 Chugani, H. (1998).A critical period of brain development : Studies of cerebral glucose utilization with PET. *Preventive Medicine*, 27, 184-188.

Kempermann & Gage, 1999.)[23],[24] Animals placed in 'enriched' environments had larger brains and many more synaptic connections.

The Learning Hierarchy

Academic Higher Level Functioning: development of the higher intelligence relationships; schooling, reading, writing, etc .
Conception: making sense of the world
Language: Development of speech
Perception: Development of oculomotor functioning along with auditory and tactile competence
Motor Patterns: development of neural patterns required for movement
Postural Reflexes: development of the ability to be in an upright position and balance with force and gravity
Primitive Reflexes: Emergence and integration of survival reflexes

23 Jones, T., & Greenough, W. T. (1996). Ultrastructural evidence for increased contact between astrocytes and synapses in rats reared in a complex environment. Neurobiology of Learning & Memory, 65 (1), 48-56.

24 Kempermann, G., Kuhn, H., & Gage, F. (1997).More hippocampal neurons in adult mice living in an enriched environment. *Nature*,386, 493-495.

Compare the atmosphere of stimulation – that is, external challenge – to the current world in which children are raised: seated. Unstimulated. Not forced to confront new scenarios. Presented with the answers in advance. Given automated toys. Allowed to sit out challenging problem-solving scenarios. Hidden from confrontation. Allowed to be afraid to fail. Deprived of practice. In short, the kids aren't overstimulated; it's just *all too easy.*

"When I was your age...." your grandfather started, finishing with an incredible story of walking barefoot to school in a snowstorm, up a mountain... but he may have been right: things aren't challenging enough to teach us the valuable lessons we NEED to cope anymore. In attempting to make our world more efficient, we've made it too simplistic; now, we confront with anxiety those situations which our forefathers wouldn't have blinked over. One of the great opportunities for insight into this phenomena is the obsession with 'perfect.' Perfectionism will be addressed later in this text, but suffice to say that "waiting for perfect" creates far more problems than "hoping for the best" ever could.

Gross Motor Control

Like trying to paint with a wet noodle, the fingers are unable to be precise without a strong and stable support system. If we are able to sit up straight, hold our heads without our hands, and maintain good head position, we are going to receive accurate information through our vestibular system because our perception of our environment is clear and balanced. If strength or stability are weak in the shoulder or trunk, the fine motor control in the hand begins to suffer, and writing skills quickly follow. Improving the strength and stability of the shoulder and trunk is not only beneficial to the writing process, but also in the development and maintenance of a strong and healthy body.

To improve the strength and stability of the shoulder and trunk throughout the day, Ignite! students participate in the exercise interventions that challenge the trunk and shoulder **before** long periods of sitting, and mobility interventions **after** long periods of sitting to maintain flexibility in the hips, chest and back.

Many practitioners of Yoga may not realize that their beautiful exercises were developed hundreds of years ago as a means to prepare the body for education and meditation immediately before and after long periods of sitting. When mindfulness and focus were required, ancient practitioners of Buddhism knew that proper physical training was required to remove the distracting potential limitations of the body.

Giving students the ability to strengthen the trunk and shoulder during lengthy sitting assignments can increase their productivity in academics; increase the duration of focus and attention during seated activities; and when they eventually do get a chance to move, they will be as limber as a leopard.

Fine Motor Control

Many actions in the classroom require the coordination of small muscle movements and the eyes to create precise and accurate actions. There are many contributing factors to the development of fine motor control in handwriting, including: the developmental environment; vision; attitude, emotion and motivation; attention and memory; and gross motor control. Insufficiency in any of these areas could be the culprit for poor handwriting. For our purposes, however, spatial awareness is frequently the main focus of practise, because it can be influenced and greatly improved through exercise. Fine-motor skills- like handwriting - have many visual-spatial interactions necessary to discern things like direction, size, shape, slope, and positioning. Difficulties with spatial awareness will result in inaccurate strokes, choppy lines and inconsistent shapes, which makes notes difficult to read. Through proper practice and appropriately-guided progressions, improvements in spatial awareness can be made through exercise.

Activities to help improve fine motor skills include colouring inside the lines; drawing straight lines and geometrical shapes with measurements; picking up small objects; using tweezers or chopsticks; following lines with scissors; using buttons or snaps; stringing beads; molding clay or putty; and playing with Lego or building blocks.

Perception

Perception is a complex system relying on the coordination of vision, comprehension and motor skills. *For the purpose of creating a program that improves perception skills in handwriting, we will only focus on the controllable factors: vision, comprehension and fine/gross motor skills. Other decisive factors in the formation of one's perception skills are shaped by: prior knowledge, cultural upbringing, environmental and developmental circumstances, and therefore must be taken into consideration when evaluating their work.* Perception is the ability to:

- use visual information and turn it into meaning
- recognize letters, recall what a letter looks like, discriminate between two familiar letters such as "b" and "d".
- identify when two images are similar, but different
- compare a problem to a previous experience or other relevant data

Aside from problems with vision, improving perception can be done through activities that challenge students to find letters and shapes in:

- ⅄ different languages/alphabets
- ⅄ objects around the room or outside
- ⅄ scrambled words
- ⅄ overlapping letters, and abstract objects
- ⅄ Copying letters, shapes, drawings, cursive words, pictures and using different fonts
- ⅄ Making letters out pipe cleaners, sand, or drawing in the rest of a partial letter.

Academic and Motor Skills Relationships Summary

Academic Skills

Focus/Attention	Reading	Math	Written/Oral Language	General Knowledge
Safety and Survival Needs	Making Connections	Deduction	Abstraction	Induction
Whole-Brain Synthesis	Sequencing	Analysis	Sequence Formation	Organization
Noticing	Visualization	Pattern Recognition	Verbal communication	Memory and Reason
Cross-Pattern Movements	Midline-Crossing Movements	Eye/foot coordination	Spatial Awareness	Hand/eye and hand/foot coordination
Autonomy / Equilibrium	Dynamic Balance	Bodily Awareness	Three-dimensional Laterality	Locomotor Skills

Developmental Motor Skills

On the bottom of the chart above are basic motor skills, developed at different stages through early childhood. Each is necessary for the development of the skill above. A child begins with tasks at the bottom of the chart, and progresses upward from motor skills toward academic skills as they learn. Different children may be at different levels of academic skill at the same age, depending on practice and fluency in motor skills.

For example, a child whose sense of dynamic balance has not been developed in the vestibular system will not be successful with midline-crossing movements (opposing limbs move) like crawling. Children who are unable to recognize patterns in their environment will struggle with math; students whose safety or survival needs aren't met will struggle with attention and focus.

Upward progress through this chart parallels the progression from lower-brain to higher-brain thinking. Using the last example, a child who bears anxiety over social isolation, hunger, or lack of sleep will necessarily prioritize those states, which are required by more basic brain functions. Recall the example from the beginning of Section II: the brain is like the internet built on top of a calculator, which is in turn built on top of an abacus. All must be operating at once, and high-level functioning is limited by the WEAKEST level of processing.

Another connection: Maslow's Hierarchy of Needs, which we'll discussion more in the "Delivery of *Ignite!* In The Classroom" section to come.

Sleep and Brain Development

Most mammals have two distinct phases of sleep: SW (slow-wave) sleep, and REM (Rapid Eye Movement,) which is the deeper phase. Most dreaming occurs during REM sleep, but not all.

In children and young adults, growth hormone is released during deep sleep. This growth hormone is necessary for the addition of dendrites, expansion of the brain, and increased bloodflow to the brain.

Activity in the parts of the brain that control emotion, social interaction, and decision-making ability is reduced during deep sleep. This suggests that optimal brain function for these tasks requires long periods of rest.

In our culture, stress created from social interaction – whether face-to-face, over the telephone, on facebook, or while texting – is completely pervasive. Personal time that was set aside for 'isolation' a decade ago – quiet time after school, alone time walking home – has now been besieged by the constant stimulus of the cell phone and smartphone.

Since the brain's systems, like human muscular systems, recover and grow stronger while at rest – that is, after a stimulus has been removed – it stands to reason that parts of the brain built for social interaction also require periods of rest in order to progress and mature.

In one study, researchers at the University of California[25] examined brain plasticity in young cats who had just been exposed to a new environment. Cats who were allowed to sleep afterward developed twice the amount of brain change as their counterparts who didn't sleep. And more animal studies demonstrate that sleep can dramatically enhance changes in brain connections: REM sleep is when the brain reorganizes its connections, says Michael P. Stryker, Ph.D. This is the type of sleep that we fall into when we first go to sleep, and accounts for about half the total sleep time of babies

(who sleep up to 3x as much as adults.)

This is called 'procedural learning,' and Dr. Robert Stickgold from Harvard Medical School concluded that REM sleep "seems to be essential for learning how to do things."[26] During the REM phase, the brain integrates information that it collected – but didn't have time to process – during the day.

A study of rat brains showed that parts of the brain that received new encoding during the day were also very active at night, suggesting that this pattern repetition may help encode memories and improve learning. This can only happen while in REM sleep; if this part of the sleep cycle is shortened or skipped, a whole day's worth of learning could possibly be jeopardized.

REM sleep also enhances emotional memory, which is a technique we use at *Ignite!* to promote the embedding of information. Essentially, data with an emotional tie is more likely to become permanently embedded, more efficiently recollected, and recalled more accurately than bland data. German scientists at the University of Bambridge Department of Physiological Psychology found that "late sleep particularly enhanced memory for emotional texts. This enhancement was highly significant in comparison with memory for neutral texts."[27] This may be because neutral texts are poorly recalled, and therefore do not require the repetition and imprinting

---

26 Robert Stickgold, PhD; Matthew P. Walker, PhSleep and Memory: The Ongoing Debate Department of Psychiatry, Harvard Medical School and Center for Sleep and Cognition Beth Israel Deaconess Medical Center, Boston, MA

27 Ullrich WagnerSteffen Gais,and Jan Born. Emotional Memory Formation Is Enhanced across Sleep Intervals with High Amounts of Rapid Eye Movement SleepLearn. Mem. 2001. 8: 112-119

necessary for information deemed worthy of long-term storage. "Results are consistent with a supportive function of REM sleep for the formation of emotional memory in humans," said the authors.

Why Change Is Exhausting

This may surprise you, but you spend most of your day on autopilot.

Imagine the last five miles you drove: can you describe anything that was different today? How about brushing your teeth - can you remember the order in which you moved the toothbrush around your mouth? Do you remember the scoops of coffee that you put in the filter this morning?

These behaviours are 'unsupervised' - they don't require conscious thought. You're free to daydream, process, and think about other things. The motions become intrinsic. They're automatic. With athletes, we strive to achieve this type of intrinsic reaction and motor control with the movements required by their sport.

However, when these automatic behaviours are negative - bad habits - they have to be changed. That requires enough 'supervision' to override the automatic tendency. Change requires more conscious control than we're used to giving. It means struggle against the default setting AND more time spent in the driver's seat.

Dozens of studies have demonstrated the exhausting effect of self-correction. In *Switch*[28], by Chip and Dan Heath, they've done a terrific job of laying out the concept in greater detail Here, though, are a few stories from *Ignite!*:

Kevin had been doing *Ignite!* for several weeks. His

28 Chip Heath and Dan Heath. Switch: How to Change When Change Is Hard. Random House Canada (Feb 16 2010)

focus and attention had reached a level that allowed him to concentrate on complex patterns. Motor patterns had been corrected (he could do more complicated movement tasks,) and cross-brain reinforcement was next. Tyler had prepared writing skills for him; after a warmup including exercises to help prime the brain areas necessary for reading and writing, they set to work. Kevin focused on nothing else for ten minutes. He completed the task, put on his coat, walked out to his mother's car, and fell asleep immediately.

After a long run-up, Coach Chris was meeting with a high-level consultant for an important meeting. Beforehand, Chris did a five-minute skipping warmup, focused with some *Ignite!* drills to make his brain more permeable and attain Beginner's Mind, and then drove to the meeting. Three hours later, bursting with information and feeling like there was a giant Jawbreaker in his brain that he was trying to chew, he returned to his vehicle. It was freezing cold and uncomfortable. But Chris still wanted to sleep.

Think about the most productive times of your life: they seemed busiest. That's no coincidence. When the brain is unoccupied, it operates less efficiently. When bored, it seeks to fill itself, and sometimes does so with bad habits, including too much drama; needless stress; or hyperfocus on irrelevant data. These are habits that the brain slips into to save energy.

Balance – The Vestibular System

The integration of sensory input is the way in which we form an image of our 'world' in our brains. The vestibular system gives us information about gravity and motion, and about our body's muscular movements and position in space.

The first sensory system to fully develop and begin

myelinating (by five months after conception) is the vestibular system, which controls the sense of movement and balance. After conception, the vestibular system is the first sense to develop in the fetus, and other brain processes organize around it as the child grows in the womb.

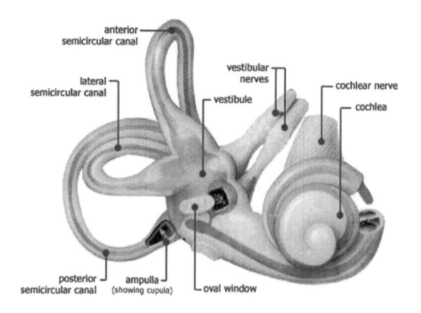

anterior semicircular canal
lateral semicircular canal
vestibular nerves
vestibule
cochlear nerve
cochlea
posterior semicircular canal
ampulla (showing cupula)
oval window

his is the sensory system considered to have the most important influence for everyday functioning – our ability to move and act against gravity. It's the unifying system that directly or indirectly influences nearly everything we do. The vestibular systems maintains both static and dynamic equilibrium and every time we move, sensory impulses shoot along the vestibular nerve to the brain. The vestibular nerve is the first cranial nerve to develop at 5 to 6 months in utero, and stems directly from this system. These impulses go through nerve tracts to the cerebellum, which monitors and makes corrective adjustments in the cortex. This system connects directly or indirectly to every muscle in the body, and triggers causes the motor system to increase or decrease its impulses to specific muscles, especially the core and neck muscles, instructing them to contract or relax.

The connection between the vestibular system and neocortex as well as the eye and core muscles is highly important to the learning process. When we don't move and activate the vestibular system, we are not taking in information from the environment.

One terrific example, already in progress: In the Forest Kindergartens in Denmark, Sweden and Germany, children have the opportunity to actively develop their vestibular systems. They roll down hills, climb over big rocks, climb ladders and trees, walk on logs and spin around to folk songs as they sing. When they enter school, their bodies are fully ready to learn.

The vestibular system collects information on inertia and spatial perception from the vestibular organs: three semicircular canals in the ears, and the Otolith organ. The canals are oriented along the x,y, and z axes and measure motion on each of the three dimensions of space.

When the head moves, tiny hair cells detect the motion of fluids inside each canal, as if you had a carpenter's level for each dimension inside your head. Tiny movements of the hairs in the fluid are used by the brain to calculate inertia (direction change, tilt, rotation, and speed.)

The Otolith Organ uses an appendage that looks like a pendulum (the Utricle) to orient the brain to the feeling of the vertical force of gravity. Without the Utricle, you'd feel as if you were always falling, or being pressed toward the ground. The Utricle helps you acclimate to the force of gravity toward the earth.

Combining the inertial information from the three semicircular canals and the Otolith organ, humans can gain a three-dimensional perspective on their world with themselves as the centre. As a child continues to develop in the womb, the other major brain systems – motor, tactile, auditory, visual – develop alongside the vestibular system, but their progress is limited by the progress of the vestibular system. If vestibular development is impeded, the other brain systems will fall behind accordingly. This is important, because improper vestibular development – which continues AFTER birth – creates problems with balance and spatial awareness can cause many other problems which don't appear related at first glance. For instance, reading and comprehension, eye tracking, and memory can all be impeded by unfulfilled vestibular development.

Multi-Sensory Integration

Quick: what are your five senses?

While you can list them separately (sight, touch, smell....) they only very rarely work independently. In order to form a complete and accurate picture of your environment, the information they provide needs to be integrated, balanced, and put in a shared context. This is how you can match the sound of a train to the large silver object hurtling down the tracks toward you; this is how you know not to eat the meat that's been in the refrigerator since last month; this is how you judge the heft of a bowling ball.

While sight can provide a three-dimensional model of the world, our senses add dimensions that help us make decisions. This data is compared to what our vestibular system KNOWS to be true, and what experience has taught us. That green thing over there, perpendicular to the ground, and parallel to our torso? Looks like a tree. But if it's pointing diagonally up and to the left, and we're standing straight....it's a tree that we've never seen before.

The vestibular system forms a backdrop, then, against

which we hold up information. It's clearly critical to develop the most advanced vestibular system possible. Training your vestibular system through running, jumping, rolling, tumbling, swimming...these are all things that will help you learn new sports later in life; have better spatial awareness; and avoid falls and accidents, even decades later.

Children who participate in dance, tennis, and particularly gymnastics have an advanced vestibular system throughout life. While the vestibular system is almost completely formed by the age of 12, some improvements can be made even as adults, thanks to neuroplasticity.

Listening, Ear Infections, and Auditory Processing

As discussed above, the vestibular system is very dependent on canals located in the inner ear. This location is protective – it's hard to reach, shielded by the skull, and in a spot not typically prone to injury relative to the rest of the head.

When there's a problem with the ear, though, the vestibular system is also affected. Consider the ramifications:

- We spend 90% of our time communicating with others on a daily basis. This includes listening, talking, reading & writing.

- Managers spend 80% of their time communicating *orally* with others on a daily basis.

- During communication, people spend more time *listening* than any other activity (e.g., reading, writing and speaking). Unfortunately, most of us are not very effective listeners.

⅄ The average listener retains only 50% of what is said immediately after hearing it.

⅄ The average listener retains only 25% of what is said 48 hours later.

⅄ The average listener retains less than 10% of what is said a week later.

⅄ Research consistently shows that the single most important skill that people need to perform well on the job is the ability to communicate effectively with others.

⅄ The two most important factors in helping graduating college students obtain employment are their speaking skills and listening skills.

⅄ One study of top executives estimated that poor communication costs organizations between 25% and 40% of their budgets.

⅄ Another study of top executives estimated that 14% of each 40 hour work week is wasted specifically due to poor communication between managers and their staff. Based on a 50 week year, this amounts to 35 wasted work days per employee![29]

Most people are good at hearing; this is not to say that they're adept at *listening*. The two terms - listening and hearing - are often used interchangeably, but mean very

29Source: Dr. Tyrone A. Holmes, Ed.D, LPC, CPT

different things.

According to the International Listening Association:

- ⌃ 45 percent of a student's day is spent listening.

- ⌃ Students are expected to acquire 85 percent of the knowledge they have by listening.
- ⌃ Only 2 percent of the population have ever received formal listening instruction.

While most children are born with the ability to hear, most are never taught HOW to listen. The majority of the population is born with the ability to hear, but not to listen. People do not – or can not – listen, and therefore remember, for several reasons: physical conditions, cultural beliefs, and just plain boredom.

Listening has been an important part of communication since the dawn of the conscious mind. Relaying of messages, retelling of history, reenactment of important stories, relay of information...all rely primarily on the ability to listen first, remember second, and repeat third. Before 3200 BC, when writing was first used by cultures such as the Sumerians or Egyptians, listening to people speak and repeating the message was the only way to communicate. In fact, some cultures in Eastern Europe still rely primarily on their storytellers to record and replay their histories.

In *"Moonwalking With Einstein,"* [30]Joshua Foer recounts his visit with one of these Eastern-European tribes. He was interested in not just the ability to recall the salient points of information as told through story, but also in variations in the story between storytellers.

The tribespeople all swore that there was NO variation; that the stories were retold verbatim, using not just the

30 Foer, Joshua. Moonwalking with Einstein: The Art and Science of Remembering Everything. Penguin Group (USA) , 2011

same tale and morals, but the precise language each time. Foer found something else, though: that the details, and sometimes even the path of the story would change from teller to teller. However, the most important parts – the message – remained the same.

Unlike a game of 'telephone,' where details in the story change between individuals in a matter of seconds, Foer surmised that the important lessons were constant between tellers...even though the details could change. These are revered men and women in their culture, and Foer wasn't eager to press too hard on details. However, it became clear that, while the story was very memorable, the specific descriptive parts weren't relevant and therefore not memorable.

What IS Listening?

Listening involves a collage of skills:

- Predicting
- Guessing
- Reflection
- Recognizing connectors
- Recognizing discourse markers
- Understanding intonation
- Summarizing
- Identifying relevant and irrelevant points
- Understanding inferences

We use the listening skill every second we're awake. We listen for our babies to cry; we listen to stories from our hairstylists; we listen to sermons and to arguments, to music and advertisements. We have the ability to listen to material presented to us in almost any form.

During a school day, students listen to material presented in different ways for several hours. They listen to directions, facts, rules; they listen to gossip, stories, announcements. Each of these situations requires a different type AND level of listening skills, which can be broken into four categories:

- *Inactive listening:* Being present when someone is speaking, but not absorbing what is being said. *Example*: Imagine attending a conference session that has no interest or applicability to you. You will be there physically, but not mentally.
- *Selective listening:* Hearing what you want to hear or what you expect to hear instead of what is being said. *Example*: Every morning, you hear a train whistle from the tracks a block from your house. One morning, the train doesn't run past, but you don't notice; when asked later if you heard the train pass, you answer in the affirmative. The brain automatically fills in the information that's missing, or glosses over the facts based on repeated experience.
- *Active listening:* Hearing what is said, concentrating on the message and absorbing it. *Example*: The Board of Education is offering bonuses to teachers that complete a required list of professional development courses. You are interested in the courses and the bonus. You take detailed notes and pay close attention to what you need to do.
- *Reflective listening:* This is one of the most complex types of listening. It involves actively listening, interpreting what is being said and observing how it is being said. *Example*: A student regularly comes to class looking sad and depressed. When you ask her if everything is o.k. at home, she responds that it is, but the look on her face and body language scream it is not. You ask her again if things are o.k., but question her body language. She breaks down and begins to cry, revealing that her parents have been arguing a lot.

A healthy vestibular system requires optimized auditory capabilities. Performing static and dynamic balance movements that require the head to tilt or turn stimulates the vestibular system, and helps re-establish nerve networks that may have been damaged during ear infections, or underdeveloped as children.

As mentioned earlier in this Section, one of the first questions asked to new clients at the *Ignite!* Academy relates to the frequency of ear infections as a child. With the information shared above, it's obvious now why this is important: with the vestibular system controlling the way in which information is received, processed, and interpreted, it's a critical piece of any of our five senses.

In order to improve these senses, it's necessary to remove limits that are present because of weaknesses in the vestibular system. In order to hear and speak accurately, we must be able to hear the full tone of the sounds presented, including higher harmonics that occur in normal speech. Children who miss regular communication with other people do not share a sense of hearing that's as well-developed as children who share conversation with peers and adults.

Communication from media sources do no produce the tones and vibrations necessary to develop sensitivities. When these capabilities are impaired, language acquisition suffers. Children with recurring ear infections in the first 5 years of life may miss these complex tones from their parents.

If you're a parent, you've likely been given the advice to play classical music for your baby, even before they're born. By using the logic above, it appears that this type of aural stimulation WILL help....but it won't automatically make your baby smarter. Rather, it will increase their POTENTIAL for intellect by fully developing their ability to listen. In turn, the vestibular system's ability to accurately receive and process information gathered by auditory cues is enhanced. It's not a guarantee of brilliance; it's just providing the best foundation possible for growth later. Children with reduced sensory acuity, poor hearing, and balance due to infections don't fully experience their environments. This means a limit on the information they receive, the stimulus they're given, and ultimately the connections they're able to make.

When a child is over-sensitive to environmental stimuli, the sensitivity manifests itself as a disability, or an inability to process the information being received. Dyslexia is an inability to break words down into sounds; link sounds into symbols; and do these things automatically.

Over-sensitivities to environmental stimuli can be exacerbated by ear infections, high-carbohydrate diets from sugar and yeast, stress, and antibiotics. These factors affect normal vestibular function in the inner ear; balance; and eye tracking, making reading and language very difficult to learn. Lack of cerebellar/vestibular development shows up in the muscles that control movement of the eyes, causing them to lose partial focus on letters and words. Other muscular weaknesses are frequently present in the posterior chair of these children. An inability to hold their heads or torsos upright for long periods of time – necessary for the reading and comprehension of text – can affect their ability to sit, listen, and absorb information. These students are frequently shifting, squirming, stretching, or vibrating.

Thus, children who balance the chair on two legs may not be misbehaving. They may be merely trying to unconsciously activate their vestibular system through a challenge of balance. These children, however, may excel at other physical skills not associated with the part of the vestibular system that's been compromised.

Having one ear become more dominant, or one ear damaged by infection or development, means that auditory processing only occurs in one of the hemispheres instead of both. This potentially limits the ability for students to process a source of stimulation – or information - with the appropriate hemisphere.

Through integrated movements, triggering and challenging senses of balance and proprioception to activate the entire vestibular system, *Ignite!* helps the student better develop hearing and listening skills. These movements involve large areas of the motor cortex and frontal eye field area; promote plasticity and greater cross-linking in the brain; and stimulate growth and myelination in the rest of the frontal lobe, including the pre-motor and superior pre-frontal cortex for high-level thinking and creativity as well as more grace, balance and control of all our muscles. That's a lot of benefit for the small investment of a few minutes' worth of somersaults, log rolls, and balancing.

Spatial Awareness

Spatial awareness is the vestibular system's sense of where the limbs are in space, and our body's position relative to the things around us. Without this system of biofeedback, we wouldn't be able to judge where to place our feet while walking; how letters flow together on a page in any order; or how to guide the fork to our mouths. Athletes wouldn't know where the ball lies in relation to the foot, or how far they are from the finish line, or in which direction their opponents are heading.

Spatial awareness requires that we build a 3-D model of our environment using information collected from all senses, and integrated into a cohesive picture. Putting together pieces of data, and using the vestibular system as a basis for context, is a skill closely related to abstract thinking.

In this way, then, do we organize our thoughts. Studies have linked a well-developed sense of spatial awareness with creativity, as well as the ability to do math that requires more modelling. Especially in 'visual thinkers,' the ability to organize and classify abstract mental concepts either enhances or limits their ability to use their visual imagination and abstract thought.

Spatial awareness is critical: while fleeing from a predator, would your ancestor know how to jump over a stream? Would she be able to gauge the depth of the cliff, or the speed of the lion?

Deficiencies in the perception of spatial awareness can restrict people from achieving their true potential – mentally, as WELL as physically. Since spatial awareness requires the efficient integration of information, activities which refine the vestibular system and enhance the integration process can refine all aspects of brain processing.

Integration Between The Two Brain Hemispheres

Imagine two computers with a cable connecting each to the other. The computer on the left receives motor and sensory input from the right side of the body; the computer on the right receives the same from the left side of the body.

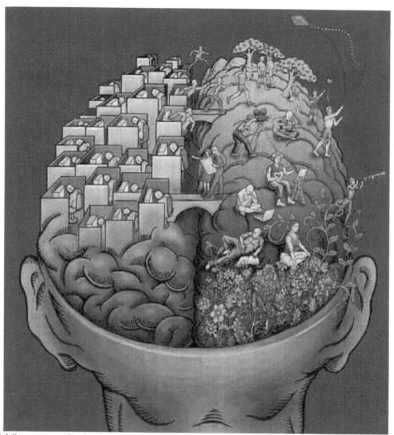

When we link the two systems, the most efficient way is to synchronize both – to achieve a standard platform on which both can operate at the same level. After all, if one computer is more powerful than the other, the lag time will slow both machines. In this way, the chain is as strong as its weakest link. However, it's not the case that both sides of the brain are automatically operating at the same level. The first step in the *Ignite!* protocol for many is to achieve a balance between both hemispheres; to ensure that the weaker link is not limiting the total potential pulling power of the entire chain.

Since cognitive tasks involve BOTH sides of the brain, a lack of physical efficiency – or integration – between the hemispheres can result in slower cognitive processing. It logically follows that some students with reading delays, auditory processing issues, language delays, or other learning delays may simply be suffering from a lack of balance between the two sides of the brain.

Many readers of this book will be familiar with the deadlift movement. Popularized by powerlifters, the deadlift is a tremendous tool for teaching the body to integrate the hamstrings, gluteus muscles, and spinal erectors (among others) to achieve powerful hip extension. When working together, the 'main' movers of the deadlift can achieve amazing weights – Rickey Dale Crain had a 700lbs Deadlift at a bodyweight of 132lbs in the 1980s – but if one small link in the chain is incapable of lifting the weight, the potential of the entire chain is less. We sink to the level of our lowest capacity. If Rickey Dale's hamstrings could pull 710lbs off the floor; and his gluteus maximus could pull 750lbs; and his spinal erectors could pull 800lbs; but his gluteus medius was capable only of 600lbs.....then 600lbs would have been his limit.

Lack of integration between the hemispheres can trigger a vicious spiral. Since the cognitive processes are so tightly entwined with, and dependent upon, the physical efficiencies of the brain, problems that appear to be entirely local (poor eyesight in one eye) may be linked to a cognitive issue.

For example, a child with less efficiency in the left hemisphere may have poorer vision in the right eye. Suppressing the right eye means that the child reads with his left eye only, and the brain networks supporting the right eye will become even LESS efficient through lack of use. Dominance develops and deepens, and exacerbates the lack of integration. And since different types of intelligence are processed in different hemispheres, a slight weakness on one side of the body can spiral into a cognitive delay over time, especially if uncorrected during the developmental years.

As a more specific example, consider a child whose left eye is weaker than her right. Since the left eye receives slightly less stimulation as the body learns to rely more on the information received through the right, the wiring in the right hemisphere (attached to the left eye) becomes less efficient. Since the right hemisphere is most closely associated with creativity and artistic endeavours, the child may receive the external feedback that she is "not creative" or "bad at art" or "not good at thinking abstractly." The implications are enormous: as you'll see in Section III, telling a six-year-old that she is "not creative" is a sentence that can shape her life's path negatively....

On the upside, all of these potential weaknesses can be overcome, just like a weakness in the posterior chain of a deadlifter. Since the left side of the brain controls movement on the right side of the body, and the right side of the brain controls movement on the left side of the body, *Ignite!* can enhance the integration between both hemispheres through activities involving both sides of the body. Addressing weaknesses first, and then attempting to achieve balance and an 'even playing field' between the hemispheres allows a more solid platform upon which to pursue higher learning.

To use a specific example, consider one part of every human's learning spectrum: cross-pattern creep (most would just call it "crawling.") This is an important part of brain synchronization, but the rush to walk is usually given priority. "She walked at 7 months!" a parent gushes, to the admiration of all around them. Though science has never shown a correlation between early ability to stand and later physical prowess, it's taken for granted that an early start at mobility somehow gives the child a head start as a runner or athlete.

This is unfortunate. Crawling is an important part of the

spectrum of learning that must occur for full, balanced and efficient brain function. When the right hand moves, the left hemisphere is activated; when the left leg moves, the right hemisphere makes connections. When one side moves, followed by the other, and locomotion occurs, the cognitive benefits start to become hardwired.

Why, then, is walking of less benefit to brain development than crawling? Think about the child's line of sight: when walking, they don't look at their feet. Sensory integration means that the feedback the child receives while crawling *(I feel the floor with my left hand. I see my hand on the floor...)* is better embedded because more senses are confirming the data. Especially since the senses and vestibular system are not yet fully developed, stimuli that occurs closer to the face is clearer and processed more accurately:

"I feel a hard object. I see a ball in my hand. It is not cold. It is not warm. I can squeeze it, but it does not conform to pressure. If I move my arm this way, the

object will go to my face. I see it even more clearly. If I activate my mandible, and move my fingers this way, I can put it in my mouth. It tastes different...."

Since the hands are closer to the head – and therefore, eyes, ears, mouth and nose – a child will typically use them more than the feet to gather information. While other primate species have greater tactile sense and mobility in their feet than humans, it can be argued that the ability is a learned trait, rather than a genetic one; their mothers use their feet to climb and pick things up, and so then do the babies. In humans, over time, the hands become much more specific and sensitive than the feet, because the information they collect is quickly reinforced through the other senses.

This is important, because as a child crawls, she looks at her hands; as a child walks, she looks where she's going instead of at her feet. Since the left hemisphere controls movement on the right side of the body, and the right hemisphere controls movement on the left side, using a biofeedback loop with sensory integration brings the two sides of the brain closer toward balance.

While crawling, the child learns to better synchronize the two hemispheres. Operating together to create forward locomotion, they develop a consistent timing system – a system in which the standards of measurement for both sides of the brain are matched perfectly. For the right arm to move forward, followed by the left arm, at the same rate and by the same degree, time and space must be perceived equally by both hemispheres.

When it IS time for the child to begin walking, a greater degree of efficiency and capability must occur evenly on both sides. Sensory integration, too, becomes quicker, as the child must learn to collect and interpret data more quickly or risk losing his balance and falling. At this point, since sensory integration between both sides of the brain is critical for improving ALL brain functions, cognitive processes also begin to become more efficient. Math skills, spatial awareness, the bases for reading, and the capacity to learn are all heightened as the child learns to walk. If sensory integration has been maximized through the crawling phase, and the child has developed a high level of synchronicity through crawling, they may focus on balance at this phase, and higher brain function will develop rapidly alongside the vestibular system.

The position of the crawl, on all fours, also challenges the strength of the posterior chain, specifically the back and neck muscles that support the proper growth and development of the vestibular system. When Therapy clients at *Ignite!* are put through their initial functional movement test, they're asked to perform the push up hold. The NeuroMotive Therapist, in this way, can evaluate how long the individual is able to hold their head and back in a straight line and still be able to communicate with the Therapist without having to focus on keeping their body upright and aligned.

Gender can play a factor when it comes to cross-hemisphere communication. A bundle of interhemispheric fibres called the *Anterior Commissure* is clearly larger in female brains and can carry more traffic *(Allen and Gorski, 1991.)* The advantage means that females are wired to tie together verbal and nonverbal information more efficiently than males. This may also be the reason statistics show why girls outperform boys in verbal and reading skills early in life.[31]

---

31 Kimura, D. - "Sex and Cognition". MIT Press, 1999

Brain Timing / Reaction Time

Integration between the two hemispheres of the brain is critical for both coordinated movement AND higher-level cognitive function. Successful integration of the two sides of the brain requires efficient timing, because the outcome will be dependent on the LOWEST level of efficiency. If the brain 'knows' how to catch the ball, but can't coordinate recruitment fast enough to move the hand to the correct spot, the ball will wind up on the ground.

Processing speed is limited by the 'weakest link' in the chain. Improving brain processing speed requires these 'weak links' to be identified and addressed; luckily, since slower brain processing is manifested in motor skill deficiency, we can test the latter to identify the former.

The greater the motor-coordination requirements, the faster the brain must process information provided by the various senses and the vestibular system, and the more efficiently the integration of the two hemispheres must occur.

Smooth, coordinated movements require efficient integration of both hemispheres. Suppression, rigidity, and uncoordinated movements are the result of slow processing speed and/or faulty integration. That provides a clue as to the same processing speeds and efficiencies available to the student for cognitive tasks. Inefficient brain timing is also a factor in ADHD, and Central Auditory Processing Disorder, in which the sufferer doesn't correctly process the information received through the sense of hearing.

Luckily, these two 'separate' capacities – the physical and the cognitive – are backwards-compatible. Improvements in brain efficiencies necessary to improve recruitment for physical purposes will also be used to help speed up cognitive tasks.

Improving reaction time by the student, and balance, spatial awareness, and rate of force development – strength – will necessarily cause greater integration between hemispheres. As the hemispheres learn greater efficiency, the brain can more quickly process information to be used either for a challenging physical task OR a challenging cognitive test.

Increasing The Difficulty Level of Activities

As we progress towards adolescence, the difficulty level of our movements becomes increasingly harder: from lying flat to rolling over; from crawling to walking; from walking to running. Each requires a higher level of integration and efficiency within the brain, recruitment of more neurons, and greater memory or 'coding' of the order of neuron recruitment. At first, we do these things tentatively and imperfectly; through practice, we shed off the unnecessary excesses in our movement, and become more efficient. The same is true within the brain: efficiency means the use of FEWER neurons and processes to achieve the same result.

When we progress toward more advanced techniques, we're forced to create more neuronal connections. Increasing the difficulty of the task increases the neuronal involvement required to complete the task. This is why you can't become a faster 100m runner simply by running more miles than everyone else: you have to wire the brain to move the limbs as efficiently as possible for a short time (as well as the different physiological requirements.)

Since different brains are at different levels of organizational capacities, it's common to find a wide range of physical capabilities among a group of children at a similar age. Some brains may not yet have reached a level where it's possible to complete a technical movement, like hitting a ball, where some in the group can consistently coordinate the movement with ease. In order to avoid a discouraging sense of repetitive failure, then, it's best to start out with easy movements and progress upward as each is mastered.

In the business world, the practice of 'promotion to the point of least effectiveness' is rampant. Take a great car salesman who loves his job, and 'reward' him by promoting him to sales manager....and you frequently have an unhappy employee. The prestige of the 'managerial' position isn't enough to make the staffer happy, because they've gone from an environment where they were comfortable, sufficiently challenged, and confident in their skill set to one in which they're faced with overwhelming stimuli they're not yet equipped to handle. True, some will overcome the steep learning curve and eventually thrive, but this isn't the rule.

In a student, the same thing occurs: today's master of the Jungle Gym is tomorrow's last-place finisher on the gymnastics rings. Gone is the confidence, the Bright Spot, and the prestige; and moving back down the ladder to the jungle gym is a further blow to confidence. However, with a planned progression that allows for new neuronal connections to occur – perhaps from jungle gym to parallel bars to trapeze to modified rings to rings – the brain can 'keep up' with the demands placed on it via the new challenge. At each stage, the neuronal connections will improve their efficiency, making them ready for the new challenges of improved spatial awareness, more precise brain timing, and improved synchronization between both sides of the brain.

Learning and Performing are State-Dependent.

Any task requires a level of arousal (willingness to act) to initiate action toward its completion. The level of arousal necessary for each task will range from very little (something you enjoy) to very high (bungee jumping.) The level of arousal necessary can differ not just by task, but also by the circumstances surrounding the task. For instance, it's much easier to jump out of bed on Christmas morning than on the Friday of a regular workweek.

Learning is state-dependent. This means that you're best able to recall information learned under the same circumstances as when it is to be applied. Learning about things in context builds relevance into the information, making it 'stick' better in the brain. This is also true for arousal level: the level of arousal at which we perform an action must match the level of arousal at the time we received the input for the task to be executed effectively.

For example, if a student learns a tennis backhand in the quiet serenity of private lessons, with a private coach, at 6am, they will be challenged to duplicate the shot with the same level of proficiency when in front of a crowd and facing a tough opponent.

When a student prepares for a test, they typically do so in a quiet and comfortable place. However, the test is typically delivered while the student is in a different arousal state: an increased heart rate; anxiety; social hyperawareness, worry about 'going blank'.... Then, they go blank. Why? When the information was being processed and stored, they were in a calm state. When it came time to recalling the information, however, their heart rate shot up, releasing adrenaline, cortisol, and other hormones that interfere with memory retrieval.

Be aware of your arousal levels while receiving input and during performance. If possible, increase your heart rate prior to receiving input. This increases alertness in the brain and mimics the conditions present during a test.

A final note: it's critical to keep demanding more of the brain to improve neuronal connections. While too much stimulation, too soon, won't help the brain progress, it's certainly better than too LITTLE stimulation at all.

Binocular Teaming

Binocular Teaming is the ability of both eyes to work together to provide an accurate picture to the brain. Binocularity and stereopsis (the way your eyes work together to provide separate information to the brain, which has to combine the two perspectives into one image) provide depth perception. These skills are critical, since they provide the ability to track, fixate, converge, and move the eyes together (visual motor integration.)

Controlling the way we use and aim our eyes together is an importing skill that keeps us from seeing double. The ability to use both eyes as a "team," or a single functioning pair, is what allows our brain to fuse the two separate pictures coming in from each eye into a single image. This skill is called binocularity. Stereopsis refers to the ability of the eyes to move in unison rather than independently.

There are two basic ways to aim or "team" our eyes:

1) The ability to turn our eyes inward to maintain single vision for objects up close is called *convergence*. It is similar to looking "cross-eyed," like this:

2) The ability to turn our eyes outward to maintain a single image for objects far away   is called *divergence*. Our eyes appear to aim straight ahead, like this:

Obviously, without these skills, reading and writing are impossible, and functioning in a classroom or social environment are a huge challenge. Imagine trying to read while letters float off the page toward you at different speeds, growing larger or smaller; or scrolling up and down while you try to 'catch' them and form words.

NOW imagine the frustration a teacher must feel toward a sixth-grade child whose reading is impaired. The child requires more help than average, but the teacher has no extra time or assistance. More often than not, the child is 'left to work at their own pace' – in other words, marginalized. It's not true that the entire class should slow its lessons to match the learning pace of the slowest, but there ARE tools available to the student that can help, as you'll see in Section III.

Vision therapy, too, is available for several different types of binocular deficiencies, IF the parent or teacher recognizes the root of the problem. There are several types of vision problems, including:

- one eye doesn't process as much information as the other;

- one or both eyes may not focus on a specific point (over- or under-convergence);

- vertical or horizontal alignment issues that cause the 'aim' of the eyes to be incorrect.

It's important to remember that sight is a piece of the 'vision' process, of which the eyes are only a part. Vision is integrated with, and dependent upon, a vestibular system that's fully developed.

Arguably, since no one has perfect vision, this type of therapy could benefit anyone; some can simply benefit more than others. And the best part: students who suffer from a binocular inequality, or slow vision processing, can benefit from the same exercises as those who are merely seeking a tuneup, or to improve cognition speed for a different task.

Below are two simple word-search puzzles. Cover your dominant eye, and time yourself while you complete the first. Then, time yourself with your non-dominant eye covered to perform the second. Is there a difference?

```
G G I L D R R M E O G P O E
R N X W Y E E E A N N R R E
R I E R M P C M H E E H R E
H T T O X E A O N T C T M C
S I R I T B L R B E T G O I
N R O F I O L Y E O R G T T
T W C G N T P P N H N E C C
E D O C R O S S F I T R G A
O N E U R O M O T I V E O R
L A N B A E E I N H T A N P
H H W E D I O G G E G D I P
E I N A E N I O N R I I R G
N A E I A R F O F O S N R I
N C E V P F H T W O R G D B
```

NEUROMOTIVE   IGNITE   THERAPY
SPEECH   COGNITION   MEMORY
HANDWRITING   RECALL   READING
NEOCORTEX   BDNF   BRIGHT SPOT
PRACTICE   GROWTH   CROSSFIT

```
T N A E C I T C A R P L
I G O V N T O R I G E L
W B R I G H T S P O T A
G N I T I R W D N A H C
D C R O S S F I T G E E
I I Y M Y P T I G R R R
N O E O D R E M H O A E
X E T R O C O E N W P A
N G I U R O B M C T Y D
H O N E A I G D E H P I
C O G N I T I O N M O N
E T I H R E O D G F I G
```

CROSSFIT	BDNF	HANDWRITING
READING	COGNITION	PRACTICE
THERAPY	RECALL	SPEECH
NEOCORTEX	IGNITE	BRIGHT SPOT
MEMORY	GROWTH	NEUROMOTIVE

Proprioception

Just as the brain is always recalculating our position in space, it tries to maintain the body's position based on the information it receives through the vestibular system. This is an ongoing, autonomic process.

Picture a satellite orbiting the earth with thrusters scattered all over the surface. When the satellite rotates too far in one direction, a thruster automatically kicks on to right the orientation of the satellite. Various speedometers and gyroscopes are necessary to measure and balance the satellite; in humans, that's part of the function of the vestibular system.

Simply stated, proprioception is awareness of the body's position and movement. Like a GPS, the body's "joint positioning system" works on feedback from a variety of the body's sensory systems, including the muscles; vision; joints; touch; and sense of balance.

Joint stabilization occurs when the tendons, ligaments and muscles that stabilize a joint are recruited at the right time, with the right amount of tension, in balance to one another. Joint dominance occurs when a muscle, tendon or ligament on one side of the joint is disproportionately stronger or tighter. Overuse injuries are largely the result of joint dominance left unchecked for too long.

Hard exercise requires a well-functioning proprioceptive

system to stabilize the joints. An athlete who has had a wrist injury may believe that she has "weak wrists" years later. What has really happened is that the brain has learned the wrong way to position the joint; what the brain believes to be 'normal' is actually unstable. This conclusion has led to the rampant adoption of physiotherapy immediately after injury, or even surgery, in recent years.

Imagine a football player dislocates his shoulder, and tears his labrum. Perhaps on the advice of his doctor, he follows the 'RICE' procedure (Rest, Ice, Compression, Elevation) until it "feels better." It may feel better for several weeks. In the meantime, the brain learns to accept the labral tear as the 'new normal.' The proprioceptive processes are sending feedback to the brain that "things are okay, thanks!" On a less dangerous hit, the shoulder is again dislocated; tendons stretch; the brain adapts again. After a decade, the player's shoulder pops in and out of its socket, virtually at will, and surgery is required to remove scar tissue and shorten the stretched ligaments.

Unless physiotherapy is introduced immediately postsurgery, the brain begins its process of 'naturalizing' the shoulder – adopting the 'new normal' – and the injury slowly builds up again. Balancing joint MOBILITY with joint STABILITY is crucial for athletes.

If a therapist can improve the brain's ability to integrate all the information it's receiving from proprioceptive sources, the athlete is less likely to suffer a joint injury in the first place, and faster rehabilitate an acute injury when it does happen.

Sensory integration activities improve the efficiency and accuracy of neural connections in the brain. As neural capability and speed increase, a variety of other benefits are realized:

- timing improves

- vision improves

- awareness improves

- reaction times improve

- proprioception improves

- speed of movement improves and becomes more efficient.

If there was ever a coach's 'wish list' of improvements for a player in any sport, it's the one right above this sentence. Can the improvements be made with gadgets like heavier pucks and BOSU balls and balance boards? In a small way. Can they be better improved through a program that combines strength training with proprioceptive training, sensory integration, and neural efficiency?

Definitely. It's time to learn how to do it.

Section III – *Ignite!* In Practise and Delivery

In this section, we describe the way we actually deliver the *Ignite!* Program – first, in a one-on-one setting; then at school; and then at our own *Ignite!* Academy. Key to the success of the *Ignite!* Program is not just the science, but also the delivery of the material. Buy-in from the practitioner or student is key, and we'll discuss ways that we use to improve the experience for both the Coach and student in this section.

Interspersed with the methodology, you'll find research references and more specific science. Rather than simply keep the biology, chemistry, and electrical science in its own section (making it a bit harder to draw connections,) we prefer to introduce or reinforce knowledge where it's most relevant. You WILL find information repeated in this section; you'll also find some information explored in greater detail; and you'll get new information where appropriate.

Some material in this section applies so broadly that we'll cover it first, without designation for environmental setting. Things like, "Bright Spots," for instance, are relevant in ALL settings where goal-setting and education are the goal.

Other material in this section is grouped where it is most relevant, but is still important to understand for delivery of Ignite! In other areas. For instance, in "The Student's Body At School," we discuss the basic functions that must be met before learning can occur. This, of course, is important in ANY setting, but most frequently rears its head in public schools. Sadly, teachers are the professionals who must most often interact with students whose most primitive biological demands haven't been met: kids who haven't had breakfast; kids who have had a stressful morning at home; kids who are unprepared for colder weather....

In short, though you may plan to use Ignite! To help a child at home, or a child out of the school setting, there's much to be learned from the way we approach classroom instruction.

First, though, please consider learned readiness (and readiness to learn, too) :

Readiness to Learn : Beginner's Mind

The practise of 'Beginner's Mind' has been popularized by Taoists, but is a shared concept through most religions or spiritual cultures. In essence, 'Beginner's Mind' is a state of readiness to learn with a permeable (or open) mind. In practise, the student approaches a lesson as if he knows nothing about the subject. Though he may be a Master of a particular martial art, he can still learn from each practise if he approaches the session as a newcomer.

This is not easy. The confidence that comes as part of the reward following long hours of practise and skill development can often stand in the way of Beginner's Mind. Arguments with teachers, rebuttal or refusal to participate, stagnation or simple defensiveness are common among those who perceive Mastery in themselves. This is a handicap: ego is a roadblock that limits progress.

In our own facility, the most impressive athletes are not necessarily the most accomplished. Rather, the true Masters are the athletes who can suspend their egos and enter Beginner's Mind. These are the people who will learn new things from every lesson, no matter their 'advanced' status in a given skill.

Perhaps more interesting is the ancient process of preparing for Beginner's Mind, which usually involved challenging physical exercise. Yoga, for instance, was developed and honed as preparation for meditation. Yogis, over the centuries, couldn't help but notice that the discomfort of their muscles could limit their meditation or prayer time; proper preparation of the body would allow for longer, deeper inward thought without limitation by the body.

While some facets of Buddhism tend more toward stillness for hours, either in a trance-like state or in an 'open' state of unfocused "noticing," others incorporate movement within their prayers. Even the rhythm of breathing is controlled as a type of metronomic beat to measure the prayer. In his 2006 autobiography, the Dalai Lama noted that upon his first visit to a Christian prayer service, he was shocked to find that Christians didn't move at all during prayer, but preferred to stand or kneel.

"Have fun screwing up...it means you are removing your ego from the problem."
- Greg Glassman, founder of CrossFit

Learning requires practise. It's not enough to simply instruct the brain to, "Be more positive!" or "Be more open to new information!" All of the concepts in this book must be practised, with all of the temporary setbacks and moments of illumination that accompany the practise of a physical skill. However, these are important parts of the *Ignite!* program, and without these tools, the scope and effect of the *Ignite!* Method is lessened.

Maintaining a 'Beginner's Mind' will allow you to find

novelty and small improvements during practise time; help keep you motivated during times when success may seem less obvious; and keep your focus on the value of the journey, rather than just a subjective destination.

This concept is so important that we've called the collective act of achieving 'Beginner's Mind' every time you practice by its own term: The Growth Paradigm. You'll read more about The Growth Paradigm later in this section.

For now, though, consider again how our brains get ready to retain information; respond to new stimulus; and choose which information to prioritize:

How A Brain Changes Itself

1. *New focus and attention is given to new subject...or increased attention is given to an old one.*

The Nucleus Basalis reacts to the increase in attention given to the stimuli. Performing focusing and attention exercises primes the Nucleus Basalis to produce acetylcholine, which instructs the brain to give priority to the memories being formed.

2. *The brain responds to the challenge and reward feedback systems.*

A tough challenge is required to stimulate the production of dopamine. Dopamine is excreted as part of a 'reward' system in the brain; therefore, the challenge must be tough enough to create a sense of satisfaction upon completion. Dopamine is necessary for change to occur in the brain (which can change its shape due to its plasticity.)

3. *Targeted training for specific subjects creates long-lasting connections with a high perceived relevance.*

When acetylcholine and dopamine have been secreted, prompting the growth of new nerve cells, conditions have been created under which the brain can change itself. Stimulating the brain in different ways determines the way in which the brain grows; exercises that are chosen for different subject matter can generate lasting improvements in those subjects. When we reinforce knowledge in those subjects with specific challenges, the brain – already primed to prioritize the new information – stores a strong connection.

Let's consider again the model of Good-Better-Best with regard to training a brain:

Good – everyday activities that stimulate neural growth, like learning a new language; solving crossword puzzles; learning a new skill. These are better than nothing, but the change that's stimulated is incidental and is less directed.

Better – daily 'interventions' or short workouts directly before the subject matter is introduced.

Best – a personalized program, delivered one-on-one by a NeuroMotive Coach or NeuroMotive Therapist. This program delivers measurable results and is targeted specifically at weaker links.

In an important study[32], scientists studied the effects of exercise on cognition in children who were lacking in exercise:

From *Conclusions*: "....a specific improvement on executive function and brain activation changes attributable to exercise were observed. The cognitive and achievement results add evidence of dose-response and extend experimental evidence into childhood. This study

---

32 ("Exercise Improves Executive Function and Achievement and Alters Brain Activation in Overweight Children: A Randomized, Controlled Trial" by Davis, Tomporowski, et al, in Health Psychology (2011: Vol 30, No 1, 91-98.))

provides information on an educational outcome." and "...physical education may prove to be a simple, important method of enhancing aspects of children's mental functioning that are central to cognitive development. This information may persuade educators to implement vigorous physical activity."

The results clearly show that, just like adults, a child's learning can be enhanced through physical exercise. The most important part here, though, is the 'dose-response' notation: researchers in this study found that MORE exercise provides MORE benefit. While specific doses or minimums haven't been studied, every study done on the subject has shown a correlation between increasing amounts of exercise and increasing cognitive benefit. In short, more is better; the benefits don't fall off after the first few bouts. This supports our notion of several 'interventions' throughout the day, which we describe in great detail later in this book.

The Practice Paradigm

We now take for granted the knowledge that the brain is plastic; that it's capable of repair, growth, and progression at any age. But this wasn't always the case; even a decade ago, scientists firmly believed that each of us was given a fixed set of neurons, and a limited ability to expand our understanding of the world.

NOW, we know that repetition of a task reinforces the motor pathways in the brain. Practice makes permanent. Learn a skill incorrectly, and it sticks with you. But practice perfect execution, and you'll be hard-wired for life.

Some children miss some of these motor patterns early in life. For example, children who largely skip the crawling stage may lack poor cross-body coordination patterns when they're older. Conversely, children who practice tumbling, gymnastics, dance, or martial arts typically perform better at complex motor tasks as adults. Reinforcement through repetitive practice makes a huge difference.

Luckily, it's never too late to improve. Even senior citizens can learn (or relearn) to move more efficiently. After a stroke, when the body's 'motor memory' is wiped out, a patient can learn to walk again; studies in Alzheimer's sufferers show that the devastating effects of the disease can be put off through regular exercise and stimulating mental tasks like crossword puzzles. Non-athletes can learn, as adults, to perform complicated movements like the Tango, handstands, or backflips.

The key is to approach repetition as practice. If you're practising, you're not becoming frustrated by failure. Failure is acceptable, because...well, you expect it, during practice, don't you?

The key to growth is constant patient practice, choosing the 'Bright Spots' in your performance, and constantly reaching upward.

When considering the success of the student in the long term, a key factor – the foundation – is the student's mindset when they arrive for the *Ignite!* session. In many instances, the student is nervous: they're entering an unfamiliar environment with social strata unlike any experience they've had before.

If *Ignite!* is being performed in their classroom, there's the social stigma of failure in front of friends. If visiting the *Ignite!* Academy, there's the awkwardness of performing in front of strangers. It's a no-win situation...unless the stage is set in advance.

The 'Practice Paradigm' is the expectation that the student will work hard at– but not necessarily succeed at – accomplishing a skill. It is dependent upon the Growth Mindset; it dies at the altar of Perfectionism.

Play, an aspect removed from our educational system, is an important part of learning. A student who is enjoying a task will stick with it much longer, be more open to forming new connections, and be more willing to stray from the 'accepted norm.'

Reading Keith Richards' autobiography, *Life*[33], it's striking to notice how much he still loves to play. He loves talking about music; playing music with friends; and experimenting with things. He posits that Blues music is popular because its beat resonates closely with the human heartbeat, and tries to write music that will trigger emotion by tapping the physiological component. When Keith figures out a piece of music by another guitarist, it's a huge moment for him.

Some have called Richards a "genius." Most would say that he has "talent." But Richards was nearly expelled several times as a youth for being a bad student. He got bad grades. He couldn't pay attention in class. He dozed and daydreamed. He hated Math and English.

Years later, Richards would once go NINE days at a stretch without sleeping – his "record" - and what did he do the entire time? Played. When Richards uses the verb, "to play," he's not just using it to describe his actions on an instrument; he's playing the guitar like a game.

How do you hold the attention of an ADD student, who loves to turn a problem around and poke at it from every

33 Richards, Keith. Life. Little, Brown and Company

angle? You give them time to play with it.

If a problem is approached with a sense of play, the judgement associated with "right" or "wrong" answers is eliminated. The self-judgement associated with "the right way" or "the wrong way" is erased.

Using an athletic example, let's examine three types of pullups: the 'strict' pullup, the kipping pullup, and the butterfly pullup. At some point, the latter two were the 'wrong' versions of the former. Many who don't understand the purpose or value of the kip still argue that it's "cheating" to swing your legs during a pullup, as if there were a moral obligation to remain rigidly vertical.

Somewhere, sometime, a person gave themselves permission to practice pullups, and found that they could successfully 'link' kips together and thereby do MORE pullups. At some other time, a person practicing the kip tried it another way, and started the butterfly movement. Did the evolution of the kipping pullup really happen this way? Probably not. However, without the practice paradigm – permission to play with a problem – evolution of movement OR thought cannot occur.

When Mel Siff (who wrote *Supertraining*, one of the most comprehensive books ever published in the field of human performance)[34] was alive, he kept a blog by the same name. In those days, the 'blogs' were called, 'Lists,' and writers would post via email. There weren't any colourful banners, but reams of digital black text on white backgrounds. In this way, Mel Siff would debate all comers on the topics of strength training, aerobic training, physiology....

Siff was way above and beyond most thinkers in any

---

34 Siff, Mel Cunningham. Supertraining. Supertraining Institute (2003)

field - if we put him on the Jaques chart[35], he'd probably be around an 8. One day, responding to a post about how "science" exists not to prove, but to disprove, Siff commented that it's our CULTURE that has that all wrong. In most cultures, a 'scientist' is regarded as an artist: they're creative, have big ideas...they're like dreamers. The TECHNICIAN is the one doing the experiments and charting the progress over months and worrying about sample size. In our culture, 'scientist' means experiments and math and charts, and 'technician' just means "junior scientist."

In other words, while most cultures hold the Practice Paradigm – and a sense of play – in esteem, we've denigrated the idea to be somehow wasteful and childlike.

In our own experience, a client – Chuck - had severe problems with balance when he began at *Ignite!*. Traditional teaching methods require a teacher or Coach to constantly correct, or overcorrect (*No, try again....*) It's important to constantly remind the learner NOT to look at the Coach for immediate feedback after a failed attempt. A true 'practice paradigm' – understanding that a task is an experiment – means that the learner knows which cues to consider for feedback after a 'mistake,' and then develop their own solution.

In Chuck's case: after progressing from a basic squat movement into one requiring more balance on the foot (a wall ball,) Chuck struggled to stay centred over his feet. He'd been receiving coaching on feedback and practice for three weeks, however; when he caught the ball off-balance, and rolled forward on his feet, he fell to his hands and knees. Then he paused; considered; walked away from the medicine ball. The Coach knew that

35 Jaques, Elliott. The Life and Behavior of Living Organisms: A General Theory. Praeger, 2001.

Chuck's reaction could go one of two ways: a blowout, with self-blame and frustrated behaviour; or an attempt at a solution.

Chuck found some open space in the Academy. He lowered his rear leg to the ground, and balanced in a 'lunge' position. Then he took a step forward, and lowered his other leg to the ground. He was doing a very slow but stable walking lunge, practising his balance. He was familiar with the walking lunge exercise, but had not chosen it on his own before; more importantly, this was the first time he'd devised his own solution. While the Coach stood by silently, providing no feedback, Chuck practised the walking lunge a few more times, and then returned to the wall ball station. He picked up the ball and executed ten wall-balls without stopping. In the back corner, his parents high-fived.

To Chuck, he'd completed a wall ball – something, in his mind, any 'normal' teenager would have been able to do easily. To his Coaches and parents, it was a big breakthrough: instead of becoming frustrated and walking away from the task, kicking things in his path, he'd found a solution and implemented it without a cue from his Coach.

As you'll read in this book, learning is anchored down by movement. Doodling, eye tracking, speaking aloud, writing things down, and practising familiar movement patterns – they're all critical, and they're all interrelated. Movement patterns help client develop better cognitive processing, and vice versa. Quick workouts prime the brain; specific cross-body patterns help the student imprint math, reading, or processing; and challenges keep it fun, which is key to reinforcing the growth paradigm.

You'll learn how to create the optimal environment for learning; how to run a session to help with specific and class-sized goals; how to measure success, and how to keep positive progress happening. A recurring theme in this text is the importance not just of memory, but understanding.

Principles of Changing A Brain

In their book, 'Switch," authors Chip and Dan Heath spend a lot of time explaining the difference between convincing the 'logical' part of the brain and the 'emotional' side of the brain. The first step, they suggest, is to 'Inform the Rider." Make a clear impression; form a clear picture of your goals or targets. Tell the elephant's rider where you wish to end up. But knowledge of the desired endpoint, alone, isn't going to get you anywhere.

"Motivating the Elephant" is the term used by the Heath brothers to describe forming an emotional bond with your goal. While a logical view is necessary to know the desired outcome, an emotional bond will provide the endurance and motivation to move – and stay moving – toward the goal.

The Heath brothers use the "elephant" example to illustrate the proportion of the importance of appealing to the emotional brain. In general, people don't do what makes sense; they "follow their heart," or "use their intuition." They react emotionally, even irrationally, when presented with logical stimuli.

The Growth Mindset

At the beginning of this text, you read the story of Kris: an autistic child whose parents dedicated themselves emotionally, financially, and socially to his ongoing development. "Can you imagine a better family for Kris to belong to?" was the comment from our third partner. What made that family so great? The Growth Mindset.

To Kris' family, every step was important – but not every step was a step forward. Instead, "setbacks" were viewed as learning experiences. No money, no time, no effort was ever 'wasted' – instead, discoveries were made into what did work, and what did not.

When Kris spent more time with male therapists, he

tended to develop his physical skills quickly. When he spent more time with female therapists, he tended to progress more socially. This may appear to be a broad generalization, but Kris' parents are also both scientists, and familiar with objective measurement. This is empirical data – their observation – but still relevant.

What was most important to Kris' success? The long-term view, and the understanding that not every session would appear to have a positive, measurable outcome.

If you've ever conducted a job interview, you've heard a common response to a popular question:

"What's one area where you're weak?"

"Well," goes the scripted line, "....I'm a bit of a perfectionist...."

This is a line rehearsed with career counsellors, student advisors, and other job coaches before the interview process. Is it a good answer?

Perfectionism, we'd argue, is detrimental to the end goal. If the goal is to be perfect - which is, of course, unattainable - then the process is flawed from the outset.

Our principal tool for encouraging adherence, progress, and forward movement: Bright Spots. (We'll write more about Bright Spots later in this book.) However, it's tough to apply Bright Spots when the goal is perfection: are you, personally, more perfect than yesterday? How would you measure 'perfect?'

With that in mind - that 'perfect' is subjective and, therefore, not measurable - we submit that 'perfect' is not valid goal, and that 'perfectionism' is a negative trait.

Perfectionism causes a tendency that we'll call *paralysis by analysis*. Rather than taking action, a participant waits for the perfect moment, or the perfect answer, or the perfect solution. "Something better will come to me," is the early iteration of a dead man walking. Dissemination of all possible variables, whether deciding where to buy gas or analyzing poll data, takes time that could be spend executing.

Try this analogy: a perfectionist walks into a room in need of paint. The paint, rollers, and tape are already in the room. "This will take at least three hours," says the perfectionist, "I'll come back when I have time." Time, of course, never creates itself, and work expands to fill the time available. That's Parkinson's Law.

The Growth Mindset is our modern-day version of Kaizen - the lifetime pursuit of 'better.' The Growth Mindset requires belief that you can never be 'perfect' - but you can always be better than you currently are. It requires a humble submission to the concept of Beginner's Mind - that there's always more to learn on any subject - and that any action toward positive change is better than none.

Let's return to our analogy above. A student of the Growth Mindset enters the room to be painted; "I have five minutes now," she says; "Enough time to tape the first wall." Slowly, bit by bit, the room grows closer to satisfactory completion.

Applied to a physical example, let's use the example of double-unders: a technical skill requiring little physical strength, but a lot of practice. The perfectionist fully expects to be able to link fifty double-unders by the end of the month. Today, though, is Deadlift day, and he wants to focus all his attention on lifting. His coach gave him a warmup - perfect for the deadlift - and he doesn't want to deviate from that process. After his max deadlift, he's "too tired" to practice well, and needs to be 20 minutes early for his next appointment, so he leaves without practising.

The student with a Growth Mindset considers that they have to do some kind of warmup, but it doesn't have to be perfect. Therefore, five minutes can be spared to practice. After a full minute, the student achieves ONE double-under - Bright Spot - but can't link two together. No matter, because partial success has been achieved, and the student can't wait to try again the next day. In fact, after deadlifting, the student is encouraged enough to try again for a few minutes, even though he risks being late for his next appointment....

We believe in the value of "good-better-best." But 'good' is not a step in the road toward 'perfect.' Perfect is the ENEMY of good, because it hampers the Growth Mindset.

The way we feel about a situation triggers specific neurotransmitters. Objectively speaking, to the body/mind every experience is simply an event. The way we choose to perceive that event, coloured by our emotions, determines our response to it and our potential for learning from it.

When a new client, Brianne, started with *Ignite!*, she had just begun a college-level course that had no relevance to her long-term goals. Her therapists, bright and well-meaning, believed that enrolment in an 'easy' topic of study would allow her to build confidence in the classroom; practice structure with scheduling tasks; and allow her to rebuild her study habits after her traumatic brain injury.

Brianne was very intimidated by the prospect of delivering a group presentation. "What if I forget everything?" "What if I mess up?" Her confidence was still very weak after performing basic movement therapy. This was the *Ignite!* approach:

First, her NeuroMotive Therapist did some warmup exercises to get her mind off the stress. This was a temporary tactic, designed to allow her to open up and talk about each potential outcome of the group presentation. She had recently had success with skipping, and bought a rope with which to practice at home – a huge Bright Spot - so the Coach had her practice that skill. Next, they used a Memory Palace (we'll include more on Memory Palaces later in this book) to help her recall the 7 topics in her part of the presentation. To make sure she knew them, the Coach asked her to run on the treadmill and repeat them; then skip and recite them; and then, perform two rounds of "Cindy" and recall them again. When she completed each task – in ascending order of difficulty – perfectly, Brianne and the Coach both knew that she could recall the subject matter while stressed. This discovery allowed Brianne to eliminate the anxiety component from her list of potential tripping stones.

The next problem addressed by the Coach was the speed at which Brianne could read. His strategy was to simulate the environment in which she had the most success reading....in her bedroom, where she was relaxed. Practising a visualization to 'put herself in her bedroom,' she read as rapidly as possible...at least as well as a normal teenager. Brianne could cross her fear of reading aloud from her list of potential trip-ups.

After removing these two sources of anxiety, the only item left on Brianne's list was her presentation plan: her actual steps for delivering the information to her group. This plan was simple: they wrote out the steps together on a large whiteboard.

By the end of the session, she had a list of 3 steps to complete. Her focus was on those steps and she never once worried about negative scenarios, because she had specific tasks that she was confident she could complete. She aced the project.

Months later, Brianne was faced with another potentially negative experience. Starting a new online class, she was asked how she felt about the prospect. Her reply: "I hope it's not hard...." sent up red flags for her NeuroMotive Coach.

His comments: "This girl was in trouble. The brain/body does not recognize negative instructions. It was the classic, "don't-think-about-the-purple-elephant game." With that mindset, she would unconsciously be searching through the syllabus for topics that were going to be hard. She would only pay attention to the information that she couldn't understand, which would just reinforce in her brain how *impossible* this would all be."

Brianne's Coach quickly intervened. "What are the steps you are going to take to make this course easier on you?" he asked.

She knew where he was going with this line of questioning. She rolled her eyes, sighed; and said, "I'll look for what I know, or can do."

"And what are you going to do about the stuff you don't know about yet?" he followed.

Like a child who knows when their parent is right, "Use the steps to finding information out of a text." she responded. Brianne's Coach had given her a two-step plan for approaching her new course: do the easy things first; then follow the steps to retrieving information that was new to her. Crisis averted. Her NeuroMotive Coach killed the negative experience before it had a chance to grow into a serious learning problem.

At least 80% of what we perceive in our lives takes shape in our mind with a heavy dependence on where we focus our attention. We can change our reality by changing what we focus on and pay attention to. If we perceive an upcoming event as a potential disaster, the neurotransmitter *adrenalin* is released and the mind, followed by the body, responds with a series of survival-oriented reactions. With increased adrenalin, we also produce the neurotransmitter *cortisol* that decreases our ability to learn and remember. However, if we choose to perceive the event as a learning experience, or an adventure; if we have a specific procedure to focus our attention, and have played out all the variables in our minds; and in such away eliminated potentially negative factors, then other neurotransmitters like dopamine, GABA, acetylcholine, nerve growth factor, interferon and interleukins are released. These increase our ability to establish or reorganize neural networks so that we may effectively think and remember. The release of neurotransmitters are intimately intertwined with cognitive function.

The Talent Myth

What did Mozart, the Beatles, and Bill Gates have in common? If you answered, "they're geniuses!," you're close. They're all masters. They've all been given great chances in life. And they've all spent thousands – tens of thousands – of hours practising.

Are students born 'gifted?' Are there really prodigies? Are some kids just destined to menial work?

In the last five years, several authors have drilled down into the myth that our fate is predetermined. The earliest to popularize the practice paradigm was Malcolm Gladwell in his book, *Outliers*, where he posits that the most elite among us have been the beneficiaries of both opportunities to practice, and a quality coaching environment.

Recently, Mathew Syed went more in-depth with the 'practice paradigm' in his book, *Bounce*. A former world champion table tennis player, Syed stresses that not luck, but practice and opportunity for coaching made him reach the top. He cites dozens of others who reached the top of their field, and are frequently heralded as geniuses, who merely had access to practice time and equipment.

For instance, Mozart had a father who was a composer, and a piano at an age where very few youth had the luxury. The Beatles took gigs that lasted 4 months at a time in Russia, where they'd play for 8 hours a day, experimenting with songs from every genre. Bill Gates lucked into a private school – the first in California to have a computer for its students. Syed lived down the street from the top Table Tennis coach in the world, and was given a table for Christmas when he was four. Each of these 'prodigies' had a series of good fortune, not an exceptional birth.

It's true that children born to wealthier parents in first-world countries have more chance of success in life than their cousins born in remote regions of third-world countries. Access to better nutrition, prenatal care, education, and sports coaching shapes the paths of generations. But this has nothing to do with a cosmic wheel of fortune; rather, the care and practice of families, access to reşources, and exposure to practice.

In the introduction to *Outliers*, Gladwell relates the story of how he became interested in the notion of 'natural talent.'

Gladwell was attending a Junior-level hockey game. At the Junior level, players are competing to be drafted into the professional ranks. Gladwell noticed that the players ranked highest – or who seemed to possess the most natural talent, and who had garnered the most points over the season – all seemed to have birthdays in the first three months of the year. The number of January, February, and March birthdays were over-represented among the top players in the league. Intrigued, Gladwell set out to explain this correlation....and try to uncover any causative link.

The cycle that he discovered is perpetuated throughout

sport: the older players are bigger at an early age. By age eight, a child who is born in January will be quite a bit larger than a December baby; the developmental difference at such a time of rapid development is magnified.

The larger child – older by months – is perceived as a player with more 'talent' or 'potential,' and is selected to play at a higher level (usually, a rep team, which gets better and more coaching.) The larger child is entered into a cycle of higher-level coaching; more practice time; competition against better opponents; more exposure to other coaches and scouts; more critique and feedback. Over the course of the next 10 years, this cycle magnifies the prospects of the player, and the opportunities afforded them help them reach much higher levels. Thus is The Talent Myth perpetuated.

Bright Spots

One of the major problems people have, when making changes or starting new habits, is that they focus too much on the negative. *"I'm fat. I'm out of shape. I have no willpower..."* we hear these all the time in the fitness practices. People perceive that they're starting to push a heavy car from a dead stop, and fail to acknowledge that, most of the time, the car is either already rolling or on a downhill slope. Chip and Dan Heath *(Switch!)* believe it's a mistake to start the goal-setting process from that negative point.

Instead, they recommend that the student identify Bright Spots first. Chances are, a new fitness client isn't doing EVERYTHING wrong; they're just doing the right things infrequently. Even if they're reading about exercise, but not acting on it, they're doing something. Your first job with a new student, or with yourself, is to identify a few

Bright Spots in the past, and then try to isolate some small bright spots in the future.

Q: *What are you doing right now that's working?*

A: Be specific. "Well, I'm walking the dog every day." "I'm trying hard" isn't specific enough. "I really WANT to this time!" is too vague.

For a student: "I'm reading my textbook on the bus ride home." The bus ride may be too distracting, but the student has already formed a positive habit, at least.

Build on that first Bright Spot. "OK, let's keep that going."

Next, try to duplicate that Bright Spot. "How do you feel while you're walking your dog? What do you think about? What do you enjoy about it? Where do you go? What do you enjoy seeing? What's the best part? Do you prefer to walk your dog at the end of the day, or in the morning? Do you enjoy seeing your dog have fun?" Find out WHY. It's important to make an emotional connection, rather than just a logical one.

For a student: "I read on the bus because I don't have time when I get home. The bus ride is boring. None of my friends are on the bus with me..." Questions to ask: what part of reading on the bus do you enjoy – the pictures? The uninterrupted time?

THEN do goal-setting. Let's say that the fitness client would like to lose 10lbs. It would be nice if a client came in and said, "I want to improve work capacity across broad time and modal domains." That doesn't happen. So let's go with what's more likely.

Q: How will that goal make you feel when it's attained? What made you choose that number, specifically? How do you think you'll look / feel / act?

You're getting the client to 'try on' the goal, and as anyone in retail knows, if they try it, they'll sell themselves on it. Practising success is as important as practising ping-pong. The phrase, "fake it 'til you make it" is relevant and effective when a student practices the art of winning.

One day, while riding the bus, you'll read the last page of the textbook. How will you feel then? Someday, you'll see something toward the end of the book, and relate it to something you read earlier. How will that feel? How will you know you've made a connection?

Q: What will be your first sign that you're succeeding? Let's say that you wake up tomorrow, and 10 pounds have melted off. What's the first thing you'll do that will be different? How will you come to realize that the weight is gone? What will change in your life? What will you have for breakfast on that day? How will you dress?

At this point, a coach is trying to establish their first milestone. Be specific. Don't accept, for instance, "I'll know I'm succeeding when I get on the scale and two pounds are gone." Instead, "I'll know because I'll feel lighter when I wake up. I'll know because my husband/wife will comment that I look better. I'll know because my pyjamas feel loose." THAT'S your first milestone : loose pyjamas drawstring. Write that down for them.

When they've achieved their first milestone, a coach can revisit the questions and establish their second. This short-circuits the three-month conversation you're likely to face if you don't break down the goal-setting process:

Client: "I feel great. My clothes are loose. I'm stronger and more flexible and my back pain is gone. My wife can't keep her hands off me. My hair is even coming in thicker! I don't drink as much coffee, I'm more alert, I'm not depressed. But I still haven't lost 10lbs!" If you're like me, this is one of the most aggravating conversations you can have.

Student: "I read the whole book! I figured out how chemicals help move a molecule across a membrane. I got an A in the class – my parents are jacked, and my University application looks WAY better! But...I still don't see how this is important to me..."

The small goals, in this case, don't even have to be objective. At the three-month checkup, you can go down their list with them: has your spouse noticed a difference? Are your clothes looser? Do you feel better when you wake up? Check, check, check. Goal attained. On to the next.

Big problems aren't solved with big solutions, but with a bunch of smaller steps. The magnitude of the solution shouldn't try to match the size of the problem. If a new client is 400lbs, they may believe that they require more change than someone who weighs 200lbs. That's not true; in fact, the opposite is true. It's easier to lose 50lbs if you're 400lbs than if you're 200lbs. You don't have to lose 200lbs, but two pounds...a hundred times. Just keep focusing on the two pounds.

It's common, if you're a teacher, to hear this distressing sentence: "I want to be a (insert scientist title here,) but I need to take physics to get into the program, and I'm SO BAD at math!"

Now, we know that the real problem isn't the grades necessary to get into the degree program at the University of the student's choice. The real problem is that the student is afraid of failure. In this case, the stakes are so high that the fear is nearly paralyzing.

Think about your fear of falling off the bottom step in a staircase: it's not terrifying. Yes, you may bruise your hands or knees, but that's the worst-case scenario. Now, pretend you're at the top of the staircase, and you fall down one stair. Much scarier? Of course: the magnitude of the fall hasn't changed, but the aftereffect changes the context. If you fall from the top stair, you're unlikely to stop until you reach the bottom. If you fail a physics test, you may not be able to recover your grade to a high enough level to be accepted into University. If you're not accepted, you'll have taken physics for nothing; wasted a semester of study; risked isolation from your social group by not graduating with them; risked your ego integrity by failing.

Later in this book, we'll talk about the practise paradigm and the growth mindset – two tools we use to short-circuit the paralyzing fear of failure that's rampant in our educational culture.   Using bright spots, though, we can encourage the student to seek knowledge from the physics course, and use that knowledge to leverage career choices later on.

The Art of Theatre

Emotion drives long-term, clear and vivid memory. Forming an emotional connection with a goal is critical for engagement. Any learning opportunity should be an emotional experience to ensure memory and adherence.

Theatrical elements of coaching require the coach to be

charismatic. When writing this text, one of our biggest hurdles was, "How do we teach people to be Tyler?" Tyler is our Director of Education, and he sweats personality. Charisma rises from him like a musk. Obviously, not everyone is charismatic, or can deftly handle students the way Tyler does. However, these are NOT genetic traits (though Tyler's parents are both kind, outgoing people with dozens of friends.)

Rather, charisma is a learned and practised characteristic. Even the shyest farmboy can overcome his squeamishness, given the proper stimulus, time for recovery and rebuilding, and consistent positive feedback. *Ignite!* Director of Education Tyler 'learned' charisma as a young child, when his parents would host frequent dinners and house parties. His brother is also charismatic, having practised interaction with people from the earliest age.

If you're a parent, you've heard this before. Your five-year-old isn't interested in Little Red Riding Hood, not really; they just want to hear the Big Bad Wolf voice. Voice inflection is more powerful than you may realize. It goes without saying that it's critical to project an enthusiastic demeanour to students, but doing the same thing all the time - same cheers, same words of encouragement, same gestures - can become monotone. Students acclimate to teachers who repeat the same words, jokes, and motions all the time. And since we already know that novelty is king, acclimatization is a negative.

If you're a coach, here are some steps to changing and applying inflection during a tough workout:

- ⅄ Get on their level - if they're on the floor, get down with them. Try to make eye contact.

- Alternate pulling and pushing, carrot and stick: "Don't Stop. Five more to go!" "Let's do another three, and then take a five-second break." "Keep your hands on the bar!" "Okay, let's try to get the first thirty unbroken."
- Use a more intimate voice when things get REALLY tough. At the start of the WOD, it's great to be loud and screamy. With three reps left on Grace, though, I'm standing so close that I'm practically sharing their shirt.
- In that same vein, a low voice - just above a whisper - adds a degree of intimacy that lets the athlete know that they are receiving your undivided, private attention at that moment. Eye contact can also work wonders from across a room.
- Building: in a crowded, noisy gym, if you see one athlete struggling, start with a calm, empathetic voice. "Okay, you're doing well. You're already over half done. Three more seconds rest, and we stand up again. 3...2....1....okay, great. Hands on the bar." Building speed and pitch into your speech can lead to a crescendo of action.
- In a quiet gym, with an athlete attempting a personal best, you can draw attention to their attempt with the slow buildup, too. Start with the personal and intimate, as above, and slowly build up your magnitude until people are taking notice. Nothing beats the private attention of a coach when you're trying hard; and nothing beats applause when you succeed.
- A deeper voice seems more sincere.
- Different scenarios require different voices (and different personalities.) Outside? loud. Max deadlift? Loud, from behind. OLY technique day? The best music, as tested in many studies by the former Soviet Union, is one which reinforces pride in the individual. The USSR lifting music of

choice? Marches. Modern-day, North American music? It may be rap. It may be southern Rock. The point is, it must be novel enough for the lifter to give it some attention, and familiar enough that it isn't distracting.

As with anything else, frequent change is best. To illustrate the technique to our interns on Tuesday night, I went systematically from one athlete to the next in a circuit during the WOD. I used a different voice every time I made a lap. It wasn't spontaneous; it was planned. The athletes didn't notice that I was always encouraging them in the same order. They didn't see the pattern. What they DID recognize was individual attention, tailored to fit their exact predicament.

Theatrical elements in your coaching can include loud praising in front of others; changing tone and pitch of voice to lessen and build excitement; using external props (like a giant clock) to build an atmosphere, or even encouraging viewership from "fans."

It's less about novelty for its own sake than it is about forming an emotional connection with students and clients. As you gain experience, you'll recognize the time to whisper; the time to talk; and the time to yell.

When using *Ignite!* by yourself, creating a theatrical environment is still fairly simple. The best stage for imagination is within your own mind, of course.

Einstein famously decreed that a person didn't understand physics until they were able to explain it to a ten-year-old. That very image is a powerful tool: take the lesson you're trying to learn, and pretend to teach it to someone younger, or someone with less background in the subject, or someone with no prior knowledge at all. Not only is it helpful for memorization purposes (changing the context and language helps create a stronger engram) but it causes you to think about a familiar concept in a new way.

Another option for creating a sense of dramatic importance around learning a new skill: do it 'for time.' For example: run through your notes, from A-F, as many times possible in 1 minute. Rest 1 minute; try it again. Record your times. Then move on to something else. Try it again next week, and attempt to 'beat' your previous score.

Some students like to study to music. A word of warning, though: the brain can only track one line of thought at a time. If you're actively listening to music, you're not actively storing other information. A simple test: can you name the last song that played before the current one? If so, you're paying too much attention to background noise.

The Social Contract

We all have an unwritten set of promises that we've made, by default, with people we meet or see. For instance, it's understood that every other driver at the stop light will wait for the green light to shine before they drive into the intersection. Yes, it's the law; but the police aren't at every intersection at all times.

Instead, the inherent trust for other humans that is implicit in every interaction is necessary for us to succeed as a society. If we can't trust one another to behave in a predictable way, we raise our defense mechanisms...and disable the ability to learn.

Most objection, defensiveness, and argument has its foundation in fear: the fear of being embarrassed in public (more serious than death for many people); the fear of rejection; the fear of being wrong, and thereby compromising the ego.

If you've ever been in an argument (and who hasn't?) you'll recall a time when your original point was defeated, and you scrambled to support your position with other 'facts' or 'data' that aren't relevant to the original conversation. Sometimes, afterward, you'll regret the argument and think, "Why did I say that, anyway?"

The amygdala plays a large role here. We call the amygdala "the Lizard Brain," because it was formed at a much earlier stage in our evolution, and lies deep beneath the neocortex. Its job: keep us safe. Run from trouble, or fight with everything you've got. Differentiate yourself from enemies in order to be embraced by the Tribe. Reinforce that you are similar to your friends...

Unfortunately, the psychological contracts we make with people occur as part of our relatively new ability to think at a high level. We experience complicated love (and not just lust,) or desire things for reasons that aren't immediately occurring (we save money to buy a new car sometime next year.) The amygdala doesn't understand 'the future,' though. The Lizard Brain only understands the immediate perceived needs of the body; and as we discussed earlier in our ice cream cone example, the Lizard Brain is always working.

Therefore, our need to win an argument can sometimes trump our need to remain on good terms with a coworker. We go too far: "You can't even spell the word! Why would we listen to you at all?!?" and insult the person, rather than debating the message. In Latin, "argumentum ad hominem" literally means to attempt to counter the claim by attacking the person behind the claim.

If a convicted murderer, for instance, told you that a Dodge Caravan was the best van on the market, would it matter that he was a mechanic before he was incarcerated? Probably not: his opinion is automatically discarded, because he's broken the social contract (and the law!) between himself and the rest of the Tribe at large.

When a new client enrols at the Ignite! Academy, we have a piece of paper that lays out their responsibilities, and our commitments as NeuroMotive Coaches. It includes a waiver, a PAD form, and a couple of other ground rules (our fifth bullet point at the *Ignite!* Academy: *"I promise to be nice to everyone."*)

But the *real* contract - the one on which we'll be judged - isn't written down. It's the *understanding* that fills the spaces between the text. The type of member we desire is the one who doesn't need the contract. They don't need the burpee penalty, because they're not late. They take off their wet shoes at the door because they don't want others to have wet socks.

You promise not to cheat on your wife. That's not in your marriage contract; it doesn't have to be. It's unwritten. And these rules also exist with your members, students, teachers, and children *(I promise not to embarrass you in front of the group,)* with other drivers *(I promise not to cut you off and potentially make you crash,)* and perfect strangers *(I promise not to spit on you.)*

Problems arise when the Psychological Contract isn't fulfilled. REAL problems - the divorce kind - happen when two partners are keeping two different contracts.

Change is uncomfortable. But if you're building a family in your box, you have a psychological contract with those members to address them like family. Changing your rates? Tell them so - but not as a corporate robot. Not as someone who reports to a Board, or appears rigid. Tell them as Coach Mike.

Dr. Shirley Glass, a renowned expert on marriage infidelity, talks about "walls and windows" - basically, the parts of your relationships that you make public, and the parts that you keep discreet. In a marriage, of course, it's important to keep some things 'behind walls' - that is, your squabbles; the bathroom tendencies of your spouse; his bad habits, her bad hair. When these things are made public - or a window is placed where a wall should be - the social contract between spouses is broken. Gossip to your best friend about his distaste for flossing? That's breaking his confidence. Tell your buddies her real hair colour? Should have kept that wall standing, friend.

I use this analogy to illustrate the opposite point: that, too often as coaches and teachers, we place walls where we should have windows. We create barriers that restrict our sphere -or bubble - of influence, rather than open windows to expand our social circle.

Example: a new client - thin, ponytailed, wearing a race t-shirt and shorts with a high cut - comes in to ask about our gym. She mentions that she coaches a running group. Is this a good response?

> ⚔ "We do POSE running. Most people do too much distance. Have you ever read CrossFit Endurance? I'm certified. Do you have bad knees? You probably have too much heel strike. You need to get stronger hamstrings...."

Count, if you will, the walls that I've erected in the above paragraph (I see seven points of difference that I've put up; seven things that tell her, "we're different than you"; seven things that identify me as "not in your bubble, missy. Not in your Tribe." If you squirm a bit, here, don't worry: I've been guilty of this type of thing for FIFTEEN years.

Is this better:

> ⚔ "I run, but I'm not great at it. I did a few races last year, just for fun; I really like cross-country stuff better. My ADHD brain tends to like variety, so distances scare the hell out of me...." ?

At this point, she may laugh and say, "Me too." When she does, you may see a small shimmer around and above you; that's the merging of two bubbles. Emphasize your windows, not your walls.

On a final note, the best way to open windows: shared love for the topic. Getting that across at the start of the conversation places you inside the same mental 'bubble' right away.

Positivity....and Love?

Emotions are generated from biologically-automated pathways and have been found in cross-cultural studies to be experienced by people universally. 6 of the most commonly studied are joy, fear, surprise, disgust, anger and sadness.

How do we know that the emotion of joy, for instance, is biologically wired instead of learned from our parents? The greatest example I've ever heard: *blind babies smile*.

The main function of emotion is to get the mind and body ready to perform an action or act that's appropriate to the emotional stimuli. Actions can be trained, and so can the corresponding emotional response. Since the emotional response occurs before the conscious recognition of a stimulus (a relic from an ancient part of our brain, developed before the modern parts) our response to new stimulus is usually pre-empted by emotion. Emotion, then, determines the backdrop (or lack thereof) and perceived importance of new information that we receive, even BEFORE we process that we've learned anything.

Feelings, on the other hand, are our culturally and environmentally developed responses to circumstances. Worry, anticipation, frustration, cynicism and optimism are all feelings that can be practised, avoided, or encouraged. The way we react to emotional stimuli, too, can help change feelings; and vice versa.

In a 1996 study, Nesse [36]suggests that natural selection shapes emotions only for situations that contain threats or opportunities. There are more threats in our environment than opportunities, unfortunately. The cost of failure to a threat could mean death and the cost of failure to an opportunity is not likely dire.[37] Therefore, the body reacts with more emotion to a threat than to an opportunity, and we're more likely to dwell on things that can do us harm than things that may give us joy: *"As soon as I get this big speech over with, I can just relax and enjoy my weekend...."*

There are many different health problems related to negative emotions: stress has strong links to heart disease, and some cancers; fear and anxiety fuel phobias and anxiety disorders. Jealousy fuels aggression and violence, and substance abuse. 17% of US citizens self-identify themselves as "depressed." The path from 'shame' to eating disorder is well documented.

Positive emotions, though, aren't hard-wired as quickly, because the brain deems them less important. They don't become automated at the same rate, and less priority is given to them since no threat is perceived. Rather, they must become automatic after much exposure through personal experience, practise, and exposure to circumstances where they're tested.[38] Yes,

36 Nesse, Randolph M. Natural selection and the elusiveness of happiness. The Royal Society. Published online 31 August 2004

37 Pratto F, John oP. Automatic vigilance: The attention grabbing power of negative social information. Journal of Personality and Social Psychology. 1991;61:380–391

38Levenson, R., Ekman, P., & Friesen, W. ~1990!. Voluntary facial action generates emotion-specific autonomic nervous system activity. *Psychophysiology,*27, 363–384.

everyone feels joy, but not everyone feels joy during the same circumstances. Some people are so caught up in failure that even when positive feelings DO occur, they're automatically tempered with, *"this doesn't usually happen," "I got lucky", "...just wait for the other shoe to drop," "it's a rare surprise," "what's the worst-case scenario now...."*

Specific action tendencies and organized plastic (physiological) change go hand in hand. We are able to change our reaction to emotions through practise, and this results in a physiological long-term change in the plastic brain.

Positive emotions:

- ⚔ Broaden the scope of attention – create a 'safe' feeling, and spark interest.

- ⚔ Broaden the scope of cognition – influence creative thinking, lower defences, open new information-processing strategies, help students perform better on standard test of creative thinking.[39]

- ⚔ Broaden the scope of action – trigger a wider range of types of play, more variations of action within play types, and longer play episodes. [40]

- ⚔ Build physical resources – through rough and tumble play, development of vascular endurance, muscular strength, fight skills and tactics, bonding, predator avoidance and hunting, survival instincts, locomotor skills, and the vestibular system as a

[39]Schwarz, N., W♦nke, M., & Bless, H. (1994). Subjective assessments and evaluations of change: Some lessons from social cognition research. *European Review of Social Psychology, 5*, 181-210.

[40]Renninger, K. A., Hidi, S., & Krapp, A. (1992). The role of interest in learning anddevelopment. Hillsdale, N. J., L. Erlbaum Associates.

whole.

⅄ Create intellectual resources – an early safe feeling from a caregiver provides a foundation for interest.

⅄ Spark inspired exploration - which can increase a child's cognitive or intellectual resources. Securely-attached children engage in more independent exploration of a novel physical space and develop superior cognitive maps of that space as indicated by their performance on tests of spatial knowledge. [41]

⅄ Build a greater interest in learning - which has been linked to greater conceptual understanding, higher levels of academic achievement, lower drop out rates, and greater psychological adjustments.[42]

⅄ Build social resources – shared smiles, laughter, social play, enduring alliances, and friendships, increasing the likelihood that an individual will help others who are in need. Cooperating and turn-taking is reinforced.

⅄ Protect health – improved heart health and some cancer risks are greatly reduced. Relaxation techniques, stress relievers, and 'happy places' all rely on positive emotions to exist. Students who report themselves as 'generally happy' or even

[41] HAZEN, N. L., & DURRETT, M. E. Relationship of security of attachment to explotation and cognitive mapping abilities in 2-year-olds. *Developmental Psychologe* 1982 18, 751-759-

[42] Deci, E. L., Vallerand, R. J., Pelletier, L. G., & Ryan, R. M. (1991). 'Motivation and education: The self-determination perspective.' Educational Psychologist, 26, 325-346.

'moderately happy' on surveys also tend to make healthier choices, accept more responsibility, and carry on the feeling of health later into life.

⅄ Undo negative effects – loosen the grip that negative emotions can have on people's thinking.

⅄ Promote the sense of 'flow' – which we'll discuss soon.

The four main positive emotions

1. *Joy.* Happiness, amusement, elation...for feelings of joy to be present, the brain must assess the situation as one that is safe, familiar, and requiring low effort. In this case, 'low effort' means that the challenge is equal to the skill level at which the student can perform the skill unconsciously, and still have full use of their cognitive processes.

Frijda [43] terms joy as "free activation" - readiness to engage in any challenge that presents itself as enjoyable. In turn, this 'free activation' creates the urge and willingness to play and be playful. This 'play' encompasses not just the physical, but also the social, intellectual, and artistic.

Starting an *Ignite!* lesson by first drawing out joy is

> Note: it's not acting. I truly love seeing each and every one of my clients walk in that door and knowing they're going to work hard and have a great session that day. Joy lasts a long time. The simple act of laughter can last up to 2 days after the joke. Arthor Stone, Ph.D at the State University of New York and Colleagues (1987) says that "having fun and pleasant experiences improve the functioning of the body's immune system for three days – the day of the event and two days after." - Tyler Belanger, Director of Education, *Ignite!*

simple: students can do so through their own thoughts; through encouraging the recall of Bright Spots (see below;) through performing exercises that they have recently mastered and are proud they can do. Coaches can encourage joy with a joke; or behaving as though see the student made the coach's day.

---

43 Frijda, N. H. (1986). The emotions. Cambridge, England: Cambridge University Press.

2. *Interest.* Curiosity, intrigue, excitement or wonder....the emotion of 'interest' shares conceptual space with challenge and intrinsic motivation[44]. Again, we should note that interest in a topic is only pursued if the skills of the individual match the challenges of the activity. If the challenge is too easy, loss of interest occurs quickly. If the challenge is too tough, a loss of interest occurs immediately because of a humbling blow to the intrinsic motivation. Interest is the emotion experienced most frequently[45]. Interest arises in environments that have been appraised by the student as safe, and as offering novelty, change, a sense of possibility, or mystery. Situations that are appraised as important and as requiring effort and attention are the prime triggers of interest.[46]

Interest is a feeling of wanting to investigate; it's the inner push that sends the individual into the exploration phase of learning. Sometimes, all it takes is the desire to feel included; to be a part of an identity. Interest is triggered when a student senses a potential increase to their RELEVANT knowledge base.

Environmental aesthetics is the one of the best examples

44Deci, E. L., & Ryan, R. M. (1985). Intrinsic motivation and self-determinaton in human behaviour. New York: Plenum.

45Izard, C. E. (1997). Eotions and facial expressions: A perspective from differential emotions theory. In J. A. Russell & J. M.

Fernandez-Dols (Eds.), The psychology of facial expression (pp. 57–77). Cambridge, UK: Cambridge University Press.

46(Ellsworth & Smith, 1988.) Shades of joy: patters of appraisal differentiating pleasant emotions. Cognition and Emotion, 2, 301-331.

of arousing people's interest. *Kaplan (1992)[47]* has argued that some landscapes encouraged human ancestors to

explore and seek new information, which in turn served to update and extend their cognitive maps. This expanding knowledge base could then be drawn on in later instances that threatened survival - e.g. finding water, food, escape routes or hiding places. Interest builds a store of knowledge. *Izard[48]* wrote that,"interest is the primary instigator of personal growth, creative endeavour, and the development of intelligence."

3. *Contentment* – tranquility or serenity..... contentment triggers the same areas of the brain as do mild or receptive joy and, to some degree, relief.[49] This emotion prompts individuals to savour their current life circumstances and recent success; experience "oneness" with the world around them; and integrate recent events and achievements into their overall self-concept and world view.[50] Contentment is the positive emotion that follows experiences such as being in 'flow' – when the cognitive capabilities match the cognitive challenges presented to them. Physically, it frequently leads to positive self-talk, which can lead to improved self-esteem, increasing self-awareness, appreciation for the self and for others.

---

[47]Kaplan, S. (1992). Environmental preference in a knowledge-seeking knowledge-using organism. In J. H. Barkow, L. Cosmides, & J. Tooby (Eds.). The Adaptive Mind. New York: Oxford University Press (pp. 535-552).

[48]Izard, C. E. (1977). Human emotions. New York: Plenum Press.

[49]Lazarus, R. S. (1991). Emotion and adaptation. New York: Oxford University Press.

[50]De Rivera, J., Possel, L., Verette, J. A., & Weiner, B. (1989). Distinguishing elation, gladness, and joy. Journal of Personality and Social Psychology, 57,1015-1023.

4. *Love* – a fusion of all other specific positive emotions of interest, contentment, and joy. Love broadens the momentary thought-action repertoire as people explore, savour and play. Love strengthens social bonds and attachments. It builds and solidifies an individual's social resources.

Flow

The state of 'flow' is one in which the student or practitioner can operate their brains freely, without consideration to the movement of their body. The 'flow' state presents an interesting paradigm: on the one hand, the body must be performing a task for which it has been well-prepared; on the other, the task must not be TOO challenging, or the brain will be required for conscious consideration of each movement.

It's necessary for the central and peripheral nervous systems to remain alert while the brain relaxes. This is best achieved through repetitive work, simple exercise, or holding a challenging static posture with which the student is well familiar.

Sitting in a posture that helps thought – as mastered by monks, Yogis, and other religious practitioners – must be practised and physically mastered before 'flow' can be present. Think about a newcomer attempting a headstand – an elite but fundamental move in some forms of Yoga. The newcomer would be completely unable to relax and focus, because all their mental and physical energy would be required to find and maintain the balance necessary for the headstand. Over months and years of practice, though, the headstand is intrinsically learned to the point where it becomes innate, requiring no conscious effort, but only reflexive physical movement without thought.

On the other end of the spectrum, it would seem as though the act of lying completely still would be more beneficial to achieve the 'flow' state, since it requires very little activation of skeletal muscle to lie flat on one's back. However, in this case, the body isn't stimulated at all, and the central nervous system isn't required to remain alert. The body is relaxed, and so is the brain; sleep usually follows. For flow to occur, there must be stimulation of the nervous system, even as the brain frees itself from the constraints of consciousness.

We've all experienced the 'flow state': that mental paradigm where we move easily from one thought to the next, making connections and staying on task. We enter the flow state while doing simple labours, like cleaning and piling wood – two actions that easily become automatic – and time can pass quickly while in that state. Most will acknowledge that they have their best ideas while in the state of flow. More examples:

- ⚔ Driving;

- ⚔ Singing in the shower;

- ⚔ Playing the guitar, after years of practice

It's important that there IS enough stimulus to challenge the CNS, but not enough to require conscious thought.

The 'Flow' state is important to major religions, who describe it in different ways; to scientists and writers who seek 'breakthroughs.' To some, the state of 'busy bliss' is, literally, their heaven, after they've acknowledged the experience.

Taoism, in particular, encourages "Thinking Body, Dancing Mind." In a book by the same title, author Chungliang Al Huang writes, "Does the body, indeed, think? It does when you cease to interfere with its deep-seated intelligence, known as instinct or intuitive physical response. Does the mind dance? It does when you free it to flow with life's natural processes, when you loosen your tendency toward critical judgement and control. A dancing mind is relaxed, visionary, and open to the full range of human possibility.

However, the 'flow' state is as illusive as it is worthy. Frequently, we're bogged down with negative thoughts, checklists, or other attention-drainers that require too much conscious effort without physical effort being involved.

For example, think about the dishes waiting for you in your sink. Perhaps a date is coming over after work, and you're worried that you won't have time to clean your kitchen before she arrives. Though the work is simple – you've done it hundreds of times – it's distracting, because the importance attributed to the task far outweighs the action required to complete the task. For the full workday, you think about your sink full of dishes waiting at home; strategize ways to leave work quickly, or even early, to get them done; consider other options (inviting her out to eat); even think about worst-case scenarios.

Meanwhile, your work goes unfinished, because you're unable to enter the state of unconscious focus necessary to work through your to-do list at the office. These tiny, day-to-day distractions, which may take little effort but can't be immediately resolved, build up into a logjam that prevents 'flow.'

Negative emotions are the largest culprits here, since your brain is hardwired to focus on threats and emotional responses to problems, rather than resolutions. It's much easier to put aside a happy memory from the weekend and 'get down to work' than it is to forget your daughter's crying before school that morning, for instance. If you're a manager, anger at an employee who's frequently late or messy may hinder your ability to do your own work.

Positivity and love are the greatest aids to 'flow;' anger, fear and hostility are the largest hurdles. As the Dalai Lama states, "Love is expansion. Hate is contraction." We'd add one more: ambivalence, or uncaring. This is the TRUE opposite of love, and it's also the largest block to 'flow' in the modern learning system. When a student can't find relevance in the subject matter, they become chemically unable to enter the 'flow' state, where ideas and connections come easily to them.

In these cases, there are several tools available to restore 'flow' to yourself, your clients, or your students. The negativity has to go somewhere; it has to be replaced by positive energy, or the awareness that forward progress is being made. We'll address both in the next few pages.

Example: Morning Pages

Writers have a solution to the 'logjam' of thoughts in the brain: morning pages. Every morning, many writers awake and write three full pages, allowing their mind to wander. They use pen and paper (as you'll see, the practice of handwriting is beneficial for integrating the hemispheres of the brain) or keyboards. The point, though, is that the 'morning pages' aren't on any particular topic, but just an outlet for distractions. Spelling and grammar don't count; subject matter is wide open.

One online service, 750words.com, presents just such an opportunity. 750 words (approximately 3 pages) are recorded every day, and writers are compiled and scored based on total words, streaks (the number of days you've done 750 words in a row,) and tendencies. Like CrossFit, it's taking a subjective skill and applying objective measures. If the writer chooses, they may view reports of their positive vs. Negative word counts, emotional words used, etc. over time.

As taught in many meditative courses, the best way to start is...just to start. It's common for the beginner to have several days in a row of very negative posts or thoughts, depending on how deep the pile of negative thoughts that must be worked through. If you start doing morning pages, and the first weeks, days or months are all very negative, don't worry...just get it out.

Having trouble starting? Write a letter to someone that you don't intend to mail. Tell them how you feel; what you like, or dislike; even how your dog's flea problem is progressing. Keep writing, though.

The 'morning pages' concept can also apply to exercises, like running (the "runners' high" many longtime runners describe is a terrific example of the 'flow' state); prayer; or other ritual that requires some automatic movement of the body without much conscious thought. The 'morning pages' exercise is a great tool to keep a habit rolling, though: there are even monthly challenges, in which you can pledge rewards or motivators for completing 30 days in a row on 750words.com.

Changing The Environment

Ignite! researchers are dedicated to finding new ways to improve cognitive functioning through a variety of interventions. However, we're also working hard to outline the circumstances that occurto form academically gifted students. There is no one worksheet, puzzle, problem or book that can take a student from a C to an A, but rather a collection of optimal learning environments in which the student receives the information and then performs the task. Students who are strong in math but struggle in English (or vice versa) do so because of the circumstances under which their development – physically and mentally – occurred. Students of any age are able to minimize their weaknesses, and the first step toward improvement is to make them aware of how they best succeed.

Different environments work best for different students. If the environment meets the student's need for success; if the student is able to create this environment anywhere; and the student participates in mass practise of a skill, we will have given any student the ability to excel at learning throughout their whole life.

In late winter 2010, we were given the chance to fulfill one of our dreams: to actually use *Ignite!* in the classroom and measure results in an objective way.

Heading into the final meeting before the study with a Superintendent and an amazing teacher/advocate, I mentioned that what we really needed was to compare the class with their peers through a standardized scoring system. This would provide a 'sample' and a 'control' group.

This amazing teacher countered: "Unless they're taught by the same teacher, you've got an uncontrolled variable in that situation." She was right. I knew that I had to find another way to create a control group.

Initially, the idea had been to allow students to choose: either they could opt into the *Ignite!* program, or they could opt out. This still wasn't ideal, since the more eager students would opt-in and create a skewed result for our research, but pragmatism dictated that since some students would opt out ANYWAY, it was fair to use their grades and classroom participation scores as a control.

And then.....they ALL opted in. Every single kid. That left the predicament of, "Who do we compare these results against? After all, maybe we just have an abnormally bright group of kids, and the *Ignite!* method just helped the best of the best a bit more?"

In the meeting, I lay my concerns on the table. The Superintendent – very quick on her toes – started thinking out loud: "You know, the kids who could REALLY potentially benefit from this are at our Camp site."

The school Board does not maintain a literal campsite, of course. What it DOES have is an 'outdoor learning centre,' where kids struggling to identify social or academic Bright Spots go to learn. Most of these kids had low grades, but were without serious learning disability. As a bonus, the same amazing teacher would be teaching these exceptional kids for the Spring semester.

I quickly agreed to involve two separate sample groups, and settle for a control group taught by another 10th-grade math teacher in the same school, with the same curriculum. What an opportunity!

When Tyler arrived at the Camp, he faced all sorts of challenges, but in the worst case scenario was still able to find Bright Spots. In a classroom totally devoid of workout equipment, and without moving the desks, Tyler began teaching with the *Ignite!* method. He started by showing the students things they could do in their seats to improve mobility. Next, he moved on to *Ignite!* drills to be performed during assignments (focus drills.) Using 'before' tests to establish a Growth Mindset, students were able to control their outcome.

By creating an environment of Practice, the teens realized that their ability to score high on a test was not up the teacher marking more easily, or guessing correctly, but was a result of a successful circumstance.

We knew that novelty, a break from routine, shaking things up, and moving around would be the only way to awaken dead heads. Tyler's next task was to make the lesson have meaning. The students had to view the lesson as an opportunity to work on reading, comprehension, problem solving, writing, complex tasks, completing work in a given timeframe, listening better, etc.

To achieve this 'best environment,' our Coaches employed these tactics (as above):

- ⚔ Bright Spot stars: writing out one Bright Spot a day before class.

- ⚔ mobility exercises while seated at the desk

- ⚔ exercising beside the desk

- ⚔ performing focus drills

- ⚔ doing assignments for time

- ⚔ Doing pre- and post-activities and comparing results

As individuals change, the system will change. The best environments don't just happen. They have to be shaped, collectively by a team with the same goals and vision. A system is only as good as its leader. In order to improve the system, we have to look at improving the people in the system.

> *"No genius ever attributed his or her success to a worksheet."*
>
> *- Bernadette Donovan, Rose Marie Iovino.*

Some things our Coaches were careful to avoid:

- ⚔ *"...because I said so."* Change is most effective when individuals take responsibility for their growth, rather than attempting to change or blame others.

- ⅄ Learned helplessness.

- ⅄ Coercion. Encouragement is much better.

Note: see, "The Change Checklist," Appendix A-2.

The 20% Bonus

When we started using CAT Testing (Appendix B-1,) as our intake vehicle for *Ignite!* clients, we told the newbies that we were trying to find both their weakest link AND something at which they were already good.

Intuitively, we realized that giving someone a bonus - a touchstone exercise at which they excelled - would keep them coming in more regularly. Teach a student to do double-unders? She'll show up for every workout where you incorporate skipping techniques, because she's already good at it. Got a tall guy in your beginner exercise group? Let him pull a decent weight before he starts CrossFit. Whenever a deadlift comes up, he'll show, because that's "his thing."

Sounds like we were onto something. Two studies quoted in *Switch* talk about the benefit of giving people a 'head start' - or making them aware that they're "gifted" before they get rolling.

In one, researchers quizzed hotel room cleaners about their daily exercise levels. Despite their high work output daily - they're moving quickly through hotel rooms, with a time limit, for 8 hours per day, with gear - most described themselves as a "non-exerciser" because they weren't members of a gym. Their work output, though, was quadruple the typical half-hour on a treadmill. CrossFit? No, but much tougher than the workout of most gym-goers. Here's the beautiful part: when researchers made the results known to the cleaners, they dropped an average of 1.8 lbs in the next month, without changing anything else. They didn't join gyms; they didn't eat better; but they worked harder, because they were exercising. 1.8 lbs doesn't sound like much, but in a huge sample, it's significant, especially when food and other variables are controlled.

In the second, patrons of a car wash were given a new punch-card to earn free cleanings. One group was given a 8-punch card; after they'd accumulated 8 punches, they got a free wash. The other group was given a 10-punch card, with two punches already tallied. They, too, had to earn 8 more punches before they could get a free wash.

After three months, the second group was twice as likely - 36% to 18% - to have filled their cards. There were no other differences between the groups, other than the 20% bonus.

If you're trying to keep someone at your Box longer, or studying more, why not exploit their strengths? Even better, brag them up in public! We use a 'like' board at our Academy to trumpet achievements by members, but pulling them into the middle of the circle during skill work is also great. Offhand praise works best in the classroom: "Anna, you're good at this; why don't you come up here and explain it to the rest of us?"

We've used this technique often, both with workouts and classroom groups. If you can find a student who believes themselves to be among the worst in the class, and make them the example of virtuous movement or knowledge for the entire group, you'll have given them a Bright Spot for life.

The Low-Hanging Fruit

When we're teaching a new client, or new student, how to perform to their full potential, it's often necessary to teach them how to win. However, 'winning' can be practised through small accomplishments, and not just on the sports field.

When we're building a habit of being successful, and achieving goals, we typically employ the 'low-hanging fruit' ideology: do the easy stuff first. Football teams often select a weak team to play before the season starts, in order to build up the team's confidence. We try to choose small, easily-achievable tasks for clients to achieve flow at the beginning of the session.

To use an example outside of the fitness or cognitive realms, let's consider an adult paying their bills. Imagine that that adult doesn't have enough money to pay all their bills; their credit cards are out of control, their light bill is late, their rent money is due, and their library fees are mounting.

While many financial experts would thump the podium in support of paying off the highest-interest loans first, we take a different approach. When a goal seems insurmountable (as a high credit card debt may,) it's better to chip off something manageable and begin to create a habit that way.

In the debt example, we'd advocate paying off the library debt (usually no more than a dollar or two) first, just to get the ball rolling. Now, it's obviously more important to pay off the rent to keep the roof overhead; the library tab just starts the ball rolling. From there, the debtor can move forward with a small victory behind him. It seems like a small thing until you're in the position, but forward motion, once achieved, keeps a body in motion until it's stopped. Inertia is the big enemy of change; any motion that starts progress on its way is a positive start.

In the classroom, beginning your math lesson with easy questions that students can quickly solve is a terrific warmup for the tougher math to follow. It's easing them into the cold, deep waters of more intimidating concepts, and it gives them forward motion. They become more focused, and many will enter a state of flow.

Lowenstein's Gap Theory

It's critical for new clients or students to know that they're not starting from Ground Zero; that they're moving in the right direction already. Bright Spots show them that they're already on the path to success; The 20% Bonus shows them that they're not at the starting line; and showing them the gaps in their knowledge makes encourages them to seek resolution. George Lowenstein's research on the Gap Theory of Curiosity has direct bearing on a student's willingness to learn.

As discussed in *"Made To Stick: Why Some Ideas Die and Others Thrive,"* by Chip and Dan Heath[51], Lowenstein wanted to know the reason people would stay to the end of a bad movie; why they'd watch a football game to the bitter end, even if they weren't fans of either team; why they'd read a mystery novel even after they'd figured out the killer.

What he discovered was that people built themselves a 'knowledge gap' and had to fill it in. To not fill it in was painful. They'd create a framework using known criteria, and then do whatever necessary to fill in the missing piece. For instance, in the case of a murder mystery, they'd paint themselves a picture using the information a clues given: the history of each character, the fingerprints found, the bloody shoe... But if there were one thing missing (the killer's identity,) they'd go to great ends to find out. To complete the picture. To fill the Gap.

This is a totally natural instinct, and it applies directly to your cognitive development. In the fitness world, where common gym 'programs' - bodybuilding set and rep paradigms, plans like P90X - fall apart is this: there's a ceiling. After 3 months, you've seen it all. The gaps are

---

51 Heath, Chip, and Heath, Dan. Made To Stick: Why Some Ideas Survive and Others Die. Random House (Jan 2 2007)

filled. Yes, you can increase weight or repetitions, but there's no longer anything to be curious about. The knowledge part of the equation is filled.

CrossFit, by demanding a diverse skillset, creates as many knowledge gaps as it fills. Every time you improve one aspect, you'll spot a weakness in another. For instance, your running skill may be terrific, but your front squat can still be abysmal. So you take a month and do some extra work on your hip and knee extension. Meanwhile, your gymnastics skills are lagging behind the best in your Box.....

Your job as teacher/coach/parent is to define the gaps. To paraphrase a famous line by George Bush: "There are known knowns. Those are the things we know. There are known unknowns. Those are the things we know that we don't know. Then there are the unknown unknowns: the things we don't know that we don't know yet." If you followed that, then you'll understand that many students aren't savvy enough to yet *know what they don't know.* Tell them.

"Hey, your Clean and Jerk should start this way....."

"Your kipping could improve a little, and you'd find pullups easier and faster...."

"Sometime, let's get together and practice your bench press technique...."

"Your stride could be a bit more efficient. Want to try POSE? It will hurt less than what you're doing now....."

This also underscores the necessity of teaching new exercises with every group before you start the WOD: to show people how much they don't know. In the classroom, it's not a bad idea to demonstrate the upper ends of a skillset. If you're a guitar instructor, play around a bit while your students are tuning their instruments.As long as you keep opening gaps, they'll keep striving to fill them.

Goals and Action Plans

Since we were very young, we've all been told that we need to change. *Stop running in the halls! Quit picking your nose! Get better at studying! Take your hat off indoors! Go on more dates! Get to bed on time! Lose weight! Strengthen your bones!.....*it's a never-ending list, because none of us are perfect.

The problem is, we're never taught HOW to change habits. No one has ever told you the steps necessary to develop long-term change, have they? It's critical that we start out the right way.

Take a minute to think about your current "to do" list. Which items on that list will be there by the end of the day? How much better would you feel if you could complete everything you write on your "to do" list?

Let's face it: the last thing we need in our lives is more visual representations of failure. What are the factors that are preventing us from completing these tasks? Poor time management skills, procrastination, interruptions, dependance on someone else for part of the project etc.: The excuses are endless. Whatever the reason may be, it is our actions that are responsible for what we do or don't do.

In the same way that we have developed undesirable habits such as procrastinating, being late, lying, avoiding difficult tasks, or quitting, we can also develop desirable habits through repeated actions. Our actions create habits, our habits form our character, and our character can ultimately determine our destiny.

Say, for example, that you set your alarm clock; when the alarm goes off you reach over, hit the button and then settle back in bed, thinking of as many reasons as possible to stay there.

It's cold out, it's so warm in here. I'm still tired. I don't want to go to school or work. Your actions are building a habit: repeat the action of hitting the alarm and settling back into bed enough times and you've strengthened that habit. It's time to get in the habit of *doing*. So how then do we motivate ourselves to take action?

Step One: Write Down Your Goal or Desired Habit. "I will get up when my alarm goes off."

The physical act of writing down a goal accomplishes two things: it actually tricks the brain into thinking it's doing that action, and strengthens the emotional attachment with the goal. Much like visualizing a skill helps to improve the performance of a skill, writing down a goal will help the brain prepare the body to complete goal. It emotional attachment is strengthened
 because the brain has deemed the information as important. When we write, we access the part of the brain used to filter relevant from irrelevant; if it's important enough to record manually, it's important enough to take action upon. Include in your goal any feelings or reasons why you want to accomplish this goal. Motivation often comes and goes, so writing down the feelings that initiated the goal and the feelings you'll have after you accomplish that goal will help keep the drive alive. Emotion is a better motivator than logic! For the reasons why this is so, refer to our Enrichment Through Exercise textbook.

Step Two: Identify Your Bright Spots
What are the things that you're already doing that will help you accomplish the goal? In most cases, you're already doing something – no matter how small – that will take you closer to success. You're already doing one thing well, at a minimum; there's some way in which you're already succeeding. This step has proved to be

the most difficult because we often perceive how far away we are from our endpoint, rather than how far away we are from the start.

Sometimes, all we need is a change of viewpoint to convert a tiresome task into a manageable task. Let's draw out a Bright Spot right now: you've already read Step One and are halfway finished reading Step Two of this handbook. Finish the next paragraph, and you'll be 1/4 of the way finished learning how to set a life-changing action plan.

Step Three: 'Chunk' your goal into smaller, bite-sized achievements.

Chunking is a method of splitting up your larger goals into smaller achievements, like waypoints on a map. For example, driving from Sault Ste Marie to Toronto is approximately 688 km. After passing a sign that says, "Toronto 300km," you know you're heading in the right direction. Each time you pass a "mile marker" you've achieved a smaller piece of the puzzle, but the main thing is that you have made progress. The more times you engage in the act of achievement, the better the chance you will create the habit of achieving. Recognizing small wins is very important to long-term success.

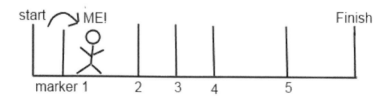

Step four: 3,2,1..GO!

The only way to really get yourself into action is to train yourself to respond to a command. As in the alarm clock example: if you don't respond immediately with a 'get up' action when the buzzer sounds, every time, you will not form the positive habit of rising immediately and starting your day.

3,2,1...GO! Is the way we start workouts and Interventions at Ignite! Since many people overanalyze – and then procrastinate – we try to eliminate the time available for over-thinking by counting down to the start. Second-guessing, over-consideration, waiting for "the perfect time to start...." these are removed at the Ignite! Academy. Try practising this command right now: pick an action (that is appropriate for the environment you are currently in); write it down; say 3,2,1 Go!; and do it right NOW! With enough practise, you will be developing the habit of responding to your own internal command and eliminating the procrastination option.

Learning and Performing are State-Dependent.
Any task requires a level of arousal (willingness to act) to initiate action toward its completion. The level of arousal necessary for each task will range from very little (something you enjoy) to very high (bungee jumping.) The level of arousal necessary can differ not just by task, but also by the circumstances surrounding the task. For instance, it's much easier to jump out of bed on Christmas morning than on the Friday of a regular workweek.

State dependance means that you're best able to recall information learned under the same circumstances as when it is to be applied. Learning about things in context builds relevance into the information, making it 'stick' better in the brain. This is also true for arousal level: the level of arousal at which we perform an action must match the level of arousal at the time we received the input for the task to be executed effectively.

For example, if a student learns a tennis backhand in the quiet serenity of private lessons, with a private coach, at 6am, they will be challenged to duplicate the shot with the same level of proficiency when in front of a crowd and facing a tough opponent.

When a student prepares for a test, they typically do so in a quiet and comfortable place. However, the test is typically delivered while the student is in a different arousal state: an increased heart rate; anxiety; social hyperawareness, worry about 'going blank'.... Then, they go blank. Why? When the information was being processed and stored, they were in a calm state. When it came time to recalling the information, however, their heart rate shot up, releasing adrenaline, cortisol, and other hormones that interfere with memory retrieval.

Be aware of your arousal levels while receiving input and during performance. If possible, increase your heart rate prior to receiving input. This increases alertness in the brain and mimics the conditions present during a test.

Always have a plan....

Jumping into a task without a planned approach can allow unplanned things to happen. We can blame our failures on external factors, or - even worse - credit luck for our accomplishments.

All successful performers have one thing in common when performing a familiar skill or task: they all have a planned approach. A planned approach is simply an action plan.

When learning a new skill or task, having a planned approach can mean the difference between frustration and forward progress. Here are some things you can use in your approach to your goal:

1. Have you made sure your most basic needs have been met? Are you safe? Thirsty? Hungry?
2. Do you have an action plan in place?
3. Have you visualized performing the skill?
4. Does your arousal level during practice match the state you'll be in during testing or competition?
5. Have you warmed up the necessary muscles to perform the skill correctly?
6. Have you switched on whole-brain functioning through cross-body movements?
7. Is your skill level in line with the challenge? Are you prepared for the level of challenge you're facing? Do you need to make the task easier....or make it harder?
8. Are you worried about result or effort?
9. How will you handle failure? What will be your next step? Just as important as your plan for eventual success is to have a plan for handling the eventual short-term setbacks you'll face.

There is always more than one way to approach a challenge. The Growth Mindset and Practice Paradigm are discussed often in this book, but they cannot be overstated: you'll need frequent exposure to the challenge to succeed. Trial and error, playfulness, frequent practice, winning AND temporarily losing....all are necessary in the pursuit of a goal.

Anchoring Activities

The 'Anchoring Activity' is like a live scrimmage or a dress rehearsal.

Earlier in this guide, you read about the ways learning is state dependant, and students are likely to perform better when their practice mimics their "test" conditions.

When a body practices a skill frequently, its brain perceives the skill as more relevant to survival. Conversely, when a stimulus is experienced once, without repetitive exposure, the brain cannibalizes the neuronal connections that are required to conduct the skill more efficiently. The physical – and, often, cognitive – memory of the skill is erased, and the next exposure to the same challenge will feel as if it's the first exposure (ie no progress has been made.) The principle of, "use it or lose it" isn't just a rhyming adage – it's physically true. Neurons that aren't reinforced with repetitive exposure to a challenge are pruned like the dead branches on a tree. If you want a lesson to stick, hit the refresh button often.

There are many ways to be creative with Anchoring Activities. However, good Anchoring Activities all have a few things in common:

1) Practice under similar environmental factors to reduce state anxiety. Factors like issuing time restraints, mimicking location, including familiar surroundings, and using the same equipment as you would during a test day or game day.

2) Practice under similar arousal levels to avoid stress as much as possible. Anxiety levels spike as soon as the teacher says, "Pop quiz!" However, when a student has practised a "Pop Quiz" environment during her homework time, she's more familiar with the stressful response, and is therefore less likely to go blank.

Some anchoring activity ideas:
- include the skill (academic OR athletic) in a workout
- talk about it with friends or parents outside the place you learned the skill
- find other situations where you can use the skill or create a mind map.

- ⌖ The most effective anchoring activity of all (and by far the most frightening) is teaching the skill to others. Practice in front of an imaginary audience, talking out loud.
- ⌖ Rephrase the ideas; pretend to teach them to a group of 10-year-olds (no matter how advanced the movement or curriculum.)

Many coaches use the term "practise like you play", which is a great model for practise. However, his should be the last step in the model. Anchoring activities should occur last because a full understanding/coordination of the skill is required before a student canpractise under the same environmental factors and arousal levels in which we might be expected to perform the task.

Praising Effort, Not Skill

In Bradenton, Florida, Nick Bollettieri coaches tennis. In his 80s, Bollettieri has been coaching at the Academy that bears his name since the 1970s. Most of the top players in the world have passed through his doors.

As Mathew Syed wrote in "Bounce,"[52] Bollettieri Academy appears a lot like any other first-tier Tennis school: rows and rows of courts; pros in white, sporting the Bollettieri logo; dozens of young athletes working on their two-handed backhand. The difference isn't obvious until you look at the faces: grim, determined. Sweaty. Jaw muscles flexed, they're clearly focused on doing better, and working hard to get there. This is NOT the case at other Tennis centres.

Does Bollettieri somehow sift out the hardest workers? Is he so tough that the top contenders self-select?

No. Bollettieri does a lot of the things common to great coaches: he keeps messages simple. "Move to the left earlier," he'll say. He only tries to correct one thing at a

52 Syed, Matthew. Bounce. Harper; First Edition edition (April 12 2010)

time. And one other thing:

He praises effort, NOT talent. "Good. You're working hard." "That's okay," he says, when a student hits a forehand long. "It's not the outcome, it's how you respond to the challenges." And kids DO respond: they work harder for Bollettieri than anyone else.

This is the main theory behind Carol Dweck's 'praise' research.[53] Essentially, kids react positively to praise...at first. Long-term, though, it can limit them.

Dweck's experiments showed that kids who were showered with praise were less likely to challenge themselves in the future (risking a blow toself-esteem,) less likely to progress much past their comfort level, and less likely to achieve a high level of accomplishment AT ALL. Praise a kid for finishing a test so quickly? They'll learn to avoid things that they can't win. Praise a kid's amazing box jump skills? They're LESS likely to try higher boxes next time. After all, we all like being praised...why risk it?

The key is not to forgo praise, but to praise the RIGHT thing. And the RIGHT thing, says Bollettieri, possibly the most successful Tennis coach in the world, is EFFORT.

EFFORT is a constant. You're either trying hard, or not. Trying hard leads to purposeful practice. Conscientious effort is the delivery service for champions. Encourage hard work. Acknowledge talent, but don't make it the frame for your praise.

One of the most common questions we get from teachers and parents: how do I get my kids to start? How do I start building a habit of building a faster, stronger mind myself?

53 Claudia M. Mueller and Carol S. Dweck. Praise for Intelligence Can Undermine Children's Motivation and Performance. Journal of Personality and Social Psychology 1998, Vol. 75, No. 1, 3 3 - 52

It's one thing to build the proper environment for cognitive growth; it's simple to start yourself when you use Bright Spots effectively. However, it can be much tougher to entice another to start, especially given an age difference. How can we encourage another to start practising exercise, or even to start studying more?

Extreme Persuasion

There are 5 elements of persuasion that, when put together, are nearly irresistible. The author of *Flipnosis: The Art of Split-Second Persuasion*, Dr. Kevin Dutton[54], created the SPICE acronym to help us remember:

1. Simplicity:

Most of the brain's processes are automatic. That means that we 'skim' information and put together puzzles with many pieces missing; we 'infer' the missing pieces based on our perception of the big picture. We automatically fill the 'gaps,' as discussed above. This is partially why so many fender-benders occur so close to home: the driver looks in their rearview mirror at the same street they've seen a thousand times. The brain 'inserts' a picture of the empty street, even if the driver doesn't actually see the street; the car behind him becomes invisible.

For our sake, the take-home lesson: keep your message as simple as possible, so there are no gaps to be filled with the wrong information.

2. Perceived Self-Interest

People decide what's important for themselves based on what similar people are doing. Of course, "similar" is

54 Dutton, Kevin. Extreme Persuasion. William Heinemann (Nov 24 2009)

determined by the individual, NOT by their coach or teacher. An example: a Beijing study[55] showed that adding the phrase, "Our Most Popular Dish" to any item on the menu would increase that item's sales by 20%. The closer the peers were related to the individual, the more likely the individual would take on the characteristics of the peer.

For us, this underlines the necessity of telling stories about the AVERAGE client, instead of just posting pictures of the genius students or athletic firebreathers. The more commonalities between the viewer and the subject, the more likely the viewer will be to take ownership of the same ideas. This is called, "social proof," and people tend to trust it more than data.

3. Incongruity

This is true of tonality of voice, "non-verbal communication," and typical cliches used in advertising. Cliches, as I've often complained, are dismissed by the brain and never permeate (partially for the reasons in #1, above.) When you're using cliches, the listener automatically "fills in" the gaps, "solving" the puzzle. And once the puzzle has been solved, it's discarded. It requires no further action and is thus not stored.

However, when we start with a familiar model, and allow people to infer what comes next....and then throw in an unexpected curve, we're demanding attention. Partially because of Lowenstein's Gap Theory, people can't stop themselves from watching until the end. Mozart was a master at this. But so was Vic Bloom, who wrote Archie comics. In a book from my childhood, Bloom was talking about writing for comics, and he used this example over

55 Fang, Hangming et al. "Observational Learning: Evidence from a Randomized Natural Field Experiment," of the American Economic Review , June 2009.

four frames: Souphead is skateboarding, and slips off. The skateboard continues down the street, unseen by Jughead, coming around the corner with a huge burger blocking his view. If you had to guess the next frame, you'd likely guess it would feature Jughead on the ground, covered in ketchup.... but Bloom's recommendation was to have the skateboard pass harmlessly between his legs. Start with the familiar, then throw a twist. In the final frame, Souphead, chasing his skateboard, rams into Jughead, and they're both splattered.

4. Confidence

There's a difference between being *in* authority (you're the boss) and being *an* authority (you're a trusted expert, often removed from the immediate situation.)

For us, this is why a client who reads our blog daily and finds information, delivered for free, to a large audience, is more likely to commit for the long term than a client asking questions in our office. Any client who accepts you as an authority, instead of just the holder of their long-term contract, will be more likely to become a part of your gym family or Ignite! Academy.

The old adage that 'a clipboard will get you anywhere,' is absolutely true. Speak with confidence, and you can talk your way into (or away from) anywhere.

5. Empathy

Empathy has more in common with similarity than sympathy. If you can demonstrate commonality ("that workout killed me, too!") it's more effective than, "good job! That looked hard!" There IS no fixed 'sales' process that works: those who are most successful are the ones who can apply situational context to recommendations for services. For instance, "Great time on that shuttle run! The only thing that helped me get better was getting some running coaching from Mike, last June."

The SPICE model makes a lot of sense. Does commanding have any place within that model....or does it take away from the messages you're trying to deliver?

Predictability

What's the best way to behave with students and children? This is a frequent topic of conversation among Coaches and teachers. How do you inspire confidence, avoid conflict, and keep people coming back to the Knowledge Table?

You don't need to be everyone's best friend. What you need to be is *consistent*.

Readers of parenting books will recognize this bit of advice: the best gift you can give someone is the knowledge that you're going to react the same way today as yesterday.

Cognitive Dissonance

In 2000, I landed my 'dream job': managing a fitness equipment store. After years of working from 6am-10pm, driving through all weather conditions, shuttling members of the 'Team' I'd been managing around like a parent, here was my chance. I could be IN the fitness industry from 9-5, making an actual salary, and still helping people. All I had to do was learn to sell stuff. How hard could THAT be?

I found out quickly. No matter how many books I read, or speakers I attended, I never once made my sales quota for the month. Two years in, I could vomit data about treadmills to anyone who came into the store...but I couldn't tell a story, and so couldn't convince anyone to buy. This is because I don't know any stories about elliptical trainers. Somewhere, I'm sure there IS a good story or two that doesn't involve a hilarious mishap...but I've never heard it.

The irony didn't strike me for years afterward: at 9am, I'd dutifully dust off the machines, and spend the next eight hours extolling their virtues to anyone who came through the door. I'd tell them that a treadmill that cost $3000 was *better value* because it would outlast all the miles they'd be sure to put on it. I'd push the $4000 home gym because it had more workout options...just follow the chart printed on the weight stack over here, see? Mindless. Simple. You can't help but exercise on this baby! *This exercise bike will even track the miniscule amount of calories you'll burn on it!*

At 5pm, though, I'd head through the back doors to the parking lot. There, an athlete would wait for his personal training session. We'd push sleds, sprint, swing plates, carry heavy stuff...but not use any of the equipment from the store. Not once. Not even a little pair of spring collars.

It's probably obvious by now: I couldn't sell the stuff because I didn't believe in it.

Jerry Seinfeld: I have to go take this stupid lie detector test. How do I beat it?

George Costanza: You're asking me how to lie better? That's like saying to Picasso, "Teach me to paint like you can."

Jerry Seinfeld (rolling eyes): Well, whatever. I gotta go.

Costanza: Remember, Jerry: it's not a lie *if you believe it.*

The best religious leaders, salesmen, politicians....they don't have to 'sell' anything, because they believe their own message. If you *don't*, people will know. Can't produce your 5k running time when a new client asks? They won't stick around. Immerse yourself, or risk being exposed.

On the other hand, if people know your best times; SEE you doing CrossFit; HEAR you raving about Paleo eating, TALK to you about books and math, and even DEBATE with you on the subjects of grammar and punctuation.......

Tapping: Testing Intrinsic Learning

If your body can 'think,' your mind can 'dance.'

Often, when you learn a new movement pattern, your biggest obstacle is your mind. A lot of the time, your body knows what to do, and it's up to you to get your brain out of the way and let your body react. A great trick I learned by Matthew Syed, author of *Bounce*: tapping. He used this game with ping-pong players; last week, I used it with figure skaters.

The game: Hooverball. Teams of two face each other across a high obstacle. We used 48" worth of plyometric boxes, so the skaters could see their partner's head, but nothing else. They'd squat and throw the ball over the boxes to their partner, who would catch it, squat, and throw it back. A simple movement pattern, limited only by the ability to catch and release the ball in a predictable way, making it easier for their partner to catch.

If the athlete caught the ball and released in an unpredictable way, their partner would have a harder time catching the ball, resulting in frequent drops. Thus, the goal of the skaters was to get as many possible catches in 60 seconds. Syed's theory, applied: the less the skaters thought about the movement, the more natural it would become, resulting in more catches. As the movement became more intrinsic, the skaters entered a state of 'flow,' and they racked up more points.

In the first round, skaters were given one minute to get as many catches as possible.

Team #1 - 26 catches; Team #2 - 30 catches.

In the second round, they were instructed to count how many times I tapped my foot during the minute. They had to focus on me, instead of their partner; I kept the tapping easy (60 per minute, on the second.)

Team #1 - 32 catches; Team #2 - 36 catches. Both were close to the correct number of taps, but that doesn't matter; the important part is that a big piece of their conscious mind was occupied while they did the game, so that the movements would have to be completed without thought.

In the third round, I warned them that I'd vary the speed and frequency of the tapping.

Team #1 - 36 catches; Team #2 - 40 catches.

Did competition and exposure to the test help?

Absolutely. But when a twelve-year-old moves from nine or ten drops to zero drops in two tries, she's not learning to catch better that quickly. That's a thinking body at work.

The problem, as we see it, isn't that we don't have enough information. The problem with teaching a subject, now, is that there is TOO MUCH information; teachers must disseminate the data available and prioritize its delivery based on:

- relevance of the subject matter

- readiness of the student or class

- average level of learning by the student or class

- timeliness of the message

- where the data fits into the 'big picture' of curriculum delivery, which may change more than once during a student's scholastic tenure.

This is also true in the fitness industry.

The Cognitive Surplus

The Personal Trainer of a decade ago is now superfluous.

Keyholder to that giant Vault of Information, the Personal Trainer was the King of 1998. He could hand out low-calorie diets, and no one would check his math. He could prescribe 4 sets of 8 reps to everyone (The Weider "Blanket" Method) without retort - after all, HE was CERTIFIED. With a frame, and everything!

Those very few with a degree, in 1998, had a monopoly on "real" information. We could (and did) refute anything said by any other Trainer, and it was good enough to get us boatloads of clients. We could be boring, and still win! We didn't even have to exercise!

The problem with the education system, though, is that teaches everyone to read. Whoops. Suddenly, that Vault is without walls. There's information everywhere, to the point that many use the phrase "information overload" to describe their biggest problem in reaching potential clients. There's just too much out there.

Not so, says Clay Shirky[56]. Since the printing press, and the creation of one more book than a single man could read in his lifetime, everyone has had to choose which information to absorb. There's been 'information overload' for centuries, says Shirky. That's the Cognitive Surplus.

The real winners, he says, are the Discriminators: the filters. Google is a filter. So was Guttenburg. Governments are one type of filter. Seth Godin, a marketing expert, has begun calling these filters "lenses," since their information is distorted by the worldview of the Discriminator.

The Personal Trainer - or NeuroMotive Coach - of 2010 is Discriminator. Also Disseminator, Chemist, and Anthropologist. He is aware, experienced, and open. Instead of attempting to protect that information through more "secrets," he is trying to be the biggest funnel possible.

Pleasure Vs. Satisfaction

When the 'pleasure centres' of the brain are turned on,

56 Shirky, Clay. Cognitive Surplus: Creativity and Generosity in a Connected Age. Penguin Press HC, The (June 10, 2010)

everything we experience gives us pleasure. However, there is a difference between pleasure and satisfaction.

Pleasure activates the exploratory reflex: it triggers the act of hunting for anything that can make us feel *more* pleasure. Satisfaction comes from accomplishing the act that is pleasurable to us.

Dopamine is one chemical reward transmitter in the brain that's triggered by exercise. After winning a marathon, for example, though they're exhausted, the winners' brain triggers the release, and they feel satisfied. The losers may still receive a feeling of satisfaction IF they've run a personal best, or feel they've run particularly well over a tough course; OR if they've conquered a novel goal for the first time.

In "*The Brain That Changes Itself*,"[57] Norman Doidge recalls Dr. Robert Heath's experiments on humans in the 1950s[58]:

57 Doidge, Norman. The Brain That Changes Itself: Stories of Personal Triumph from the Frontiers of Brain Science. Viking Adult

"An electrode was implanted into the septal region of the limbic system and turned on... these patients experienced a euphoria so powerful that when the researchers tried to end the experiment, one patient pleaded with them not to. The septal region also fired when pleasant subjects were discussed with the patients. These pleasure centers were found to be part of the brain's reward system, the mesolimbic dopamine system. When the pleasure centers are turned on, everything we experience gives us pleasure. When the pleasure centres are switched on when teaching a task, it is learned more easily because learning felt pleasurable and was rewarded."

Doidge goes on to discuss how negatively-associated emotions provided only short focus; likely, long enough to avoid danger quickly, and then clear the mind for new threats in our forebears.

58Olds, James (1956) Pleasure centers in the brain. Scientific American. 105-116.

Skilled Vs. Unskilled Performers

We'll use the phrase, "performers" here to encompass the broad array of practitioners and learners that a coach will encounter through classrooms, gyms, homes, and other institutions. To help a beginner performer progress to an expert performer, a Coach must seek to understand the psychological components that differentiate skilled performers from unskilled performers.

In 1952, Guthrie[59] defined a 'skill' as:

"...the ability to bring about some end result with maximum certainty and minimum outlay of energy or of time and energy. A novice could conceivably execute a flawless motor skill, yet not be able to perform it consistently, or with as little effort relative to an expert performer."

Forty years later, Boutcher[60] hypothesized that an individual is limited to perform one complex task at a time, and thus may have to divert all of their attentional capacity toward a NEW task, with which they have little intrinsic knowledge. As performers practice a novel motor skill, they eventually become more efficient. Muscles coordinate automatically over time, and less thought is required to complete the task. This means that skilled performers can pay attention to other stimuli, instead of the task at hand.

Since a less-skilled performer has to consciously juggle more information when learning a new motor skill, they have less capacity for attention to other details. Beginners are also much more likely to

59 Guthrie, E.R. (1952). Psychology of learning. New York: Harper

60 Boutcher, S. H. (1992). Attentional and Athletic Performance: An integrated approach. In T. S. Horn (Ed.). Advances in Sport Psychology, (pp.251-266).

have anxiety during new situations, and the emotional arousal that results can narrow the capacity for attention, and the ability to respond to peripheral stimuli *(Boutcher)*. Expert performers are more likely able to perform optimally at a higher arousal level than novice performers *(Abernethy, 1993)*[61], because they've been exposed to the stimuli many times before, and have also become more adept at dealing with any anxiety associated with the task. While the phrase, "nerves of steel" may not be quite accurate, the 'hardening' effects of practice will definitely calm the student for each specific task.

Adding the element of competition creates a new layer of anxiety for beginner performers. Novices attempt to consciously track the progress of the performance, and this detracts from their ability to maintain good muscle control. Obviously, this can trigger a downward spiral: as the player becomes more anxious, they're far more likely to make mistakes. As they make more mistakes, they become more anxious.

Expose a child with ADHD into this situation – a beginning learner who tries to share concentration among several stimuli at once – and the seeds of poor motor control are planted.

Channel search is the ability of skilled performers to pick out the most relevant cues for the most important task at hand. As the baseball nears the outfielder, she attempts to perform 'channel search' to move into position, lift the glove, and squeeze at the correct movement. Beginners, though, are less adept at channel searching, which complicates the

---

61   Abernethy, B. (1993). Attention. In R.N. Singer, M. Murphey, & L.K. Tennant (Eds.), Handbook of research on sport psychology (pp. 127-170). New York: Macmillan

matter further: not only are they unfamiliar with the correct motion required to catch the ball, but they're also anxious about dropping it AND not equipped to choose the BEST motor response.

Expert performers specifically know what information to attend to, and are better able to focus in on these cues. Picture the cool-as-a-cucumber basketball forward as he approaches the free-throw line: hundreds of fans are waving towels and yelling in the background, and he completes the complicated movement correctly about 50% of the time. Interestingly, expert performers are better able to detect false cues as compared to novice performers *(Abernethy, 1993).* Free-throw practice, with or without crowd noise, better prepares the athlete to make the throw, whether the crowd is for him or against.

Since a skilled performer is more adept at recognizing the correct channel, they can wait longer before making a decision – sometimes, the last possible moment, as in the case of hockey stickhandling. Their experience – their practice time – makes them better able to predict probabilities than the novices.

Behavioural Prospective

Ignite! NeuroMotor Coaches can aid performance development by altering the environment:

- ⋏ using social reinforcement strategically
- ⋏ praising effort, not reward
- ⋏ using praise strategically, or withholding praise strategically
- ⋏ heightening association of the skill with a positive

emotional cue.

- ⅄ altering the individual thoughts – cognition – of the performer.

With regard to the last, the *Ignite!* NeuroMotive coach recognizes the individual's beliefs, memories, and biases may also influence the development of proficient skills. It's inherent upon the NM Coach to teach the performer to focus on particular cues, rather than emotions, in order to better improve their motor skills.

Ecological Prospective

The student, her environment, and her behaviour within her environment all interact. They also change over time. Control is distributed throughout all three of these components, and different emphasis is granted to different elements at different times.

Take, as a crude example, a student who finishes a very tough workout; feels dizzy; and is going to vomit. Ordinarily, he would never disgrace his coaches or himself by throwing up in public. However, the environment – a dizziness, low blood sugar – is rapidly beginning to dominate the equation; vomiting is imminent. As the environment takes priority, consideration to the performer's self and behaviour begin to diminish. He makes a dash for the washroom – a last attempt at salvaging his self-esteem – but doesn't make it. He settles for a large trash can because it's available; satisfies the harsh demands of the environment; upholds the small value placed, at that moment, on his behaviour; and avoids throwing up on himself.

The student interprets the information from the

environment differently depending on their skill level. They may perceive that avoiding embarrassment is very important, or they may be comfortable enough with the coach to be satisfied with a quick run to the trash can, and then return to the field ready to learn again.

The silver lining: whichever of the three (self, environment, or behaviour) take priority, a learning and exploration opportunity will still further the learner's path toward information. Even if all the performer learns is that his Coach is patient enough to change the garbage bag without complaint, the level of trust with his environment is strengthened. When the performer eventually returns, he will face the challenge from a position of heightened experience. This should underscore the importance of creating and maintaining a positive atmosphere around the learning process.

The Perspective of The Elite Athlete

Elite athletes, at the top of their individual sport, are

reported by *Mahoney and Gabriel (1987)*[62] to have distinct characteristics that differentiate them from their less-skilled peers. They:

1. Experienced fewer problems with anxiety

2. Were more successful at deploying their concentration

3. Were more self-confident

4. Relied more on internally referenced and kinesthetic mental preparations

5. Were more focused on their own performance than that of their team

6. Were more highly motivated to do well in their sport.

Meanwhile, other scientists have noted other characteristics:

1. Morgan demonstrated that successful athletes possess more positive mood states than their less successful counterparts *(Vealey, 1992)*.[63]

2. *Morgan & Pollack (1977)*[64] have shown that elite runners were less likely to use dissociative strategies when running as

62Mahoney, M.J., Gabriel, T.J., & Perkins, T.S. (1987). Psychological skills and exceptional athletic performance, *TSP, 1*, 181-199.

63 Vealey, R. S. (1992). Personality and sport: A comprehensive view. In T. S. Horn, (Ed.),Advances in sport psychology (pp. 25-60). Champaign, IL: Human Kinetics Publishers.

compared to non-elite runners *(Boutcher, 1992)*.

3. Elite shooters exhibit different patterns of left and right-brain cortical activity than do less elite shooters *(Boutcher, 1992)*.

64Morgan, W.P. & Pollock, M.L. (1977). Psychologic Characterization of the Elite Distance Runner. Annals of the New York Academy of Sciences, 301, 382-403

Part IV– Applying *Ignite!* In A One-On-One Setting: At Home, Or With A Coach

What a Session at Ignite! Looks like

When Peter arrived in his new 'classroom' – the *Ignite!* Academy – he was a bit surprised. Familiar with the therapy setting – small rooms, quiet receptionists – he was initially overwhelmed: here was a huge room with mats, free weights, and a bit of gymnastics equipment. The chalkboard was painted on the wall...but seemed to bear a workout that had nothing to do with him. Where were all the weight machines? Where was the 'cardio' equipment? His favourite machine – the elliptical trainer – was nowhere to be seen....

Understandably, Peter was a bit defensive. He'd been working out with a Personal Trainer at another facility, and enjoyed the two-hour workouts. He liked elliptical trainers because there wasn't any risk that he'd fall off (his head injury had given him a poor sense of balance.) He liked the bench press because....well, because he's a teenaged boy.

When faced with a typical CrossFit-style gym, most newcomers are naturally taken aback. Lacking familiar cues, it sends a strong signal of novelty – easily confused with 'danger' in the brain – and defense mechanisms kick in. While most folks can overcome their inhibition if they stick around for a half hour, teenaged hormones, anxiety, and egocentric risk are sometimes enough to turn people off.

Peter's NeuroMotive Coach met him at the door; his Speech Language Pathologist had driven him there. While he knew that he couldn't just turn and leave, his next defense was to close the door emotionally.

Peter is an interesting case: following a car accident, most executive functioning of the brain was completely intact. However, he needed some help speaking clearly, and all limits on his ego had been erased. He simply had no filtering system. As he once told his Speech Language Pathologist during an interview rehearsal for a job: "Amber: I'm AWESOME. The interviewers are gonna see that. I don't need to practice." Needless to say, the *Ignite!* Coach couldn't wait to get his hands on Peter....how far could a kid without inhibition go?

On his first visit, the NeuroMotive Coach knew that he had to establish rapport quickly; find and reinforce Bright Spots; and have Peter project a future Bright Spot to interest him enough to return for the next session. Rather than jump into a monologue about the virtues of *Ignite!*, or decry the "chest and triceps" style of training that Peter currently employed with his Personal Trainer, the NM Coach said, "Hey, Peter! Wanna bench press today?"

Peter: "Okay."

Coach: "How much do you think you can do?"

Peter: "I've never done a max before. Probably about 300 pounds."

Coach: "Sounds good. You ever use bumper plates before?"

Peter: "No. But they look cool."

After a session of bench pressing, where Peter DID excel (not to the point of a 300lbs bench press, but well for a teenager,) his Coach asked, "Hey, have you ever deadlifted before?"

Peter: "No. What's that?"

Coach: "Picking up a heavy weight from the ground. I'll show you what to do, and as long as you can keep your form the way I'd like, you can go as heavy as you want. OK?"

Peter: "I'll try it." He glanced around nervously, aware again of other exercisers. The NeuroMotive Coach was taking a small risk by introducing novelty into the first workout. However, he was confident that Peter would do well at the deadlift; he was also careful to emphasize the 'practice' or 'experiment' ideology.

"Let's just try it." The Coach demonstrated with a medicine ball; then PVC pipe; and then Peter tried a bar with 10lbs bumper plates on the end. Slowly, the Coach increased the weight, until Peter reached 200lbs. He struggled, but succeeded. The Coach had reinforced his

Bright Spot (the bench press,) given him a new Bright Spot (deadlift) and had earned his trust. Peter was back, two days later, and was able to overcome the anxiety of adding a balance drill by recalling the trust he had for his NeuroMotive Coach.

A one-on-one session at the Academy typically begins with a Pre-Activity. First, we have the student or class attempt the cognitive task that's chosen as the goal of the session. The goal is developed by the teacher, coach, therapists, or parents. At the end of the session, this activity will be repeated for anchoring and for progressive evaluation.

Second, we *Ignite!* the production of neural-growth hormones and open the brain to whole-brain functioning through fun, functional, sometimes complex, heart-pumping movements. In this step we can also use specific cognitive developing movements to turn on the parts of the brain directly related to goal of the teacher or student.

Third, we have a cool down. We rehydrate the body and brain with water and engage the brain in positive thinking (self-esteem boost). We also perform a few focus drills which is very important to the success during the next step.

Fourth, we work on the cognitive task desired – for example, the math lesson. Now that the brain is primed, lessons are learned more quickly, and retained more easily.

Fifth, we practice the goal in a workout. By simulating a 'stressful' situation through increased heart rate, the student will be forced to focus, breathe and relax to be able to successfully complete the goal. When we attach an emotion to the learning process, the connection is much stronger and the student also learns how to 'notice' when they aren't focused. Using the focus drills that engage whole-brain functioning are encouraged if the student makes a mistake.

The *Ignite!* Approach to Practising a New Skill

1. Set an intention
2. Increase heart rate or create the necessary arousal level for the task; warm up the muscles that will be used.
3. Try the skill
4. Using Brights Spots and chunking, come up with an action plan for improving proficiency
5. Switch on whole-brain functioning
6. Practise with your planned approach to the problem in mind.
7. Perform an anchoring activity

The *Ignite!* Approach to Lectures

1. Create the appropriate arousal aevel
2. Perform trunk stability, hip mobility, vestibular exercises
3. Switch on whole brain functioning
4. **Take in the lesson, working to find relevance as you do so**
5. Execute your post-lesson action plan
6. Perform an anchoring activity.

The *Ignite!* Approach to Improving Comprehension and Summation Skills

1. Increase heart rate or set arousal level
2. Perform trunk, shoulder stability, handwriting interventions
3. Write an action plan
4. Switch on whole-brain functioning

5. Take in the lesson
6. Highlight key points (summarize the 'meat' of the lesson)
7. Perform an anchoring activity

The *Ignite!* Approach to Preparing for Note-Taking

1. Increase heart rate or set arousal level
2. Perform trunk and shoulder stability, handwriting interventions and eye tracking
3. Switch on whole-brain functioning
4. Take in the lesson
5. Highlight key points by recording them after the fact
6. Perform an anchoring activity

The *Ignite!* Approach to Preparing for Math Problems

1. Increase heart rate or set arousal level
2. Perform body-awareness movements
3. Set up a plan to approach the problem
4. Switch on whole-brain functioning
5. Take in the lesson
6. Practice problems
7. Perform an anchoring activity

The *Ignite! Approach to* _____
1)
2)
3)
4)
5)
6)
7)

Eventually, goals from earlier sessions start appearing in the warm-up phase. Then more complex movements are added as the students show signs that they have learned a new skill and are performing it at an intrinsic level.

Once the student notices which focus drills work for them, they are able to manage their stress and open their brains to function as a whole *anytime they are having difficulty focusing, understanding or performing.*

Since our goal is to give the student tools to use outside the gym, it's part of our program to share these personal cues and exercises with their teachers, parents and educational assistants.

Earlier in this book, you read about Kris – an autistic child who went from a nonverbal diagnosis to competing in a weightlifting meet; from the inability to concentrate on a single instruction to succeeding in a job interview.

It's time to consider another case. The *Ignite!* Team was approached by the mother of a teen with autism. Sam had been removed from school after being labelled as 'violent' in the seventh grade. Sam was very socially unsure and self-aware, and when faced with a social challenge, he'd perceive himself as "failing," grow angry, and bite himself.

During one particularly bad episode at school, Sam bit his own arm out of frustration.

Backing up a bit: teachers in the modern school system aren't taught how to deal with a child who bites himself; they're taught how to restrain a violent child.

When he bit himself on the arm, Sam was physically restrained for a prolonged period. He resisted. He was removed from school, and remained in a home setting for three years.

When Sam began *Ignite!*, he was unable to execute a squat without falling over; he couldn't write his last name. His skills had deteriorated without both physical stimulation and cognitive practice. He was sold on the notion that it was "him against the system," and that he was incapable of change or improvement.

Sam's case was an especially interesting one. Tyler faced many challenges, but used our principles from Section #3 to establish rapport; develop Bright Spots; and ultimately provide the student with a different path...

Prerequisites: Setting the Environment

In the previous section, you read about the characteristics of a positive learning environment. Creating the right context for learning is critical for the storage and recall of information; creating relevance, and encouraging the brain to link pieces of information to create a 'bigger picture.' Now we'll go through a sample case step-by-step:

1) Start with a 'sure thing'– on his first visit, Sam showed up in jeans and a sweatshirt. Obviously, he wasn't ready for movement; he was sceptical and defensive. But in thirty minutes, he was shown that he could execute a complex motor skill – the Squat – after practising some eye-hand tracking on a portable whiteboard. He was amazed, and on the NEXT visit, he was eager to try a handwriting task.

2) Set the intent of the lesson before each skill- Sam required constant reminders that his time at the *Ignite!* Academy was practice time: without judgement, just exploring and experimenting. However, even with an atmosphere of play and

self-discovery, planning the reaction for failure and for success before they happen may be required to eliminate the hardwired, or learned impulses or reactions that may be undesirable. In Sam's case, a review of actions to be taken in the result of success or failure with an exercise occurred before anything new was introduced.

This led to longer-term strategies for dealing with perceptions of failure. Reviewing the intention of the exercise, and then practising the outcome: "If you fail on this rep, what are you going to do? Are you going to be upset? How are you going to control that feeling? Specifically explain your reactions..." led to strategies to address larger issues, like biting his own arm.

3) Visualize a physical skill as harder than it really is – this technique worked with Sam. The trick was to perform a movement as if there was more weight on the bar or the box was higher than it actually was. The cues, "faster!" or "more power!" didn't mean anything to him, and he would get frustrated if he failed. But in the mindset that the skill was harder than it actually was, Sam would accomplish the task more easily and be encouraged to move up to the harder task.

*note: this is often confused with making a mountain out of a molehill, which is obviously undesirable. The difference is in the intent: it's critical to provide a skill that's perceived as a challenge worthy of great effort. At the same time, it's also essential to choose skills or objectives that the coach or teacher can be certain the student can accomplish. In this example (which always raises questions at our   seminars,) the coach walks a thin line between building up the student's self-esteem and making a task seem TOO challenging. It's useful to use this trick in a novice exerciser who hasn't yet practised enough to be familiar with his own body's capacity.

4) Reinforce the Growth Mindset through exploration and positive practice. Positive practice comes from having a plan to succeed. In a group, it may mean that students will be performing a different level of the same movement, but it should always be a skill that they CAN accomplish with effort. Establishing joy, interest and an expectation to complete the content in the warm up was critical with Sam.

5) Add an academic skill to a physical skill to demonstrate autonomic ability. Coordinating a skipping movement was very challenging for Sam, but when he would get 10 in a row without stopping, his coach increased the goal to doing 10 in a row as many times as possible. Following success on the rope, we had him solve simple addition questions WHILE skipping to see if the skipping had become intrinsic. Then we would continue to have him skip to 10 while answering math questions. A BIG feeling of accomplishment surrounded him because he understood that skipping was a part of him now; he had internalized the skill. He could do it without thinking, and that meant more cognitive space available for the storage of other skills.

6) Switch on the "Zone". The previous step is a method of switching on "the Zone" without the help of focus drills. After a few months, it was no longer necessary to incorporate specific focus drills with Sam. This is the result of a long-term process, of which familiarity and trust play a huge role. If Sam just wasn't "on" that day, or took longer to accomplish the task, he always knew he

had a back up plan: the focus drills. However, he really wanted to progress farther and farther into the workout without relying on any focus drills, because that meant he was "fixing" himself (in his terminology.)

7) Allow students to choose their 'favourite' focus drills: the figure 8, or the cross crawl, the X, tracking shapes with the eyes, drawing in chalk on the gym floor... Sam would often choose the figure 8, but other times would draw an X in his line of vision so that he could reference a focal point while performing the squat or while running on the treadmill.

8) Make the exercises scalable to encourage 'flow' in the workout or lesson. Use Bright Spots, frequent the podium, and never lett them stay at a particular stage for too long. Keep things moving.

9) Praise effort, not outcome. Sam never had weight goals at the beginning of the session. Once, Sam said, "I want to squat 150 lbs because my cousin bet me that I couldn't." This is a red flag for *Ignite!* practitioners: this could have been tragic, as Sam's back squat max was around 90lbs at the time. However, the cycle of self-comparison had led Sam to the conclusion that his peers would consider him more credible if he could back squat 150lbs. We reached an agreement with Sam: we would only evaluate the speed, balance and efficiency of the movement. When the weight compromised any of these factors, we would reach consensus with Sam that we wouldn't increase the resistance on the bar until the movement was fast, even and efficient. This is an expectation that has to be established from the outset, and reinforced with phrases pertaining to

quality like, "Can you do it better?"

10) Avoid CNS fatigue on test days – change is exhausting, as we noted in Section II. Having a student push a sled to improve running form also taxes her CNS, because it requires SO much concentration to change her internalized running form. In Sam's case, after about 8 sprints, Sam was exhausted; he looked tired, said he was tired, went into his car and just fell asleep. His mother commented that she had never seen him do that before. He'd been taxed! That was good news and bad: we had been working on his running form and coordination, but we didn't get to complete our academic part of the session. Experience goes in both directions.

11) Add movements together to increase difficulty. Sam was never allowed to become complacent. One way to evaluate if the movement has been intrinsically learned is if the student can perform other movements before and after, *and* maintain the same accuracy/proficiency from when they practised the skill by itself.

12) When the student shows proficiency at a physical skill, select it as the focus of the workout and try to distract them through fatigue or stress induced by multiple secondary tasks.

13) Make the student aware of movement efficiency through exploring. When Sam would think his performance was 'good enough', Tyler would ask a body awareness question: *Try doing it with your feet closer together; is that better? Try them wider apart; better yet?* Approach it the way an optometrist performs an eye exam.

14) Catch the student in a "zone moment" to complete an academic task or learn a new one. A couple of cues to help identify the times when the student is in "the zone":

    I)   They fail multiple times, but keep on going without frustration.

    II) They ask to try a new movement, higher weight, taller box, etc.

They are oblivious to other people, noise, and distraction in the gym. For example, typically when a bar is dropped, everyone turns in the direction of the loud noise to look. But not when they're in the zone.

They want to show everyone what they've just accomplished. In Sam's case, one particular instance sticks out: after a session of maintaining focus, he was shown how to juggle a single ball with one hand. This was a very challenging skill for Sam, since his eye-tracking and depth perception, as well as fine motor control were poor. Sam alternated periods of practice with periods of using his focusing drill of the day – tracing figure 8s – and finally succeeded at juggling two balls with one hand. Elated and proud, he was eager to demonstrate his new skill to gym staff and members alike, and when other gym staff COULDN'T duplicate his new skill, he wanted to give the whole world a high-five.

15) Anchoring down – remind them about the mass practice rule: the more good practice you can do, the better you can get. With Sam, the coach would often choose an easier version of a skill and ask him to log as many minutes of practice as possible until next session or next class.

Focus Drills, Transitions and Rewards

We refer to the action of "switching on" whole-brain functioning prior to learning quite often in our books. Focusing is a critical part of the *Ignite!* curriculum. The act of focusing is an essential step in the learning process; the ability to filter out distraction permits the student to better perceive information. Better perception means better understanding, and better action as a result. When we are gathering new information, we tend to use only our dominant (best-developed) senses. We believe what we see, for example, over what we hear. Worse, we have a tendency to select sensory data based on the input from our dominant eye, ear, hand, or foot.

This creates a potential learning limitation: a mismatch between the sense to its corresponding brain region. For example, the right eye is controlled by the left side of the brain. If a student is right-eye dominant, but has developed a right-brain dominance, the data collected through that eye isn't stored well. It's as if the data is riding a clunky airplane that manages to pull off a safe landing...but in the wrong country. However, if we perform a few minutes of midline-crossing movements with our eyes, ears, hands, or feet, we'll be in a better position to receive and integrate information into the more appropriate side of the brain.

Midline-crossing movement also means improving the communication between left side and right hemispheres of the brain. When we perform a movement that necessitates the use of both hemispheres of the brain, we improve functioning by making the brain more efficient. This can be achieved through activities that draw out creativity and logic at the same time, such as writing a poem or playing a musical instrument. However, we can also practise interhemispheric coordination by using the exercises below, which require the coordination of the whole brain into one unit. The more time we spend using both sides of our brain, the better and stronger inter-brain communication will be. Strengthening the communication between hemispheres will also improve other cognitive functions, like memory, because recall will become more efficient.

How to use focus drills

A quick review of the order of the *Ignite!* Method:

> 1)Warmup - The warmup increases the heart rate, releases dopamine and acetylcholine (neurotransmitters involved with learning and memory); creates a positive environment through success, joy, contentment, and love; and provides an opportunity for the student to receive positive reinforcement (Bright Spots) if they haven't yet that day. The warmup is also a chance to practice some movements from the Weekly Challenge for extrinsic reward.

> 2)Lesson goals and intentions -After the warmup,the lesson and the goals of the lesson are

introduce. Setting a clear direction for the lesson is going, and what prior knowledge is to be accessed, creates relevance in the minds of the students.

3)Focus Drill - Making sure that the challenge is equal to the skill level will ensure the students' participation in the drill. If you ask them to touch their left foot with their right hand and they struggle with balance, this is not going to be an effective focus drill. Time domains for focus drills can be varied; however, the student must be engaged for no less than 1 minute, and have an opportunity to use both sides of the body, clockwise and counter-clockwise, during that time.

Pre-Reading Focus Drills: Examples

Tracking inside objects– around chalk boards, door frames, in straight lines, from toes to the ceiling, in x-shapes or circles, far away, and then close practise, tracing outlines of letters, books, desks, posters, weights, tracking left to right, jumping over words, doubling back, peripheral items, pursuits while moving...these can all be implemented as part of a comprehensive visual practice session. For best results, include a lot of variety. The following are several examples of drills you can create to improve visual evaluation:

Track a square 10 times alternating directions (Left and right)	From tip of nose track each object between you and the end of the room and back. 10 times.	Track as far left and as far right as you can without turning your head. Look at each object between the right and left. 10 times	Track an X from the top right corner to the bottom left corner of the room. Track from the top left corner to the bottom right corner and each object in those lines 10 times	Track up, down and around shapes of objects in the room from left to right. 10 times
Track around a circular object 10 times, alternating directions.	Track from left to right using only the bottom of your vision. 20 times Track left to right using only the top of your vision. 20 times	Track up and down using the far right peripheral. 10 times. Track up and down using the far left peripheral 10 times	Track letters on a page backwards for 3 minutes	Track words on a page and skip over every second word. Then double back and read right to left the words you skipped over.

Tracking outside– tree lines, distance to tip of nose, trace buildings, objects, watch a moving object try and catch license plates at high speeds, track a bird, a squirrel, etc, left to right...

Track the horizon from side to side going up, down and around the shapes. 10 times	From the tip of your nose to as far as you can see, track every object between you and the horizon	Search for squares and track around each square. (windows, buildings, etc.)	Track as much of the branches and leaves on a tree in 3 minutes	Track side to side a power line without turning your head. 10 times alternating directions
Try and read the license plates of the passing cars.	Track a bird's flight for as long as possible.	Track the shapes of clouds.	Outline the shape of every (colour) object you see	Track around every round object you can see.

Tracking inside the classroom or home:

Circle the picture that is exactly the same as the picture on top. Use a comparing picture activity	Using something in the classroom that everyone has, construct an image have the class make the same thing. Building blocks	Show the students a picture for 5 seconds then take it away. Try and recall as much of the image as possible.	Word search of the day for time	Incomplete pictures and have the students fill in the rest for time, or as many
Circle the picture that is different. (Use a	Take the object and identify what it's mirror image would be.	Using a facial expression page, identify what emotion	Match the letters of each font with its	Using these shapes decide what the picture

comparing picture activity.)	What an opened cube looks like, etc.	is being portrayed. For time	block letter for time.	is (puzzle) for time.

Eye tracking the infinity symbol (or tracing with pens or markers:

Brock's String (The class can make these themselves with 3 beads and some string.)

From Wikipedia: A **Brock string** (named after Frederick Brock) is an instrument used in vision therapy. It consists of a white string of approximately 10 feet in length with three small wooden beads of different colors.

The Brock string is used to develop skills of convergence as well as to disrupt suppression of one of the eyes. During therapy, one end of the Brock string is held on the tip of the nose while the other is tied to a *fixed point. The three beads are spaced out a various distances. The patient is asked to focus on one of the beads, while noting the visual input of each eye and sensation of convergence.*

Word searches or letter searches with both eyes then each eye independently
Word meaning (matching charts)
Dictionary Bingo using new terms
Eye bingo: pick objects in the classroom, place them on a bingo card and have the students find it with their eyes. Students write down the location of the object within the room. Try it with one eye, and then both.

Pre-Handwriting Focus Drills: Examples
Alphabet 8s
8s
Double doodling (2 hands at the same time. Can be mirror images or same direction)
Constant cursive words, letters, both hands, eyes
Signature copying ("Forging")
Writing out full sentences in cursive that contain every letter in the alphabet.

For example: *The quick brown fox jumped over the lazy dogs.*

Draw the shape shown at left in each of the boxes.

Y	Y						
M	M						
S	S						
+	+						
Z	Z						
9	9						
8	8						
W	W						

Draw the shape shown at left in each of the boxes.

8							
9							
5							
0							
3							
7							
6							
2							

Scissors Practise: Cut along the dotted lines

Scissors Practice

Pre-Math Focus Drills: Examples
Counting and Cross-crawl combinations
Mixing in the lesson with the different body parts and movements.
Agility squares and counting.

Transitioning Between Subjects: Examples

These focus drills (above) can also be used as transitions between subjects. Since different subjects and activities require different cognitive demands, performing a focus drill helps the brain segue from processing one task to another. When a subject transition happens too quickly, a student may not be ready to receive input into a different area of the brain. It's important for the coach, teacher or parent be ready for a whole new combination of stressors and environmental demands. Students often must be given separate mental strategies for different tasks, depending on strengths and weaknesses. It's critical to allow time for closure: thinkers must be able to close one 'gap' before pursuing a new one, or risk distraction.

Rewards
Frequently, students will find success with a specific focus drill, and that success will trigger reward centres in the brain. They will derive pleasure from using that drill to enter a focused state. The drill, then, becomes a reward unto itself. Especially in cases when the student has just gone through a difficult session or struggled to learn a new skill, the ability to perform an enjoyable focus drill can be a huge relief. At the *Ignite!* Academy, our reward system is based around movements or exercises at which the student has recently achieved a new level of success. 'Playing' at movements which the students can perform easily, and has a history of joy when performing, is an effective reward mechanism.

Anchoring Activities

The 'Anchoring Activity' is like a live scrimmage or a dress rehearsal.

Earlier in this guide, you read about the ways learning is state dependant, and students are likely to perform better when their practice mimics their "test" conditions.

When a body practices a skill frequently, its brain perceives the skill as more relevant to survival. Conversely, when a stimulus is experienced once, without repetitive exposure, the brain cannibalizes the neuronal connections that are required to conduct the skill more efficiently. The physical – and, often, cognitive – memory of the skill is erased, and the next exposure to the same challenge will feel as if it's the first exposure (ie no progress has been made.) The principle of, "use it or lose it" isn't just a rhyming adage – it's physically true. Neurons that aren't reinforced with repetitive exposure to a challenge are pruned like the dead branches on a tree. If you want a lesson to stick, hit the refresh button often.

There are many ways to be creative with Anchoring Activities. However, good Anchoring Activities all have a few things in common:

1) Practice under similar environmental factors to reduce state anxiety
   Factors like issuing time restraints, mimicking location, including familiar surroundings, and using the same equipment as you would during a test day or game day.

2) Practice under similar arousal levels to avoid stress as much as possible.
Anxiety levels spike as soon as the teacher says, "Pop quiz!" However, when a student has practised a "Pop Quiz" environment during her homework time, she's more familiar with the stressful response, and is therefore less likely to go blank.

Some anchoring activity ideas:
- include the skill (academic OR athletic) in a workout
- talk about it with friends or parents outside the place you learned the skill

- find other situations where you can use the skill or create a mind map.
- The most effective anchoring activity of all (and by far the most frightening) is teaching the skill to others. Practice in front of an imaginary audience, talking out loud.
- Rephrase the ideas; pretend to teach them to a group of 10-year-olds (no matter how advanced the movement or curriculum.)

Many coaches use the term "practise like you play", which is a great model for practise. However, his should be the last step in the model. Anchoring activities should occur last because a full understanding/coordination of the skill is required before a student canpractise under the same environmental factors and arousal levels in which we might be expected to perform the task.

Coaching In A One-On-One Setting: Tips From Tyler

1) A NeuroMotive Coach must convey confidence. The greatest builder of confidence – in the coach AND the student – is experience. A good NeuroMotive Coach must frequently experience the process of change and take note of each step and mile marker.

2) Keep in mind that the goal is not the workout. The workout is the stimulus; the trigger; the anxiety to be overcome. It is a lever, or a fulcrum. It is not the object to be moved.

3) Always evaluate and assess. Ask the student to "ask their body" to determine when a skill has been learned intrinsically. Self-evaluation means that the student has begun to intrinsically learn the skill, and can measure success against previous

performance or the viewed successes of others.

4) Demonstrate context for all new information. What does a shape resemble? If a student were required to do one pushup for every letter value (A=1, B=2, C=3 pushups, etc.) how many would they do for the new word?

5) The buy-in phase must include a strong icebreaker component. As in the story above, students must find reasons to trust their NeuroMotive Coach, find and reinforce Bright Spots, and overcome anxieties before starting the work.

6) Frequent the podium: create many small goals or milestones for the student to achieve throughout the session. Rather than, "Today, we'll bench press 200lbs; then we'll memorize ten numbers in a sequence; then we'll do 100 wall ball throws; then we'll do some skipping...." use "First, we'll bench press. Let's go." When the bench press is complete: "Okay, let's try to memorize ten numbers in a sequence." Since the student can concentrate on only one stimulus at at time, creating worry about a future challenge will sabotage the efforts on preceding tasks.

7) Keep instructions short, as above.

8) Demonstrate knowledge through the introduction of language terms daily. For example, "Hip drive means....", "Active Shoulders means...." etc. The Coach is reinforcing his position as 'expert,' but also illustrating that there's no ceiling to knowledge; there's always more to learn.

9) Use a LOT of visuals, including a white board; chalkboards; and demonstrators.

10) Use as many analogies as possible. Tell a story. Create context around new knowledge. Give examples, make references, and reinforce connections.

11) Watch for the 'blank face.' Don't leave the learner struggling; suggest hints using contextual cues.

12) Don't gloss over mistakes. While it's crucial to keep the atmosphere positive, earlier development of a 'practice environment' and 'growth paradigm' will create better reception of corrective cues from the Coach. A client needs to know when their technique is incorrect so that they may improve. One terrific tool here is the video camera: record the student's movement, and let them watch the playback. Especially with ADHD and autistic students, external cues to movement are important since their feedback loop may not operate perfectly.

13) Review pre-workout knowledge: set out the overall, broad goals for the session before it begins...but don't dwell on "how we'll get there." See #6: Frequent The Podium.

14) Always perform an end-of-session evaluation. Review Bright Spots, areas for improvement, and then Future Bright Spots.

15) Achieve mastery in small steps. The Russian system of coaching the Olympic Lifts, for example, mandated that only one small improvement in technique could be made at each session.

Attempting to focus on more than one stimulus OR result will lessen the effect of either. Avoid cramming the session.

16) Go with the flow. A student's attitude may change depending on the day; time; what they ate; what they're feeling... etc.

How many strategies are you already using? Are you already 20% there?

Finding a Successful Formula:

When we learn a new task, the steps necessary to complete the activity slowly become wired into our unconscious mind. Practice, the right mentality, the right environment, movement and context help these skills – cognitive OR physical – become hard-wired. Our intention is to create this environment on purpose, for all learners, towards all skills. Whether we are practising practice, or practising a specific skill, we want to give the learner the best possible chance at success and long-lasting memory formation.

The *Ignite!* Approach to Coaching the Practice Paradigm

1) Set intention

2) Increase Heart rate

3) Skill introduction/pre-practice

4) Verbal cue/connection/chunking Team effort/confidence/bright spots

5) Focus drills

6) Perfect practice/ slow, taking time, bright spots and mistakes evaluation

7) Anchoring, increase difficulty

The *Ignite!* Approach to Priming The Student to Receive Instructions

1) Increase heart rate

2) Perform pre activity

3) Perform auditory focus drills

4) Verbal cue/Bright spots/notice

5) **Lesson**

6) Post activity Practice

7) Integrated workout- anchoring

The *Ignite!* Approach to Improving Comprehension and Summation Skills

1) Increase heart rate

2) Perform pre-activity

3) Perform comprehension focus drills

4) Verbal cue/ Bright spots/ notice

5) **Lesson**

6) Post activity practice

7) Integrated workout – anchoring activity

The *Ignite!* Approach to Preparing for Note-Taking

1) Increase heart rate

2) Perform pre-activity

3) Perform hand writing and eye teaming focus drills

4) Verbal cue/bright spots/ notice

5) **Lesson**

6) Post activity practice

7) Integrated workout – anchoring

The *Ignite!* Approach to Preparing for Math Problems

1) Increase heart rate

2) Perform pre- activity

3) Perform math focus drills

4) verbal cue/bright spots/ notice

5) Lesson

6) Post activity

7) Integrated workout – anchoring

The *Ignite! Approach to* _____

1)

2)

3)

4)

5)

6)

7)

Example: Talking To Students After School Ends

The common refrain, heard by every parent at the end of a school day:

Parent: How was school?

Student: Fine.

(Curtain.)

This is an important time of the day. Parents can gauge the student's attitudes about learning; uncover any social fears and successes; find Bright Spots and forecast future Bright Spots; use feedback to provide encouragement; and realize ways to encourage continual learning after school. Some tips from Tyler:

1) Avoid questions that activate episodic memory. "How was your day?" is a nice question to ask your wife to make sure she's not in a bad mood. For a teenage girl, though, it could trigger a lot of social and academic failures from that day. These questions are the easiest to ask because they've almost become as automatic as, "hi," "'bye," "please" and "thank you." They become part of a system of interaction that doesn't require inflection, but reaction. Instead, ask her something specific about a particular class, teacher, or assignment. "Did Mrs. Roberts do a good job of teaching you science today?" You may even be able to develop some inside jokes with her about the teachers, classes or students in the class. If you get her to narrow her focus to a specific time at school, she'll be more open to talk, because she won't have added up all of the day's episodes in her mind (most of which, she doesn't want to talk you about. Sorry, mom and dad!)

2) Since you're mostly interested in helping her academically, the best opportunity you can create for her is to be a student yourself. Asking her to "teach" you what she learned that day is an amazing anchoring activity. Even though you already "know everything," if you allow her to be the expert about a subject in school she'll be more open to sharing. She's been given instructions all day from people who presume to know more than she does, and when she gets home she's

dealing with people who presume to know what's best for her (parents). She needs an opportunity to teach you something she learned that day.

These need not be formal. Simply finding key words and asking questions about those subjects can be a great conversation-starter.

For example:

Parent: "What are you doing in science right now?"

Student: "Cells..."

Parent: "I don't remember much about cells. I think animal cells have a membrane, right? But plants don't?"

Student: "They have cell walls."

Parent: "Oh yeah. I think there are a bunch of other differences, too, but I can't remember what they are...." (pregnant pause.) The parent is giving the student a gift here: a 20% bonus (she's already correctly recalled information,) and employed the Gap Theory: she's dying to fill in the missing information. It's a slow, easy pitch, right across the plate, and most students can't resist demonstrating their knowledge superiority over their parents.

Section V: *Ignite!* Program Delivery In The Classroom

When Jane took over as Principal in a poorer-district Elementary school in Alabama, she inherited a real basket of problems: some of the worst test scores in the nation, high absenteeism, no parental support, and a high staff burnout rate. Students were frequently arriving at school without breakfast, and already agitated after a stressful morning at home. Jane personally witnessed a lot of yelling at student drop-off in the morning. She realized that, to succeed, she'd have to set the stage for optimal learning.

She recruited teachers for the Student Valet program. First thing in the morning, when parents arrived to drop their children off at school, Jane – or another

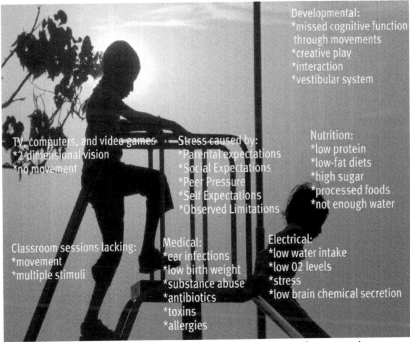

Developmental:
*missed cognitive function through movements
*creative play
*interaction
*vestibular system

TV, computers, and video games
*2-dimensional vision
*no movement

Stress caused by:
*Parental expectations
*Social Expectations
*Peer Pressure
*Self Expectations
*Observed Limitations

Nutrition:
*low protein
*low-fat diets
*high sugar
*processed foods
*not enough water

Classroom sessions lacking:
*movement
*multiple stimuli

Medical:
*ear infections
*low birth weight
*substance abuse
*antibiotics
*toxins
*allergies

Electrical:
*low water intake
*low O2 levels
*stress
*low brain chemical secretion

member of the Valet program - would open the car door right away, welcome the student to school, and greet the parent by name. This curbed the yelling right away. Then the students were herded into the cafeteria, where they'd hear a short presentation on a specific character attribute, chosen each week. Then they'd be off to class by 9am, in the proper mindset to learn.

Jane's priority was to create a 'separate space' – change the environment of the home to the positive, forward-moving school environment. To do so, she needed to draw clear distinctions between behaviour at home, and that at school; she needed to create an atmosphere of love; she needed to encourage the Growth Mindset. These things don't happen by accident, and students don't assume that they exist by default. Students must be SHOWN, daily, that they are welcome, encouraged to practise, and entering a place where they can freely explore without social risk.

Is that happening in your school? We hope so. Before we rush to judgement in the other case, though, let's consider the school 'tradition' itself.

The Traditional Education System in North America

Built on the structure of the Prussian military model, the modern school 'system' hasn't changed much since the Industrial Revolution.

Though early educational systems emphasized four areas: Logic, Rhetoric, Memory, and Language, the military model was embraced by the early funders of a public education system as a means to prepare farmers for an industrial setting. In other words, kids who were used to running free and working in a task-specific way had to be coached to embrace the 'new' work: factory work. The 'new' rules of work: sit or stand still. Follow instructions. Don't ask questions; repeat information back to the speaker.

While there are some brilliant products and producers within the educational system, they continue to be the exception, not the norm. In a culture that continues to deviate more from 'average' all the time, however – with more diagnoses of 'weakness' or 'disability' – combining the individual needs of the student with the bureaucratic, "everyone is the same" approach has become a big challenge for classroom teachers. More Individual Education Plans (IEPs) than ever mean that a teacher must prioritize his time, favouring the students who lag behind rather than the ones who excel.

The current model fails to identify or celebrate multiple intelligences: the idea that different students are good at different things. While efforts have been made to identify and differentiate "visual learners" from "kinesthetic learners," for instance, the realities of the classroom structure, the school budget, and the bureaucracy of the system means that real, effective change at the student level is sporadic and short-lived.

Teachers are taught how to lecture, but not necessarily how to interact, and perhaps not how to motivate. The best teachers will inherently appreciate these values, or work to develop them. However, the system of "one teacher for all subjects for a full year" means that a good teacher must still teach subjects they don't personally enjoy, and bad teachers are given enough exposure to do long-term damage.

The structure of discipline in schools is very simple: do this, or be punished. Tragically, punishment is frequently in the form of less outdoor play time, reduced physical activity, or the suspension of more exciting learning opportunities. This vicious cycle encourages only less attentiveness and more feelings of entrapment by the student.

No one can possibly have all the answers, but like the students in our classrooms, we must continue to relentlessly seek betterment as educators (even if we're parents and coaches.) At *Ignite!*, that pursuit takes the form of research: in the classroom, in studies on adherence and motivation, in developing tracking software and workbooks.

Reading the data from an *Ignite!* study on attention, adherence, attendance, and interaction, the NeuroMotive Therapist entering the teachers' comments from the students' rubrics was struck by the irony of one teacher's comment:

"He just <u>DOESN'T GET IT!!!</u>"

Obviously, the teacher was frustrated with a student's lack of progress or apparent failure to listen and follow directions (in this case, to remove his hat in the gym area.) Consider, though, how effective that teacher can be at delivering information to the student in question for the rest of the day.....

"When am I ever going to *use* this stuff?" is the common whining refrain in any 10th-grade math class in North America. At a loss, the teacher may sometimes react with defensiveness, give a rehearsed example, or respond negatively to the student. In the best case, the teacher can find a real-world application that is directly influenced by the lesson "You want to be a welder? You're going to have to be able to figure out the length of the third side of a triangle!"

Unfortunately, the student's mind is still largely closed; though they may be remotely interested, or forcing attention, they're still not likely actively engaged. After all, on its own, the Pythagorean Theorem doesn't appear to offer much in the way of novelty: it's just a rehearsed chorus (*'the square of the hypoteneuse....etc.'*)

To be successful, the student must be in an environment that encourages learning, memory, and thought. That means novelty, challenge, Bright Spots, and engagement.

The *Ignite!* Intervention and Weekly Challenge Approaches

Ignite! packs a one-two punch in the classroom:

1. Subject-specific 'Interventions' that last only 1-5 minutes; and

2. Weekly physical challenges designed to trigger broad-based brain growth and improvement.

Movement and Learning – A Recap

"The sensory and motor systems form the foundation for later development of both verbal and abstract thought. Skills like reading and writing require complex coordination of these systems" - Linda Verlee Williams.

As we discussed in the first two Sections, the proprioceptive senses include the vestibular, kinesthetic and visceral systems. The vestibular system registers information such as movement, direction, speed and our body's position in space. Kinesthetic senses are related to our muscles and movement, and the visceral system takes in sensations from our internal organs. In a perfect world, all of these systems coordinate data to create a 3-D picture of the environment surrounding the body (and the environment within the body) in the brain.

If any of these sensory channels are limited, and our perception of an experience is, by definition, limited, then our complete picture of the environment is incomplete. Imagine plugging your nose while eating a pizza, and missing the taste. When someone's mouth is frozen at the dentist, they can temporarily not sense taste, temperature, or touch in the affected area.

Movement is critical to learning and thinking. A study involving more than five hundred children in Saskatchewan showed that the children who spent an extra hour in gym class each day performed better on certain cognitive tasks than less active children. Movement activates the frontal lobes of the cerebral cortex, a part of the brain involved in higher-level reasoning, planning, problem solving, fine motor development, self-control, altruism, empathy and compassion. The cerebellum and basal ganglia, once associated exclusively with muscle movement, are now known to be tied to thinking and emotion through their connections with the frontal cortex and limbic systems.

Movement helps us process and anchor our thoughts. When your body is functioning in an 'autopilot' mode, your brain is free to think more creatively. It is this sense of 'flow' that creates space for the cognitive processes to operate within the brain. This was discussed more in Sections II and III.

Movement activates our mental processes and is likewise necessary for storing memory and improving processing time and recall. Exercise can also help mediate anxiety, which aids the learning process.

Georgi Lozanov, developer of *Superlearning*[65], used an integrated body-mind approach to help dissolve fear, self-blame, cramped self-images and negative suggestions about limited abilities. He postulated that intense left-brain learning can increase tremendously when the body and right brain abilities are in harmony, are lending their support, are working together properly.

Specific directed movements, such as those found in the Dennisons' *BrainGym* exercises, not only have a positive impact on stress and anxiety, but also bring different parts of the brain into an integrated state for maximized learning and efficiency.

Raising or lowering arousal level to improve focus or

65Lozanov, Georgi, Suggestology and Outlines of Suggestopedy, New York: Gordon & Breach 1978 (Translation of: Nauka i Iskustvi, Sofia 1971)

attention can be difficult. Matching the task with the ideal arousal level or learning state requires practice and experience from the NeuroMotive Coach, and provides a huge challenge to a classroom teacher. To that end, an early goal of a Coach in a class or group setting is to teach the students to self-regulate: to identify times of stress, flow, engagement or disengagement, and take corrective action on their own.

Ignite! gives the student the ability to control which direction on the scale of 'aroused' to 'calm' they may shift toward. Sometimes, learners may be required to change position on the arousal scale several times during one session.

Students in a classroom setting who are bored will seek input from their environment. Though they're required to listen, they may seek stimulation from other senses when they're not being engaged verbally:

1) oral motor output – touching mouth, chewing gum

2) movement- rocking, squirming, tapping, stretching, bouncing, doodling

3) tactile input – touching, drumming

4) visual input – looking around, looking at a phone

5) auditory input – singing to self, background noise

Teachers will frequently notice that their students will act these out these actions, and take it as a sign that the student is misbehaving, or that they are incapable of stimulating the student. In reality, the desire to move is not the same as the desire for stimulation; it's a specific desire to use a sense that's been neglected for too long. It's the body crying out for the stimulation necessary to keep it healthy.

Ignite! provides an outlet to the students: practice a skill in the corner, away from focused students, and then return to work. Even better, perform a class-wide "**Intervention**" to stimulate the senses in the best way to enhance learning in each particular subject.

Some students may develop a spot where they have had success with a physical skill and want to perform in the same area, because it's their "lucky spot." Sports and superstitions usually work together in this same way. Anytime a player has success, they try as hard as they can to maintain the same environment for as long as possible. For our purposes, we'll embrace these changes early in the program as the student develops Bright Spots, and then attempt to gradually eliminate the need for a specific location or habit as the course progresses. Giving students the opportunity to channel or develop these strengths is more important than trying to force one way upon them.

The Role of Emotion in Learning

Educational researcher Claude Beamish writes, "*Since the brain is developing or myelinating over a period of so many years, teachers are dealing with students who have brains that have differing levels of development.*"[66] This creates a gap that can be bridged, successfully, by

---

66 Beamish, Claude R. "Knowledge About the Brain for Parents, Students, and Teachers: The Keys to Removing the Invisible Roadblocks to Learning and High Self-Esteem for All Students." Conference paper, The Oregon Conference Monograph. Vol 7 (1995).

Ignite! Methods - Talent Myth, the Practice Paradigm, and the Growth Mindset - in the classroom.

In a school setting, the sheer quantity of information available to the brain is staggering. Students will vary in their sensitivity to sensory data, and different students will be more sensitive to different stimuli. At every second, there are sights, sounds, odours, itches...all things that can distract OR enhance concentration. Those are the physical senses; emotional undercurrents or overt energy from the teacher or other students, or even past experience in the room can influence the ability to learn.

The Reticular Activation System is a built-in "blocking system" in the brain which ranks incoming data based on perceived relevance. While the brain is moving data in and out of consciousness for consideration, memory, or recall, it spends most time working on stimuli that it deems most important. If, for instance, a student has been teased because of his fashion sense, she will spend the majority of class time dwelling – consciously and unconsciously – on her shirt. Attaching an emotion – anxiety – to the shirt also 'spills over' into her environment, and the classroom becomes a place of stress.

After being sorted by the Reticular Activation System, information deemed important is moved to short-term memory, lasting about 30 seconds. The information is subconsciously evaluated and, if the experience of the student adds relevance to the data, it's moved into working memory – the next level of storage – for conscious processing. At any time, the incoming signal could be dropped from the storage process. The lower-priority data is still stored in the unconscious, but is unavailable for conscious recall.

"When we feel safe we can play. And when we play we can learn." - Carol Stock Kranowitz

When it comes to self-esteem, the teacher or NeuroMotive Coach must demonstrate that effort is what determines character. Earlier in this book, we mentioned the idea of 'praising effort, not skill.' Teaching students to value the practice that they put in, and the result that they achieved, were a direct result of the circumstance they created for themselves. A student can't always have the most ideal circumstances for success, but to give them the opportunity to change their circumstances, and overcome obstacles, is one of the true joys for any Coach.

Changing The Environment By Building a Growth Mindset

Seligman's research demonstrates that optimism is a learned skill, is influenced by practice, and is an integral part of the Growth Mindset. The best part: the path to a growth mindset is lit with Bright Spots.

External support – from family, friends, extracurricular events, and community activities – can also build optimism. A strong intramural program within the school helps create a camaraderie that allows a student who may be weak in the classroom to gain esteem. Church activities, community assistance...these are all optimism 'assets' that can reinforce a student at a time when self-doubt is high.

Internal support – Bright Spots, motivation, empathy, assertiveness, planning, joy and hope...these are all necessary to facilitate optimism. In Section III, we reviews the four Positive Emotions (Joy, etc.) - these are the important parts of an growth mindset.

The question, then, is how to best develop these support systems. Prevention Specialist and resiliency researcher Bonnie Benard notes that resilient individuals are characterized by traits such as: social competency, well-developed problem solving skills, autonomy, and a sense of purpose and future[67].

Seibert notes the importance of internal attributes such as: curiosity, playfulness, adaptability and strong self-esteem, as well as the ability to learn from unpleasant experiences, value paradoxes within the self, trust and use intuitive hunches, form good friendships and loving relationships, practice empathy for difficult people, and expect good outcomes.

To back up even further, how can the NeuroMotive Coach or Therapist reinforce the values above? The answer: through implementation of the *Ignite!* Curriculum. In the Delivery section of this book, the development process for playfulness, adaptability, and self-esteem are laid out like tools in a toolbox. There are always new ways, and we're delighted each month to learn about novel ways that NeuroMotive Coaches are using the *Ignite!* Curriculum in their own cities across the continent.

Example: Mantras

Several years ago, we were approached by several ladies in our gym community to launch a class where they could learn to lift weights. These ladies were familiar with our philosophy that women should be strong, and do the same exercises as men (we eschew the pink-dumbbell triceps kickbacks of most mainstream media, and celebrate REAL strength, of which women possess a

---

67 Benard, Bonnie. Fostering Resiliency in Kids:Protective Factors in the Family, School, and Community August 1991.

natural reservoir.) They knew that we encourage women to deadlift; do pullups; do pushups with their knees straight...all the things that many 'fitness centres' tell them they can't do. These were bright women. However, they still needed us to tell them that it was okay to be strong; that squats wouldn't make their butts look bigger; that it was GOOD to be different from 'the norm.'

When we started our Barbell Bettys program (www.barbellbettys.com,) Tyler had the brain wave to start programming these ladies to create their OWN values. He had them decide for themselves what strength was, and wasn't; what was acceptable in the gym, and what was not. He gave them a mantra: "I am strong, I am beautiful" to repeat while they performed their lifts. Over and over again, they were to repeat their mantra while they exercised.

Three years later, the "Bettys" are stuff of legend. The program continues today, and many members refer to one another as 'Betty' when they meet, even outside of the gym space. They have t-shirts, facebook groups, and cocktail parties. They also have 300lbs deadlifts, and beyond. They're strong. They moved the weight; we just created the right environment for them to reset their own values, and the mantra helped with the internalization procedure.

The *Ignite!* Curriculum: A Path Less Travelled

As mentioned before, early experiences map our neural pathways as children. Every person's circumstances and experiences, whether environmental, biological, chemical, or emotional, allow for vast differences in talent, ability, temperament, personality, and cognition. In a school setting, students carry in these advantages and disadvantages and use them depending on the environment in which they are asked to perform.

Sometimes, a highly-stimulating learning environment is not enough to completely fill in the gaps for missed cognitive functions during development. Because the brain is plastic, though, a therapeutic approach implemented in school can strengthen weaknesses and strengths for any student.

Play is a form of therapy AND a form a practice. Alice is a twelve-year-old with a brain injury....but first, she's a kid. She hates the word, "therapy" and any activities associated with the word. This became an issue with other healthcare professionals on her Treatment team; Alice was refusing to cooperate during sessions, and sometimes used immature tactics to avoid participating in the therapy. These tactics even included ignoring the therapist; hiding under tables; and other extreme avoidance tactics. However, she *loved Ignite!. Ignite!* was playtime to Alice; it was practise. It was a chance to challenge her abilities, and improve. From a professional standpoint, it was part of a therapeutic treatment plan, and was, by definition, an important part of her therapy. To Alice, though, it was play. Soon enough, all therapy goals were given to her NeuroMotive Coach, and delivered via the *Ignite!* method.

These goals included part of Alice's Speech Pathology treatment, AND her physiotherapy. Of course, the NeuroMotive Coach was not trained to administer those types of therapy, but was able to convince her to practice the activities she was avoiding with other therapists. The approach was key: as soon as an optimal learning state was established, the Coach was able to give her any type of seat work and she would participate. Sometimes, she would have quick success; other times, immediate failure. However, she was always engaged; focused, learning, making new neural pathways; re-shaping her brain; she was participating in therapy, she was playing....

Ignite! offers a "balanced sensory diet" that includes a combination of alerting, organizing and anchoring activities - nearly all of which involve some movement or tactile experience.

Ignite! is different from other brain-training programs. *Ignite!* is designed to increase the electrical activity between different parts of the brain, develop neural pathways, and restore an integrated, balanced energy flow throughout the brain and body. This integration is necessary for successful brain functioning and learning.

The various movements of *Ignite!* put the students into a "state" that is better prepared for learning. The exercises improve learners' ability to take information in through all their senses (not just their preferred modality channels); help anchor new learning; and increase myelination, dendritic branching and new nerve growth throughout the brain.

By encouraging more communication between the different parts of the brain, the *Ignite!* method moves neural focus away from the survival centres in the brain to allow for better intellectual, emotional, motor and creative processing. Further integration of the *Ignite!* program can interrupt the hijacking of cognition by emotion, calm the body, and prepare the brain for more rational thinking. It can improve attention, self-regulation and formal reasoning and decrease hyperactivity.

Ignite! can also repair underdeveloped areas in the vestibular system and help kids who may have missed important developmental stages to 'catch up'. Integration activities have also been shown to improve concentration, memory, organization, listening, coordination, communication, academic performance, achievement and test scores with students of all ages.

The Student's Body At School

Most of the efforts to reform a student's behaviour, attitude, and ability to learn are focused more on the intellectual, emotional and social aspects of our students' existence; the needs and responses of their actual bodies are often overlooked or ignored.

As demonstrated at the beginning of this Section, hydration, mobility, posture, balance, coordination, stamina, body composition, agility, endurance, and strength can have a significant improvement on academic performance.

When a learner is taken out of 'survival' mode – that is, the defensive - they become more alert. They may freely focus on work rather than a tight or sore body. They have the opportunity to begin to develop trunk and shoulder strength; coordination and stamina to perform fine motor skills; balance for eye tracking and reading; agility and coordination for problem solving; and laterality for writing. They gain the confidence to stand up in front of the class, better working memory, better posture, improved screening for irrelevant stimuli, and lower stress levels.

Even one of these potential benefits alone would improve the student's experience – and their grades. They may even seem obvious; why, then, aren't they regularly implemented in schools?

In one *Ignite!* Session, while speaking with a Gr. 7 teacher, she explained to the Coach that students 'have a really difficult time remembering information from week to week.' She found that she really had to prompt the students with, *"Remember from last week, we talked about...........?Now using that information, how can we....?"*

The response was usually blank faces. And it's not just her students, she says; it's happening at all levels and to all students. So what's going on?

Based on what we know about triggers for long-term storage (and the reasons we'll explain below), we may form a few hypotheses:

1) Arousal at the time the information is presented could be low.

2) Prior knowledge of the information is too vast to make a specific connection to the new information.

3) Information isn't anchored down with movement after the initial presentation.

4) The students didn't have the opportunity or didn't use the opportunity to internalize the information through inner speech or thoughts.

5) The students only used the information once. Perceiving information as only relevant in history class, for example, they would never shape, mold or use the information in context; they would just try to recall the information later on the History Exam.

6) Working memory practice isn't valued unless the student displays a learning disability or cognitive delay.

The last idea goes back to the idea that physical education could mean, "training the physical self to use the brain more efficiently." 'Gym class' could provide a terrific opportunity – not to learn rules of various games, but to actually perform exercises that will help students learn better.

Creating the Optimal Learning Environment In The Classroom

Setting the stage for success is critical to the outcome of *Ignite!*.

Maslow's Hierarchy of Needs

For a student to reach a state of self-actualization – ready to learn, confident in their capacity, and in a positive state of mind – their most basic needs must be met first. This point may seem moot, but consider:

- some students arrive without having had a meal

before school;

- some students aren't receiving adequate sleep, or undisturbed rest at home;

- some students arrive in a state of anxiety that is caused by their home environment;

- some students arrive in a state of anxiety that is caused by the SCHOOL environment;

- some students don't feel safe at school.

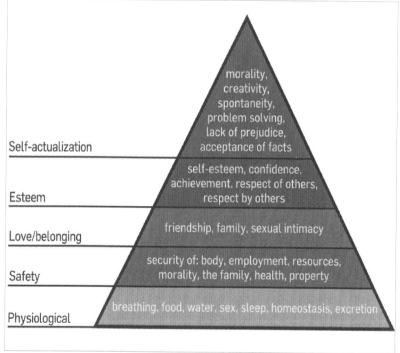

Potential Barriers to The Best Environment

High School Barriers:
- Attitudes (adolescent)

- ⚴ Excuses for being unable to move or exercise
- ⚴ Uniform or clothing restricting movement or not wanting to get them dirty
- ⚴ Lack of equipment

- ⚴ Teacher not motivated to integrate the workouts
- ⚴ Students unmotivated to practice on their own time
- ⚴ Movement limitations due to injuries or physical disabilities

Elementary Barriers:
- ⚴ Excuses for being unable to move or exercise
- ⚴ Lack of equipment in the classroom
- ⚴ Teacher not motivated to integrate the workouts throughout the day
- ⚴ Teacher who has used or is using exercise as punishment
- ⚴ Clothing restricting movements or not wanting to get them dirty
- ⚴ Movement limitations due to injuries of physical disabilities

Scenarios and Recommendations:

1) The energy level in the classroom is low

It's a hot day, and no one feels like moving and getting even more sweaty. It's cloudy and rainy and students just want to sleep. It's the last block of the day. They didn't get a lot of sleep last night. They just had a heavy lunch...... There are lots of reasons for the energy level to be low in a students' day, especially in the era of high carbohydrate lunches, inconsistent sleeping patterns, unpredictable weather conditions and social distractions, but these situations are all manageable. There is ALWAYS an opportunity to practise something, whether it be handwriting, eye tracking, or mobility; giving the students a choice when their energy level is low will motivate them to do something rather than nothing. **Recognize the energy level and adjust your lesson.** Just be cautious about adjusting the lesson too often, because students will take advantage of your empathy. **Tip from Tyler:** *I have asked students in the past to write a reflection paragraph discussing the circumstances that led to them feeling this way.*

2) A student's limitations prevent completion of the whole workout

A student is has an injury. A girl is wearing a skirt or kilt. A student is wearing new clothes that they don't want to get dusty or dirty from being on the floor. A student is wearing tight jeans and won't allow proper depth. A student is having difficulty with a movement.... Saturate them with Bright Spots and you'll soon see the students' defences breakdown and they might not care as much that their new white jeans may get dusty. The pleasure sensors in the brain will recognize that the student is performing at a lower level than usual, causing intrinsic motivation to take over; they will look for ways to keep up to the rest of the class. **Tip from Tyler:** show them they can perform a lower progression to accommodate for their restrictions. Praise their efforts when they become unsatisfied with this easy challenge and strive for something more rewarding.

3) A student just won't move or participate

After repeated attempts at trying to get a stubborn student to participate, know when to stop wasting your time and the time of the students who DO care. Don't show disappointment, but express enthusiasm for other students' participation. If that student eventually decides to participate, thank them for jumping in. Threatening a student or dictating to them is an ineffective motivation strategy. All you can do is create the best circumstances and a positive environment. You can't make everyone like it.

4) A student is emotionally distracted

They had a fight with their parents. They woke up late and didn't eat breakfast. They had a fight with another student. They experienced failure. They're overwhelmed....

Whatever the case may be, **get the student performing an easy, repetitive, automatic skill and allow them to talk it out openly or internally**. Grab a ball, sit on the floor and roll it back and forth, or stand and play catch to allow them time to process their emotions.

Example: "Campfiring"

Students see and experience a lot outside the classroom. One in two students will have to deal with the separation of their parents; many will be part of a bullying situation; all are still learning how to deal with emotional issues in appropriate ways. Talking doesn't come easy, because many students haven't established a solid social contract with their teacher or coach.

When performing a skill that provides a small challenge, but is easily managed, the student can more easily enter a state of 'flow.' Like sitting around a campfire, where anonymity is assured by darkness and the primal sense of well-being allows for shared intimacy, playing a simple game encourages the student to 'open up' to the teacher. Common movement encourages sharing; the brain relaxes while the body moves. A therapist's couch attempts to provide the same secure environment; we just achieve it more quickly through movement.

5) There was an unexpected interruption in the schedule

A presentation in the gym ruins your plans for a workout. A field trip means lower-than-normal attendance.

Equipment problems cause a delay.... Many things can go wrong in a day, but it's a game of adjustments. The *Ignite!* Program has many activities to fall back on in case your plans are interrupted. There's always a plan 'B' possible. It's important for both Coaches and Students to remember that just because something isn't *perfect* doesn't mean it's not *good.*

6) A student quits in the middle of workout because they "can't do it"

A student dealing with a lot of failure will naturally avoid stressful situations. Earlier in the book, you read about 'learned helplessness' – the brain's remarkable ability to avoid stressful situations. Even constant reminders of the Growth Mindset can begin to sound repetitive and cliched, if used too often. **In this scenario, it's important to remind the student of past accomplishments and Bright Spots; offer extra help; and then leave them to decide for themselves**. *"Remember when you got your first double under? I know you'll get this triple under, it's just a matter of time, with the amount of practise you've been putting in. Let me know if you want any tips or extra time to work on it."* Then leave them be.

7) A student isn't doing the homework.

All you can do is provide the best environment; create the right circumstances; offer expert knowledge when asked; praise effort; and point out the relationship between success and practise. Avoid emotional blackmail (*"I'm disappointed,"*) threats (*"You'll stay in at recess.."*) and comments supporting their perceived lack of control (*"Life's not fair."*) Show them that they can't move through the exercise progression charts until the skills preceding the desired outcome have become intrinsic. **Tip from Tyler:** *I've used the exact same session plan with a client 3 weeks in a row because I knew they didn't complete the homework. They became bored, obviously, and discovered that if they practised,* *each session would be different from the one preceding it.*

Setting Intentions Before Each Skill

Beginner's Mind, as we discussed earlier, is a Taoist concept in which even the greatest Master takes the mindset of a new student. Since it's impossible to know everything on any given subject, a Master learner takes any opportunity to learn as much as possible. As the learning curve tapers, new information is harder to find, and greater attention must be paid to details.

As an example, scientists studying the work behaviours of ants may continue to learn new things after decades of research. But when interacting with biologists who have little experience, they should still attempt to approach the situation with a Beginner's Mind, in case the new biologists offer a new perspective, seen with fresh eyes.

When applied to physical training, higher-level skills sometimes require the context offered by a different coach. When an adult client is trying to achieve their first muscle-up, for example, they may possess the strength, flexibility, and power to do each individual part of the movement independently. They may have the capacity to do a chest-to-bar pullup in the rings; they may have the strength to perform a very deep ring dip. They may be able to demonstrate a muscle-up transition with their feet on the ground. Their coach may have shown great success in coaching the muscle-up to others; but the athlete just can't put it all together.

One day, a visiting coach happens to be watching the athlete practice the muscle-up; the athlete tries, over and over, but can't get their head through. "Pull yourself to the rings, and then pretend you're Clark Kent ripping off your shirt to show the Superman crest underneath," she says. The athlete succeeds on the next try.

Is the new, visiting coach a level above the old coach? Of course not. Different cues work for different athletes at different times, spurring progress. Likewise, different data, or different iterations of the same data, or different context may change the way data is perceived.

Two people, looking at the same butterfly, will see things differently. It's impossible to see everything at every angle. And thus, it's important to maintain an air of humility, avoid an egotistical 'expert' perspective, and try to see things through the mind of a Beginner.

Visualizing a Skill As Harder Than It Is

Western cultural values hold that anything that's easier must be better. Ironically, most of the things we do to make our lives 'more efficient' actually make things more complex. Consider Twitter: you can make your thoughts known to all your friends instantly, in 160 characters or less. However, do we NEED Twitter? Are our thoughts always so earth-shaking that they MUST be heard, and as soon as possible, by everyone? Or does Twitter demand constant attention? Do your 'followers' need to be 'fed,' and does that mean that you're sometimes willing to compromise the quality of your Twitter content to keep their attention?

When the brain perceives a task as difficult, it prepares itself to give more attention to the challenge. A movement or skill that's easy requires little attention, and the conscious mind prioritizes other things.

For example, if math problems appear too easy, the student will be distracted *(Am I hungry? Why does that girl keep looking at me? Do I have new messages on my phone?)* and become disengaged. Challenge is a positive motivator, IF the student has positive experiences working on challenges.

Unfortunately, a culture of failure – where improper completion of a task results in a negative reaction – can turn the benefits of Challenge off for the student. If I'm punished each time I fail, I won't want to make the attempt. If there's too much risk for the small reward, it's not worth pursuing.

Imagine a new gymnast learning to walk on a balance beam. Each time she stumbles, her coach smacks her feet with his hand. The negative reinforcement won't succeed in making the gymnast more cautious on the bar, but WILL make the gymnast avoid practising on the bar altogether...

Creating A Growth Mindset Through Exploration and Practice

The idea of 10,000 hours of practice to create mastery has been popularized by several books lately. First, Malcolm Gladwell's *"Outliers"*[68] made the theory accessible to the wider audience; then Matthew Syed (*"Bounce"*) put forward the notion that it's 10,000 hours of QUALITY practice that counts.

Regardless of the number, approaching a task as 'practice' instead of as a 'test' carries a host of benefits:

1) less 'state anxiety' beforehand

2) an atmosphere of 'play'

---

68 Gladwell, Malcolm. Outliers: The Story of Success. Little, Brown and Company 2008.

3) more room for trial and error

4) less focus on the outcome than the experience

5) no reward or punishment to create distraction

6) no 'self-forgiveness' issues afterward.

'State Anxiety' is the stress created by a situation on which the outcome carries a risk of reward or punishment. For example, a certain level of stress, both negative and positive, is created by any task that can create a positive or negative outcome. By creating an outcome-neutral situation, the student's focus can remain on the task.

Even the verbal reminder to consider the session 'practice time' has positive value. "Practice" means that it's permissible to try, and fail, at a variety of methods. "Quiz time!" means that the formula must be rigidly followed, and any deviation will result in the punishment of a lower grade.

Adding academic skill to a physical skill to demonstrate autonomic ability

Everyone is good at something. Students – young and old – who have demonstrated poor academic ability may have a physical skill at which they're proficient.

One of the first goals of our classroom groups is to identify a Bright Spot – an exercise at which the student is already very good – and use it to leverage more challenging skills.

For example, a female teen who was a bit overweight had trouble with box jumps. Stemming mostly from fear, she couldn't bring herself to leave the ground with two feet at once, no matter the box height used. Her group was particularly athletic, and so we had to find a Bright Spot quickly to keep her engaged. On her second week, noticing that she was struggling, the Coach moved the athletes around to a wider variety of exercises in an effort to find one at which the student would excel. Eventually, she found her way to the rower....and broke the gym Youth record on her second attempt at 500m. Other teens cheered, smacked her on the back, and half-pulled her over to the Record Board to record her time and initials.

Her group was an evening one, and the time of year meant that it got dark early, and cooled off quickly. At 8pm, when her parents were due to arrive, she waited outside, alone; and practised box jumps on our giant tire for an hour. At nine, when the gym was closing, she came inside and asked to call her parents. "Jasmine!" I said, surprised; "I didn't know you were out there in the dark all this time! You should have come in to warm up!"

"I did 7 box jumps," she said. "I was practising."

Conversely, a student who is particularly good at math may struggle at pushups; combining movement with academia in one session allows each student to demonstrate mastery in front of his or her peers at least once per week.

How Focus Drills Help with Class Management

How do you encourage students to *want* to learn what you're about to teach? How do you capture the attention of a "problem" student, a group of talkers, or the whole class?
Loud noises, threats, 'the silent treatment': these are all methods that are used by teachers who aren't sure which actions will put the student into the desired mode: *"I want to learn this."* Maintaining silence until the class becomes calm can lead to feelings of guilt and

disconnect (*"I don't care about this..."*) Loud noises and threats trigger self-survival instincts, which sabotages the pre-learning environment.

Conversely, focus drills (as laid out in the previous section of this book) encourage the environment in which students are ready and WILLING to learn. Students enter the early stages of the 'flow state,' in which full attention to a task is pleasurable and rewarding for them.

Switching on the "Zone" in the classroom

In this situation, we define the "Zone" as the optimal level of focus and arousal for learning. This typically means, in our culture, a 'peeling back' of layers of distraction.

- no cell phones

- focus drills (allow students to choose their favourites)

When the students have been introduced to several focus drills, they can choose which to use most effectively. We always advocate a 'good-better-best' mindset: any focus drill is better than none, but some will work better for than others for a particular student. Some variety should be kept, however, to keep the technique novel and fresh.

- mentally recreate past successes – review Bright Spots

- build a routine (as discussed in the section on Characteristics of Elite Athletes.)

Making the exercises scalable for all students

One of the primary reasons we use CrossFit is that the exercises "vary by scale, not by intensity." That means that each exercise in a given workout can be modified to make them easier or more difficult, in order to accommodate a wide variety of capabilities and skills.

At a given CrossFit class, you'll find a broad spectrum of body types, skill levels, strengths, and fears. At first glance, it may appear chaotic, but it's been carefully scripted by Coaches to allow everyone to perform the same type of workout, at around the same timeframe, with maximum effort.

The simplest example of 'scaling' exercises is to change the weight used. A beginner may perform the same movement as a pro using very light weight, or no weight at all (PVC pipe) to mimic the movement and rehearse technique. There are others, however:

- time: place a 'time cap' on the workout

- modify the exercises downward on the exercise progression charts (see included)

- modify the exercises upward on the exercise progression charts for the advanced

- reduce the number of repetitions

- substitute 'alternate' exercises – like wall balls for thrusters, for instance – to accommodate those whose skill level isn't as advanced

Praising effort, not result.

Let's back up for a minute: what is the #1 priority in the classroom? What is the goal of every fitness program, first and foremost? To increase adherence. If a student or athlete doesn't have a great day, the most important thing is that they return tomorrow and practice more. That is a truth that overrides every test score, every competition, every workout, every exam: the most important thing is what happens the next day; is the athlete encouraged to try again and, most importantly, learn from the experience?

To that end, the most important feedback a student can hear is, "You worked really hard today." Praising effort refocuses the session back onto quality practice, and means that a session has been successful if hard effort has been made, regardless of the score.

Avoiding CNS fatigue on test days.

Your Central Nervous System plays a critical role in production of speed and power. Rate of Force Development is the ability of your CNS to recruit individual strands of muscle quickly and efficiently, in the right order, to the right level of activation. It's a very complex job, and it makes the difference between athletic success and failure most of the time.

Force Development occurs every time you move to a measurable degree, but higher RFDs fatigue the Central Nervous System. The CNS is NOT a muscle, and recovery time isn't as intuitive; after a max-height jump, sprint start, an explosive gymnastics move, or heavy lift, the CNS needs a lot of time to recover. At world-level Powerlifting meets, for example, lifters frequently have up to 20 minutes to recover between single lifts! You can't "feel" the CNS recover, and so it's better to rest longer than necessary than to under-rest between attempts, as long as the muscle doesn't cool off. There are several redundant systems of 'brakes' on the CNS (called inhibitors) and muscle that's cooled will limit the potential of the CNS to maximally recruit muscle fibre to produce force.

Your Central Nervous System can be improved through exercise: it can become more proficient at recruiting the correct muscles, in the correct pattern, at a higher rate, with less wasted recruitment on muscles that aren't necessary for the action.

The very systems that benefit high-level cognitive function are affected by intense exercise. While frequent exposure to intense challenge is necessary for CNS development and high-level thinking, it's also true that longer periods of rest are necessary between "maximal effort" bouts.

Doing explosive plyometrics, heavy lifts, or very fast running may cause CNS fatigue that will effect a test score. However, many athletes find a CNS "rebound" effect a few hours after maximal-effort exercise. These reports are largely unmeasurable, and so can't be applied scientifically, but exercisers who are experienced with max lifts or plyometrics seem to recover more quickly than others.

Of note: most exercisers, especially those following a bodybuilding-style routine of higher repetitions and lower-to-moderate weights, never tax the CNS very much. This is nice for muscle growth and recovery, but don't create the stimulus necessary to induce cognitive progress OR athletic skill.

Adding movements together to increase difficulty

Linking different tasks together forces the brain to 'switch gears' while the heart rate is elevated. We can call this 'brain agility': the ability to change directions while operating at a fast rate.

Athletic example: running a pattern in football requires the wide receiver to switch direction while running at full speed and arrive at a predetermined location at the precise time as the ball.

Academic example: a student must switch from visual comprehension to mathematical problem identification and solving during a timed exam, as in the case of a word/graph problem.

A progression for adding new skills to increase the dexterity of the student's attention stream:

- 1 simple movement (squat)/ 1 simple skill (addition of single digits) by itself

- A more complex movement (overhead squat) / a more complex skill (addition of double-digits) by itself

- Two simple movements paired together in a binary format (do this, then this) – 10 squats, then 10 pushups / two simple skills paired together in binary format (add 10, then subtract 7)

- Two simple movements paired together in a repeating pattern (10 squats, 10 pushups, 3 times through the pair) / two simple skills paired in a repeating pattern (add 3, subtract 1, three times.)

- A complex movement paired with a simple movement in a binary format (five overhead squats, 10 pushups for time) / a complex skill paired with a simple skill in binary format (add twenty-two, then subtract seven)

- A complex movement paired with a simple movement in a repeating pattern (10 overhead squats, 10 pushups, as many times through as possible in 5 minutes) / A complex skill paired with a simple skill in a repeating pattern (add 15, subtract 3, as many times as necessary until you reach a sum of 100.)

- Two complex movements together (10 overhead squats, 10 burpees)/ two complex skills together in a binary format (add a two-digit number, then subtract another two-digit number)

- Two complex movements or skills together in a repeating pattern

- Two complex movements or skill together, one easy movement or skill....etc.

Targeting one skill on which to focus

Following the 'practice paradigm,' it's beneficial to use physical skill development as a warmup for the cognitive work. For example, "Use the next five minutes to practice your pullups," or "You have five minutes to work on your front rolls; how close to perfect can you make them? Can you stand up afterwards without using your hands?"

This reinforces the session as "practice time," helps the student identify their own weaknesses with relation to a particular skill, and fosters improvement – creating a Bright Spot – before the cognitive work starts. It also allows for comparison between peers, with or without the interference of a coach.

Keep the movements simple if the students appear to need positive reinforcement at the beginning of the session, or more complex if the overall attitude of the class is more excited. This may change daily, or even hourly; a session beginning later in the morning can often do more complex tasks as the CNS and brain become more fully awake and aroused.

Making the student aware of movement efficiency through exploration

A wall ball is a simple task: squat, and then throw. Catch. But there's always a faster way; a simpler way; an easier way, even. Holding your elbows under the ball makes it easier to catch and propel the ball upward; dropping into your squat, instead of sinking slowly, makes the legs less fatigued; attempting to hit the same target each time makes the movement more fluid and doesn't waste extra energy for odd catches or throws that are too high.

In a front roll, it's at first acceptable to finish merely with your head in the right direction. As time goes on, though, the student should practice first finishing smoothly; then aiming in precisely the right direction; then rolling up to their feet; then linking two together, etc.

In a double-under, it's a huge Bright Spot to land upright after the rope passes underfoot twice, no matter the form, energy cost, or even noise. But to link two together, the student will need to modify their jump to land more softly, and be ready for the next turn of the rope. To link 100, the athlete won't be able to jump as high, and therefore must improve their timing to near-perfect consistency.

There's value in teaching a math lesson in the same way. If a student is primed to identify solutions in a "good-better-best" way, they'll gain more contextual insight into the problem, make the lesson 'stickier,' and be able to identify the real-world application.

The *Ignite!* Intervention

The Intervention is used immediately before a lesson in

the classroom or group setting. Its goal is to prime the student for learning and retention.

The implementation of the *Ignite!* Intervention will depend on the goals for the session. For instance, a Math class will use a different warmup and focusing drills than will an English class; a class experienced in the *Ignite!* method will use more advanced exercises than a new group.

Step #1 – Mobility.

A 'mobility' warmup will include movements of all joints in all planes. Mobility includes – but is not limited to- stretching and unweighted rehearsal of the movements to be used in the workout.

Step #2 – Increase the Heart Rate

Challenging calisthenics, running, or other exercise is introduced to elevate the heart rate. This is a trigger for chemicals like BDNF and IGF-1, and has the effect of sprinkling Miracle-Gro on the neurons.

Step #3 – Perform the NeuroMotive Intervention designed for the subject matter.

In the chart below, you will find specific skills for eye tracking, hearing, speech, memory, and handwriting. Appendix 'C' has 50 sample Interventions for each sensory input, and there are many more examples of Enrichment Interventions at the end of this book.

Step #4: *Create The Optimal Mindset and Learning Environment*

Using the methods from earlier in this text, reinforce the Growth Mentality, the Practice Paradigm, and other of the several points made here.

Step #5: Teach the Lesson

Step #6: Perform Anchoring Exercises

Using contextual-generating tools, writing 750 words, journalling, or other memory techniques (below,) make the lesson 'stick.'

Step #7: Cool Down with Easy Stretching and Water Intake.

The *Ignite!* Weekly Challenge

Every week, a teacher may elect to give his class a Weekly Challenge: simply, perform as many repetitions of exercises X,Y, and Z over the course of the week.

The goal of the Weekly Challenge is to teach students to self-initiate exercise. They may elect to work toward their Weekly Challenge numbers when they've done their homework; when they need a cognitive break; when they're returning from recess; or any other time specified by the Teacher.

The Weekly Challenge can also be folded into math lessons (addition/subtraction, or even predicting outcomes) or any other subject. Students are to track their Weekly Challenge points themselves, and Teachers are recommended to leave them outside of reward or punishment plans (please don't take away 10 squats if Allison hasn't finished her homework.)

10-Week *Ignite!* Weekly Challenge Schedule

Each week, the NeuroMotive Coach or classroom teacher will deliver an exercise challenge, which increases in technical difficulty and exertion level as the weeks progress. A Weekly Challenge is performed each day of the week before class begins in the morning or at other times specified by the teacher.

Included below is a sample 10-week cycle, using the exercises from this chart:

Lower Body Movement	Upper Body Movement	Midline Stability	Mobility	Complex Movement	Agility Movement
Pistols walking lunges squats kb swings overhead squats front squats box jumps	Push ups	hollow rocks	couch stretch	Bear crawl	Dots
	Stink bugs	deadbugs	z stretch sink stretch	Skipping	Squares
	Dips	sit ups v ups planks	butterfly lunge	Burpees	Speed ladder
deadlift	Jump to support	side pillar knees to elbows	paleo chair squat and hold toes	Broad jumps	T drill
	Handstand holds	L sits L raises	sit and reach bridge	Forward roll	Shuttle run
	HSPU		pvc stretching splits calf on wall	Bounding	L drill
	Pull ups			Skipping	
	Rowing			Rolling pistols	
				Inverted	

				burpees	
				Clean	
				Snatch	
				Ground to Overhead	

Many more options exist (*see Appendix C: Sample Challenges.)*

Creating Complex and Agility Movement Progressions is a perfect opportunity to include drills from as many different sports as possible. Football footwork drills are a great way to improve eye to foot coordination, change of direction, power and speed. Soccer drills also improve eye to foot coordination and add a manipulation component as well.

Below, you'll read a sample 10-week progression that we use for beginners to the *Ignite!* Academy. The goal, at first, is to increase "buy-in" for the program: to share with students the reasons that they should want to try physical exercise as part of learning.

Included with each Weekly Challenge below is a way to introduce the program, the weekly challenges, and the benefits and expectations of each. This has been a very productive model through the initial stages of classroom delivery. Keeping the theme of frequenting the podium, we want to have students experience and explore the question of "why am I moving so much during school?", one day at a time. We have found that practising the mental approach for a week gave the students enough time to practise their self talk, notice successful behaviours in others and work on changing their habits one at a time. Permanent change needs time.

The list above is a small percentage of the movements that can be incorporated into your *Ignite!* Program and space as well as equipment will create the opportunity for you to be creative and flexible. The introductory notes below can be modified by the NeuroMotive Coach or classroom teacher as necessary.

Week 1: Movement's Effects On The Brain

- The two sides of the brain, and their role.

- How their brain is developed through movement; how their reflexes led to lifting, turning, reaching, standing, and feeding, which allowed for exploring. "Physical movements allowed your brain to develop the necessary skills to learn about your environment."

- Sensory tendencies and dominance which lead to their current cognitive map.

- How functioning can be improved by being aware of using both sides of the brain when listening, reading, writing, exercising, daily activities.

- The Practice Paradigm. Practicing trying to write with the wrong hand will spark a novel, focused, engaged experience, for example, and can still be mastered at any age.

- How to switch on their 'focus' using cross patterning drills

- How Bright Spots work.

Week 1 Challenge of the week: **Lower-** spend 1 min in paleo chair **Midline –** 1 min plank **Upper –** AMRAP push ups in 1 min **Mobility –** couch stretch – sink stretch **Complex Movement –** burpee **Agility –** 1 foot hopping and skipping	

Week 2: Mobility and being Old

- Do a quick review of last week and Bright Spots

- Show the students the effects that negative thoughts have on performance.

- Make a chart of words describing OLD vs YOUNG

- Make a plan to avoid being old, getting old etc.

- Discuss ways to include mobility throughout the day to build up hours

- Discuss the importance and benefits of mobility.

Week 2 Challenge of the week: **Lower** – Squats **Midline** – hollow rocks **Upper** – pulling of some sort **Mobility** – spider man complex, sink **Complex Movement** – walking lunges **Agility** – carioca. or criss cross jumps	

Week 3: Mindset – Growth vs Fixed (Talent Myth)

- Review last week's Bright Spots

- Introduce the ways to build a Growth Mindset

- Opportunity and time management

- Discuss the ways to overcome (or reinforce) negativity

- How to learn from mistakes

- How to create circumstances

- Reinforce the Practice Paradigm

Week 3 Challenge of the week: **Lower** – chair pistols **Midline** – Supermans **Upper**- Stink bugs **Mobility** – z stretch, calf stretch, sink **Complex Movement** – broad jumps **Agility**- forward hopping, lateral hopping	

Week 4: An Optimally-Functioning Environment

- Review Bright Spots from last week.

- List things that hinder or help the learning environment.

- Make a connection to the emotions involved during the classroom times.

- What can the student control? What can't they control? Make a list.

- Learning is state-dependent. The student's environment plays a major role in determining their state. How do you identify positive or negative environments?

- How can you apply the last 3 weeks to help your learning environment?

- Introduce 'noticing' this week if they aren't aware of the factors that help or hurt their learning environment.

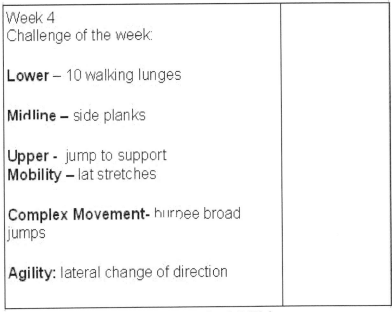

Week 4 Challenge of the week:	
Lower – 10 walking lunges	
Midline – side planks	
Upper - jump to support **Mobility** – lat stretches	
Complex Movement- burpee broad jumps	
Agility: lateral change of direction	

Week 5: Finding Relevance In All Things

- Review Bright Spots from last week

- How to create an emotional attachment through arousal

- How to create an emotional attachment through personal experience

- How to make connections to things already known

- How to make connections with the Growth Mindset and Practice Paradigm

- How to use 'chunking' - write out the steps, relate it to learning a movement

- Using the lessons learned in the last 4 weeks, find relevance in classroom subjects

Week 5	
Lower – front squats hold onto an object, **Mid-** hollow rocks	
Upper – wall walks	
Mobility – sink stretch, lunge/spider man complex	
Complex Movement- bear crawl, forward rolls	
Agility - cone drills – T, L, etc.	

Week 6: Goal-setting

- *Review Bright Spots*

- Set one goal and do it. NOW! Discuss 'low-hanging fruit' and the characteristics of Elite Athletes.

- Frequent the podium

- Review the differences between objectives and goals

- Build smart goals. Make sure they're measurable, specific, and tell your body what to do.

- Give an example of performing a movement as fast as you can vs completing each step mentally (use 'chunking' from last week to tie things together.)

Week 6 **Lower** – overhead squats **Mid** – V ups **Upper** -pull ups, pulling **Mobility** – squat and hold toes, sink **Complex Movement** – ground to overhead **Agility**- dot drill series	

Week 7: Managing Goals and Objectives

- Review from last week and highlight Bright Spots

- Discuss the management of failed goals and objectives

- Review 'noticing'

- Discuss self-awareness, and staying on track

- Discuss 'belief in the plan'

- Compare "Hope" vs "I hope," and their effects on the brain

- Compare "I hope" and "I will"

Week 7	
Challenge of the week: have each student choose their own, one student choose 1 each day for the class etc. Many options here.	
Lower- Choice	
Mid- Choice	
Upper- Choice	
Mobility - Choice	

Week 8: Getting to know your Optimal Environments

- Bright Spots

- Students: use noticing and evaluating skills on their own to list warmups and skills that work best for them

- Discuss nutrition that's best for learning

- Compare Intrinsic and Extrinsic motivation

- Find phrases that work to create more positive environments

- Make a class-wide list of external factors that can interfere with positive environments

- Stress that this week is a BIG self-awareness week

Week 8 - You can cycle back to week 1 and watch the students who have put in the time blow their old scores away! **Lower-** spend 1 min in paleo chair **Mid** – 1 min plank **Upper** – AMRAP push ups in 1 min **Mobility** – couch stretch – sink stretch **Complex Movement** – 1 min of burpees **Agility** – 1 foot hopping and skipping	

Week 9: Creating Optimal Environments Anywhere

- Review from last week and highlight Bright Spots

- Plan to create as many scenarios of your optimal environment anywhere.

- Rolling with the punches when the environment isn't what you want

- Using the *Ignite!* method anywhere

- Practising in an uncomfortable or unfamiliar environment.

- How to anchor learning down in the brain.

-

Week 9 Challenge of the week: **Lower** – Squats **Mid** – hollow rocks **Upper** – pulling of some sort **Mobility** – spider man complex, sink **Complex Movement** – walking lunges **Agility** – carioca, or criss cross jumps	

Week 10: What has worked, what hasn't, and how to continue

- Review from last week and highlight bright spots

- Have students write out the recipes for success and the times where failure occurred

- Have students write what failure has taught you in every failed experience

- Have students write a schedule that they can stick to

Week 10 Challenge of the week: **Lower** – chair pistols **Mid** – Supermans **Upper**- Stink bugs **Mobility** – z stretch, calf stretch, sink **Complex Movement** – broad jumps **Agility**- forward hopping, lateral hopping	

- Discuss how to make optimal functioning available as many times as possible throughout the day. At the end of 10 weeks, students will have their *Ignite! Student Handbook* full of accomplishments; strategies to create their own successful environment; and have the proper mindset,along with strong practice habits, needed to accomplish their goals.

In the classroom, students will notice that they spend more time throughout the day 'in flow;' that they are less anxious; and that they retain information more easily.

Suggestions For Using the *Ignite!* Method During an Elementary School Day.

Good Morning Motor Movements: Using the Weekly Challenge chart, the class performs every movement for a full minute at the beginning of each day. This will allow the students to get a head start on their weekly objectives. The teacher or NeuroMotive Coach may want to track 'points' per repetitions or successful completion as a way of tracking progress.

The Weekly Challenge exercises can then be used as transitions between subjects. For example, "While I write this note on the board, choose one movement from your Weekly Challenge chart and go for 1 minute." The teacher or Coach may also encourage the students to practise during recess, or after they finish an assignment and are waiting for other students.

Using the Weekly Challenge from Week #1, above:

Week 1

Challenge of the week:

L- spend 1 min of squats

M – 1 min plank

Up – AMRAP push ups in 1 min

Mob – paleo chair and sink

CM – burpee

Ag – 1 foot hopping and skipping

....our *"Good Morning Motor Movement"* workout would be:

1 min AMAP of each

Squats

Push ups

Plank

Burpee

Agility squares

Depending on the fitness level of the class, one round is sometimes enough; at the discretion of the Coach, the rounds performed may be increased to 2 or 3. Total time: 5 minutes.

Next, perform one minute of each mobility stretch for the week. Total time: two minutes.

Total *Good Morning Motor Movement* time: 7 minutes

Begin the introduction to the day's activities and lessons. Having students write out their Bright Spots from the day before, and their goals for the day, is a terrific way to start. Including a motivational quote or an opportunity for students to verbally communicate their Bright Spots may spark up some positive communication between classmates.

During our second study with a local School Board, the NeuroMotive Coach involved had to present the concept to the students. He had to create relevance in their minds, and that meant discussion on much of the program's content. To make things easier, he broke the course down into specific weeks – the result of which are above - to prevent cognitive overload. Included above is a 10-week discussion checklist to help teachers,

Coaches, and students form good habits and a growth mindset.

Ignite! Coaches used these discussion guidelines to motivate students in a Math class to get down on the dirty floor in their uniforms and hold a plank. Helping the students see relevance was critical: they had to appreciate not only the goals of the Coach, but to make the connections of the ways *Ignite!* would help them in academics and in life. Initially, the idea of dirtying the elbows on their uniform shirts was met with great resistance, and the discussion topics were sometimes the only participation the Coach could draw from the students.

The breakdown of the *Ignite!* method into several weeks is more effective, because it allows the students time to create relevance to the material by thinking about how it affects them.

To take it further, a teacher could spread the individual points out through the week to allow each to sink in independently.

Example:

Week 1: Movement's Effects On The Brain.

- The two sides of the brain, and their role.

- How their brains developed through movement; how their reflexes led to lifting, turning, reaching, standing, and feeding, which allowed for exploring. "Physical movements allowed your brain to develop the necessary skills to learn about your environment."

- Sensory tendencies and dominance which lead to their current cognitive map.

- Functioning can be improved by being aware of using both sides of the brain when listening, reading, writing, exercising, daily activities.

- The Practice Paradigm. Practising trying to write with the wrong hand will spark a novel, focused, engaged experience, for example, but can still be mastered at any age.

- How to switch on their 'focus'

- How Bright Spots work.

Next, the class would perform the necessary neuromotor movements for the particular academic task. These are listed in subsequent pages in great detail. If they are reading next, ask the students to perform the Visual WOD. If they are going to be doing something involved with handwriting, perform the Handwriting WOD.

As the class progresses through the day, use the *Ignite!* method before each subject, with specific Interventions for reading, language and math workouts to increase focus, attention and memory.

Again, during any transition time or time spent waiting for others to finish a worksheet, teachers and Coaches can encourage the students to repeat the Intervention or the Weekly Challenge.

Suggested Use During A Secondary School Day

As above, the teacher or Coach would have the class perform the Weekly Challenge, followed by the neuromotor skills necessary for the class. The Weekly Challenge should be posted somewhere in the class where the students can see it; they should be permitted to log points anytime they have a spare moment.

In 2006, Catalyst Fitness (the parent company of *Ignite!*) launched a two-year study into exercise adherence and retention. The findings were significant. The major problems with obesity and inactivity in our culture are caused not by lack of motivation, but by lack of continuance: people give up too early. This is true beginning in adolescence, and so the study has some relevance in motivating teenagers.

The Secrets of Sticking With It

It started with a scientific experiment about "fitness adherence."
It ended as another CrossFit success story.

Chris Cooper

This is the story of how you get your clients off their butts.

Or, if you insist on more polite conversation, we can talk about a fitness adherence study I conducted to try to understand what makes people stay with an exercise program. Among the key factors identified were intensity, novelty, accountability and competition. Sound familiar?

Subscription info at http://journal.crossfit.com
Feedback to feedback@crossfit.com

Let's back up. By 2006, I had already been in the fitness industry for a decade. It had been decade of constant study, research review, professional discussion and painstaking exercise prescription. I had coached, trained, sold fitness equipment and competed as a powerlifter. Thanks to a Canadian Forces research project, I had been able to take a chance on opening my own facility.

The empty box:
a product of laziness, fear, apathy and a lack of motivation.

The problem:

80 percent of my clients weren't doing their homework. I don't mean they weren't bringing any intensity to their workouts or skipping parts. I mean they weren't doing any of it.

By that point I was writing the best programs of my life. Or so I thought. I could talk about linear periodization and rate of force development and insulin sensitivity for hours. And I did. I was tough and creative. I gave clients crisp, point-by-point workout prescriptions other trainers wouldn't. I stayed up all night building food plans and tapering programs.

But there was a big problem: 80 percent of my clients weren't doing their homework. I don't mean they weren't bringing any intensity to their workouts or skipping parts. I mean they weren't doing any of it. The obvious exceptions were the hardcore athletes, who had something to lose if they didn't train. But how could anyone expect to make progress if he or she only spent an hour per week exercising?

Ditching Workouts:
Finding the Why Behind the Whining

We were a small personal-training facility called Catalyst. We didn't sell memberships. Our clients were to do their workouts at home or at other local gyms. We wrote programs that were easy to follow and could be done anywhere. But our clients still they weren't doing their workouts. My clients could generate plenty of intensity when I was with them. They were excellent at keeping appointments with me. So why couldn't they work out on their own? With our reputation on the line, we decided we'd better figure out why. After all, no workout is more important than the next workout.

Step 1—try to determine average adherence rates for gym members and people working with personal trainers. We had to make sure it wasn't just us. That took three months.

Most of the data available was from physiotherapy, and the statistics weren't good. We expected a high adherence rate from people who used exercise to alleviate pain and get back to work. That wasn't the case. After two weeks of being left on their own, physiotherapy patients were less than 70 percent likely to do the prescribed exercises— even if they were only stretches. After 30 days, fewer than half were actually doing exercises that would help.

Trying to find more data was tougher. Gyms aren't keen to divulge membership numbers. Most don't track attendance rates. Or maybe they know the numbers but don't want to report them. We turned instead to government-sponsored exercise programs and non-profit organizations.

Subscription info at http://journal.crossfit.com
Feedback to feedback@crossfit.com

Government programs in Canada operate on a grants-based system. Unfortunately, with three levels of government and dozens of bureaucratic agencies funding these projects, there's a lot of overlap and very little objective measurement. Take a look at the mission statement of any government-funded or non-profit program and you'll see something like this: "To increase participation in our community and encourage active living." Talk about non-specific, immeasurable goals! As a private business owner, these programs make me cringe.

It was time for us to do something.

Volunteers Needed:
Must Be Able to Quit Working Out

I put an article on a local news site asking for 12 volunteers who weren't currently Catalyst members. They were told we were studying the efficacy of a workout program, not the adherence rate. The volunteers were split into two groups.

Group 1 got a booklet with exercise descriptions and pictures. The booklet detailed a month's worth of workouts, written day by day. Group members were told to check off the workouts they started, even if they didn't complete them. Group 2 was given the same booklet without the workouts included. Instead, they were e-mailed the daily workout and asked to reply with times or weights they had used.

The groups came in and met with us. We ran through the dozen exercises with them, answered their questions and gave them instructions. They were told do as many of the workouts as possible.

After a month, we asked for their tracking logs. Group 1 had completed about 30 percent of their workouts, which was average for us. Group 2 had completed over 50 percent of their e-mailed workouts, and they were posting their scores. At this point, we didn't reply to their postings. We just logged their scores when they did their workouts. At the end of the month, three out of the six requested to keep getting the e-mailed workouts!

Group 2's adherence rate of 50 per cent doesn't seem that great, but it's much better than the industry average. Our original plan was to end the study there and just start e-mailing people their workouts daily, but one of my partners thought the results were interesting enough to keep going.

Courtesy of Catalyst Fitness

Tyler Belanger (jumping) was the first guinea pig in the CrossFit experiment at Catalyst Fitness.

We applied for government funding through one body and were redirected to another. In the end we were given a 50 percent reimbursement allowance. That meant for every dollar we spent on the research, we'd be given 50 cents back, provided we developed a product for sale and created jobs. That started a two-year research and development process. More importantly, it changed the way we approach fitness.

Get With the Program:
Keeping the Slackers in the Gym

Using a rickety platform we built called MorningCatalyst.com, we videotaped a few dozen exercises and started signing up trainees. We manipulated variables monthly in an attempt to increase adherence. Some of the results were startling.

---

3 of 6

dovetailing with the CrossFit program. Every time we thought we'd found a weak spot, our own daily workout feedback pushed us toward CrossFit.

The time had come for me to stop thinking about lions and throw myself into the den. I was still fairly competitive in powerlifting. I worried about losing weight, so I offered the project up to our team.

> Let's make this clear: we didn't set out to prove CrossFit works. Heck, we were originally skeptical of CrossFit. But we couldn't ignore the way our research was dovetailing with the CrossFit program.

In early 2008, more than two years after starting research into exercise adherence, one of my trainers, Tyler Belanger, volunteered to do CrossFit for a month. His first day was a 10 km run. Tyler is a football player. He gutted it out. Day 2 was more to his strengths. He completed Isabel's 30 snatches of 135 pounds in six minutes.

Tyler published a blog. Another trainer volunteered to go next. Tyler opted to continue. Clients reading the blog asked if they could be thrown into the mix. I opened up our one-on-one PT facility for an hour every day for "open CrossFit time." We didn't charge or coach. We just let people use the space. They had to come in at 6 a.m., but they still came. In ten days, we had a waiting list for the next month. We were excited, to say the least.

I started in May. I was pretty intimidated. Both of our trainers were setting the bar very high.

My first workout was a dream come true: CrossFit Total. Coming out of a four-year stint in competitive powerlifting, I thought I'd dominate. I had good lifts, but unbelted my numbers suffered and I barely made 1,000 pounds. Linda, a.k.a. Three Bars of Death, was in there that first week. A ten-to-one triplet of deadlift (1.5 times bodyweight),

bench press (body weight) and clean (three-quarters body weight), Linda had me collapsed on the floor after reaching eight deadlift reps. I wasn't sure I'd continue.

Luckily, May 2008 featured a lot of strength work, and my deadlift actually made a small increase. I was getting hooked. Our clients were asking for more group workouts. We started the affiliation process soon after and opened a second facility to accommodate our new CrossFit habit.

The latest update? We continue to grow, based largely on referrals. We now practice the "tricks of the trade" we learned from our research on encouraging adherence. It's working.

✦

About The Author

Chris Cooper is president of Catalyst Fitness in Sault Ste. Marie, Ontario, in Canada. Split between two facilities—a private personal training centre and a CrossFit box—Catalyst Fitness is engaged in research, athletic development and the pursuit of all things fitness. Chris has two small kids, a 14-hour workday, a 2:51 Diane and a 520-pound deadlift PR. He also has an incredible staff of trainers, therapists and coaches, as well as a probable case of mild ADD and a very patient wife.

Reach him via email at catalystfitness@yahoo.ca or on the web at www.catalystgym.com.

CrossFit

The author discovered people want a challenging workout. CrossFit just might be able to help them find it.

Lesson learned:
People try to get their money's worth.

Even if they hate the workouts, people will do them if they perceive they'll waste money by not doing them. They may not come back the next month, though. The stick works, but the carrot is better.

At this point, we were nearly a year in. We'd already learned things that seemed intuitive but ran counter to the instruction we'd received in university. Celebrate success? Hold people accountable? Be challenging and quick? In hindsight, it seems obvious: why is everyone else still doing three sets of eight on the ambiguous bi machine?

At the time, though, we were challenging the very foundations of our educations in the field. Think about this: after spending tens of thousands to learn what works, you're invested in the idea that your teachers were right. You know the list. Calorie-reduced diets plus cardio equals fat loss. Women don't want to lift weights. Thirty minutes of walking per day will get you somewhere.

Did we really want to be wrong? Hell, no. We fought it every step of the way.

A year in, we revisited the idea of bringing a group together to do the workouts at our gym. We wanted to test the effect that group interaction and achievement would bring. We called it our Morning Catalyst Live Group. We met every night at 7 p.m. for a month.

The adherence rate was well over 80 percent for our eight enrolees. Score one for group interaction. There was a charge for participation. In hindsight, this may have limited enrolment and boosted attendance by people looking to get the most for their money. But the group setting allowed us to better coach more complex lifts.

> Even if they hate the workouts, people will do them if they perceive they'll waste money by not doing them. They may not come back the next month, though. The stick works, but the carrot is better.

Lesson learned:
People enjoy group settings.

Finally, after learning the lesson that complex tasks will help keep people coming back for more, we started to incorporate Olympic lifts and powerlifting movements. Unfortunately, adherence dropped. In subsequent feedback forums people admitted they were unlikely to do a movement they weren't comfortable performing. One participant booked private training to learn the lifts, and her adherence rate rebounded.

Lesson learned:
People are motivated by live coaching.

If It Looks Like CrossFit and Smells Like CrossFit...

By this point, the link between our research and CrossFit's methodology and philosophies was becoming very obvious. Let's make this clear: we didn't set out to prove CrossFit works. Heck, we were originally sceptical of CrossFit. But we couldn't ignore the way our research was

Subscription info at http://journal.crossfit.com
Feedback to feedback@crossfit.com

First, we started reporting people's adherence rates on a weekly basis. We'd send an e-mail on Sunday saying, "Bill, your weekly adherence rate is 60 percent. Good job." At first, we used the same comments for everyone automatically. Later, we'd change the feedback to a personal note from a Catalyst trainer. Letting practitioners know their adherence rate bumped their success up a bit, but the personal note had far more impact.

Lesson learned:
People relate to a personality better than to a program.

Next, we started providing a weekly and monthly ranking —anonymously, of course. The weekly Sunday e-mail would say something like, "Bill, your weekly adherence rate is 60 percent. That's better than last week! Sixty percent puts you in fifth place among men!" Adherence improved again.

Lesson learned:
People compare themselves to other people, whether they admit it or not.

Next step: increase the intensity of the workouts. We used the same workouts we'd used the first month and added weight or repetitions or inserted goal times to increase

the challenge. This produced mixed results. But we had hypothesized that adherence would decrease, so we were surprised again.

Lesson learned:
People want to be challenged. But how best to do it? We learned the answer later.

The variable that produced the biggest result was novelty. We'd always taken great pride in never giving a client the same workout prescription twice. When we applied this tenet to our study, we found that not knowing what would come next improved adherence nearly 15 percent alone. We also mixed rest days so participants couldn't count on days off beyond knowing that they'd rest two days per week.

Lesson learned:
People like variety and surprise.

Next, we thought, "What if people have to pay for it? Will they be more likely to complete the workouts?" We added a $30 monthly fee to continue with the program. Our subscriptions fell when we ended the free service. But those who stayed were more likely to do the prescribed workout, even if they dropped out at the end of the month.

Chris Cooper found the transition from powerlifting to Linda to be a struggle—but he made it.

Subscription info at http://journal.crossfit.com
Feedback to feedback@crossfit.com

Improving Adherence – *Ignite!* Research

In 2011, *Ignite!* Coaches partnered with a local School Board to begin research, in three phases, on the *Ignite!* Method's effect on standardized test scores.

In the first study, students identified as "at-risk" for early departure from school (dropping out) were graded on subjective measures: Attention, Effort, Independent Work, Self-Confidence, Initiative, Participation, and Conflict Resolution.

Considerations

First, these are subjective measures, obviously. However, this is the same process used for grading all students (the '*rubric*') in Ontario, and we wanted to stay consistent with the system used by the School Board. To make the study relevant, it had to reflect measurable difference on their terms, not ours.

Second, the weekly score in each category for each student is actually the average of TWO scores: one given by their regular teacher, who participated in each WOD; and one by another teacher, who usually did not participate. The second teacher involved rotated among 4 teachers each week. Again, this type of grading is subjective, and frames of reference among teachers varied. How else could you explain, on a scale of 4, two teachers grading Johnny with a "1" and a "3.5"....while watching during the same 30-minute window?

The above observation underlines the importance of creating the proper environment for students. In one telling example, an issue arose with a teenager who didn't want to remove his hat. He'd been told that he couldn't wear his hat in school; though the class was at our gym, he was scolded that he had to abide by the same rules as if he were in school. Since other gym members present would be wearing hats at the same time, our Coach was loathe to enforce the rule, and it was up to the teachers.

When he arrived at a class in the gym midway through the semester, he went through the warmup with his hat on. One teacher barked, "Get that hat off!" he did. His regular teacher scored him a '3.5' in conflict resolution, because he removed his hat the first time he was asked. The visiting teacher – the barker – scored him a '1' in the same category, because she'd been forced to ask in the first place.

Third, we included only the students who completed a minimum of 6 weeks out of the 8-week (twice weekly) course. This meant that two students were disqualified from the data. Among this group, though, which features a greater-than-50% dropout rate, finishing the semester was an achievement. Did the more eager students self-select for *Ignite!*, or did *Ignite!* actually improve their attendance?

Unfortunately, we aren't permitted access to the students' scores for any of the categories before or after the study period for reasons of confidentiality. This history may have affected both the grading teacher's opinion of the student AND the Coach's first impression.

Fourth, our exposure to these students was a mere 30 minutes per day, twice per week – as much as their school schedule would allow. Several of these students are semi-homeless; several still struggle with chemical dependance. Once or twice, a student arrived intoxicated. Following the second session, when the students asked to go outside to smoke, their teacher yelled to their backs, "Just cigarettes this time, guys!"

One sad story underscored the value of improving adherence and giving the students Bright Spots in their education. Toward the end of the semester, a student who had been making regular progress in all categories – probably the most consistent of the group, without a high variability in scores between weeks, but solid progress throughout – was facing a return trip home. Home, for him, was a very remote reserve in Northern Ontario. His background there included a number of things that were extremely unpleasant, and a return tip home likely promised more of the same abuses. On the last day of the semester, he reportedly came to school under the influence of a cocktail of drugs, and committed a few misdemeanours. Since he was on his 'last strike,' he was removed from the system forever. THIS is the client we're trying to help. Banned from school for life, what options are open to this seventeen-year-old?

Student 1 – T

Skill	Week 1	Week 2	Week 3	Week 4	Week 5	Week 6	Week 7	Week 8	Week 9	Week 10
Attention	2	2.5	2.5	2.5	3	2.5	3	2	3	3
Effort	2	2.5	2.5	2.5	3	2.5	3	3	3	3
Independent Work	1	2	2	2	2	2.5	2	2	3	3
Self-Confidence	1	2	2	2	2	2	2	2	2	2
Initiative	1	2	2	2	3	2	3	2	3	3
Participation	2	2	2	2	1	2.5	2	2	3	3
Conflict Resolution	2	3	3	3	3	2.5	3	2	4	4

Student 2 – LS-K

Skill	Week 1	Week 2	Week 3	Week 4	Week 5	Week 6	Week 7	Week 8	Week 9	Week 10
Attention	2.5	2	3	3	4	4	3	4	3	4
Effort	2.5	3	3	3	4	4	3	3	3	4
Independent Work	2.5	3	2	3	3	4	3	3	4	4
Self-Confidence	2.5	3	2.5	3	3	4	3	3	3	4
Initiative	2.5	2	2	3	3	4	4	3	4	3
Participation	2.5	3	2	3	3	3	4	3	3	4
Conflict Resolution	2	2	2	3	3	3	3	3	3.5	1

Student 3 – SB

Skill	Week 1	Week 2	Week 3	Week 4	Week 5	Week 6	Week 7	Week 8	Week 9	Week 10
Attention	2	3	2	2	2	2	3	2	3.5	2
Effort	3	3.5	3	1.5	2	2	2.5	2	3	2
Independent Work	2	3.5	2	2	2	2	2	2	3	2
Self-Confidence	4	3.5	4	2	4	4	2	4	3	4
Initiative	3	3.5	3	2.5	3	3	2.5	3	3.5	3
Participation	2	3.5	2	2	2	2	2.5	2	2	2
Conflict Resolution	1	3	2	2	1	1	2	1	2	1

Student 4 – AL

Skill	Week 1	Week 2	Week 3	Week 4	Week 5	Week 6	Week 7	Week 8	Week 9	Week 10
Attention	2.5	4	3.5	2	3	4	3	3	3	3
Effort	2	3	3.5	4	4	4	3	3.5	3.5	3
Independent Work	2.5	3	3.5	3	4	4	4	3	3.5	3
Self-Confidence	2	3	3.5	3	4	4	4	4	3	3
Initiative	2.5	3	3.5	2	4	4	4	3.5	3.5	3
Participation	2.5	3	3	3	4	4	4	3.5	3.5	3
Conflict Resolution	2.5	2.5	3	2	3.5	4	4	4	3	3.5	3

Student 5 – AZ

Skill	Week 1	Week 2	Week 3	Week 4	Week 5	Week 6	Week 7	Week 8	Week 9	Week 10
Attention	1	1	3	3	2	2	3	3	2	2.5
Effort	1.5	1	2.5	2	2	1	3.5	3	2.5	2.5
Independent Work	1.5	1	2.5	2	1	2	3.5	2.5	2	2
Self-Confidence	1.5	1	2	2	1	2	3	2.5	2.5	2
Initiative	2	1	2.5	2	2	1	3	2.5	2	2
Participation	2	1	3	2.5	2	2	3	2.5	2.5	2
Conflict Resolution	2	1	3	2.5	1	1	3	3	2.5	2.5

Student 6 – VS

Skill	Week 1	Week 2	Week 3	Week 4	Week 5	Week 6	Week 7	Week 8	Week 9	Week 10
Attention	2	2	2	4	4	3	3	1	3.5	4
Effort	1.5	1	2	4	4	4	3.5	1	4	4
Independent Work	1.5	1	2	4	4	3	3	1	4	4
Self-Confidence	1.5	1	2	4	4	3	3	1	3	3
Initiative	1.5	1	2	4	4	3	3	1	3	3.5
Participation	1.5	1	2	4	4	4	3	1	3	3
Conflict Resolution	1.5	1	2	4	4	4	2	1	3	4

Improvements in the seven categories listed above were sporadic, but all showed a general trend toward personal growth in every student. Behaviours can be understandably erratic for various socioeconomic reasons in this group, and the reader may notice a few aberrations: a student making notable progress may 'slip' in scores for a week, and then return to normal the week after.

	Week 1	Week 2	Week 3	Week 4	Week 5	Week 6	Week 7	Week 8	Week 9	Week 10
GROSS AVERAGE	**2.00**	**2.24**	**2.54**	**2.70**	**2.89**	**2.89**	**3.00**	**2.44**	**3.06**	**2.90**
Attention Average	2.00	2.42	2.67	2.75	3.00	2.92	3.00	2.50	3.00	3.08
Effort Average	2.08	2.33	2.75	2.83	3.17	2.92	3.08	2.58	3.17	3.08
Independent Work Average	1.83	2.25	2.33	2.67	2.67	2.92	2.92	2.25	3.25	3.00
Self-Confidence Average	2.08	2.25	2.67	2.67	3.00	3.17	2.83	2.75	2.75	3.00
Initiative Average	2.08	2.08	2.50	2.50	3.17	2.83	3.25	2.50	3.17	2.92
Participation Average	2.08	2.25	2.33	2.75	2.67	2.92	3.08	2.33	3.00	2.67
Conflict Resolution Average	1.83	2.08	2.50	2.75	2.58	2.58	2.83	2.17	3.08	2.58

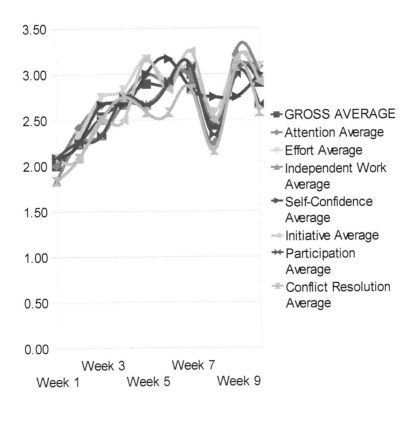

In our second study, currently underway, we're comparing grades of 10th-grade math students. There are four classes involved, with two teachers, in two different classroom settings: three classes indoor, one outdoor. In this study, we've been granted access to EQAO (standardized test) scores comparing the students using the *Ignite!* method with their peers, and against their own history.

Section VII: The *Ignite!* Academy

Ignite! works best when tailored for the environment in which it's to be used. But what if we could BUILD the precise environment that we feel would be best for delivering a program for cognitive development, and all of the other great things we mention in this book?

We imagine it would look like this: no chairs or desks, but plenty of open space. Places to write things without restriction. Flooring that's hard enough to support jumping and running, but soft enough to also support tumbling and vestibular exercises. Audio/visual equipment for feedback, but no obvious screens to distract. Books. Markers, pens, pencils, and chalk to match the plyometric boxes, gymnastics rings, and foam rollers.

In short, it would look something like this:

The *Ignite!* Academy at Catalyst Fitness is the original delivery facility for the *Ignite!* Enrichment program; for various *Ignite!* Therapies, including those for Acute Brain Injury like stroke; and for the *Ignite!* ChemoBrain program, for those who have survived chemotherapy and are beginning the long road back to full functionality.

This is the laboratory for our daily challenges. This is our centre for research; this our our petri dish and our library. Part of a much larger gym that includes gymnastics, martial arts, and CrossFit, we have access to a great deal of space...or private, smaller areas like this one:

At the Academy, we have the space to offer a wide variety of Enrichment programming. Our own Coaches research and deliver some of the subject matter, and we also frequently go outside of our own circle to include the expertise of others in our local community with uncommon knowledge.

Some of our Enrichment courses at the Academy:

- ⋏ Public Speaking for Kids

- ⋏ Money Management (Family Class)

- ⋏ Campfire Guitar

- ⋏ Creative Writing

- ⋏ Brain Training for Sport

- ⋏ SuperMemory

On our website, **www.IgniteGym.com**, we frequently post the games, challenges, lessons and contests that we use within our own Academy for your review. You'll find Tall Tales contests, Working Memory Word Searches, three-dimensional problem solving games, and more books by the *Ignite!* team there.

Already, others across North America have inquired about starting their OWN *Ignite!* Academy (the founder of our first Affiliate, JR Thomas, graces the dedication page of this book.) We license our knowledge to teachers, coaches, and therapists who want to provide a similar experience to their clients.

Affiliation of an *Ignite!* Academy provides access to more than just the *Ignite!* Academy brand. It also allows Affiliates to interact online; download and upload lesson plans; receive business AND NeuroMotive Coaching; be updated on current research; schedule webmeetings with other NeuroMotive Coaches and Therapists; and receive discounts on continuing education credits. The *Ignite!* Academy offers Enrichment-based classes, as well as one-on-one training for clients. If your facility does any programming for Youth, it's a very simple addition.

This is a sample *Ignite!* Academy Enrichment schedule used during school programs to strengthen academic prowess with subject- specific movements.

Cognitive and Neuromotor Skills: The *Ignite!* 7-day practice cycle.

Handwriting

1) Cursive fundamentals

2) Copying

3) Perception

4) Fine motor skills (manual)

5) Trunk/shoulder stability

Visual

1) Perception

2) Eye Tracking

3) Focusing

4) Binocular Teaming

Auditory (sub-disciplines: inactive, active, reflective, selective.)

1) Detection

2) Discrimination

3) Identification

4) Comprehension

Language

1) Grammar and Vocabulary (slang, buzzwords, acronyms, fillers)

2) Reading aloud, Articles and Facts (pace, projection, pronunciation, enunciation)

3) Storytelling (expression, confidence, pace, stance, eye contact, jokes)

4) Active listening, Eye Contact, Responding

5) Argumentation and Debate

Memory

1) Working Memory and Manipulation

2) Remembering Simple Lists

3) Remembering Ordered/Procedural Lists and

Steps

4) Remembering Lengthy Lists

5) Remembering Grouped Information

6) Remembering Long Numbers

7) Remembering Structured Information

Week 1

Monday	Tuesday	Wednesday	Thursday	Friday
H-1	H-2	H-3	H-4	H-5
A-1	A-2	A-3	A-4	A-1+2
V-1	V-2	V-3	V-4	V-1+2
L-1	L-2	L-3	L-4	L-5
M-1	M-2	M-3	M-4	M-5

Week 2

Monday	Tuesday	Wednesday	Thursday	Friday
H-1+2+3	H- 4 + 5	Performance	H- 1	H-2
A- 3	A- 4	Day	A- 1	A- 2
V-3	V-4		V- 1	V-2
L- 3	L- 4		L- 1	L- 2
M- 6	M- 7		M- 1	M- 2

Adjust table row

Balance for Pre-Reading Movements

Balance and dynamic balance are the motor functions that lay the foundation for reading and comprehension. If we: 1)practise a dynamic movement until it becomes automatic, 2)perform an eye scanning exercise, then 3) perform a focus drill we activate the nucleus basalis creating state dependant learning, and make room in the cerebral cortex for processing.

Monday	Tuesday	Wednesday	Thursday	Friday
Static -postural	Dynamic looking/reaching	Static follow a line	Dynamic external force	Game
Dynamic postural	Static looking/reaching	Dynamic follow a line	Static external force	Game

All Dynamic Postural Balance Workouts will include:

1) Locomotor movement

2) Complex movement

3) Jumping and change of direction/hold component

All Dynamic Looking and Reaching Workouts will include:

1) Locomotor movement

2) Complex movement

3) Jumping and change of direction/hold component **PLUS** looking R/L and reaching with L/R hands in multiple directions. Cue instructions using time domains.

All Dynamic Follow a line workouts will include

1) Locomotor movement

2) Complex movement

3) Jumping and change of direction/hold component **PLUS** all while staying on a line, or square

All Dynamic External Force workouts will include:

1) Locomotor movement

2) Complex movement

3) Jumping and change of direction/hold component **PLUS** having a partner add resistance - bands

All Static Postural Balance workouts will include:

1) Locomotor movement: walking lunge, skipping, bear crawl, running,

2) Complex movement: mountain climber, dots, side hops, skipping ropes,

3) Static hold: plank, squat, overhead, arms out, handstand

All Static Looking and Reaching workouts will include:

1) Locomotor movement: walking lunge, skipping, bear crawl, running,

2) Complex movement: mountain climber, dots, side hops, skipping ropes,

3) Static hold: plank, squat, overhead, arms out, handstand **PLUS** looking R/L and reaching with L/R hands in multiple directions. Cue instructions using time domains.

All Static Follow a line workouts will include:

1) Locomotor movement: walking lunge, skipping, bear crawl, running,

2) Complex movement: mountain climber, dots, side hops, skipping ropes,

3) Static hold: plank, squat, overhead, arms out, handstand **PLUS** having to stay on a square, line with hands and feet, 1 or both.

All Static External Force workouts will include:

1) Locomotor movement: walking lunge, skipping, bear crawl, running,

2) Complex movement: mountain climber, dots, side hops, skipping ropes,

3) Static hold: plank, squat, overhead, arms out, handstand **PLUS** having a partner challenge their balance with light resistance.

Body Awareness and Coordination

Pre-Math Movements and : problem solving and body awareness are the motor functions that lay the foundation for problem solving, pattern recognition, math skills.

1) Issue a problem solving movement, workout 2) plan, practise and perform it until success.

3) Draw conclusions and make connections. Anchor.

Monday	Tuesday	Wednesday	Thursday	Friday
Comparing lower body	Goal Setting upper body	Comparing midline	Goal Setting complex	Game
Goal Setting lower body	Comparing upper body	Goal Setting midline	Comparing complex move	Game

All Comparing BA/Coordination workouts include:

1) Locomotor movement

2) 3 variations of a complex movement Ie. (Squat – narrow stance, wide stance, toes out)

3) the complex movement (squats)

All Goal Setting BA/Coordination workouts include:

1) Locomotor movement

2) Coordination skill

3) Pose a goal setting question using the coordination skill

Laterality

Pre-Language Movements

(bi lateral, coordination) In written and oral language it is the responsibility of the muscles involved in writing and speaking to perform fluently and automatic. Conscious thought for ideas and communication happen effectively when the motor movements involved are performed unconsciously.

1) Perform laterality movements 2) Practice the non dominant side until similar fluidity is achieved with dominant side. 3) Check how automatic or learned the movement is by adding another task. Capability to multitask and keep the movements fluid means the student is ready to proceed.

Monday	Tuesday	Wednesday	Thursday	Friday
R hand,eye	L hand, eye	R foot-eye	L foot-eye	Game
R hand- L eye	L hand- R eye	R foot- L eye	L foot – R eye	Game

All laterality workouts will include:

1) Locomotor movement

2) Perform the locomotor movement laterally

3) Bilateral complex movements and agility drills

All laterality workouts can also include the use of manipulatives like a ball or stick. This table shows which subject areas can benefit from performing specific motor movements prior to the subject.

Motor Movements Academic Subject	Laterality	Balance Dynamic/ Static	Body Awareness/ Coordination
Reading Comprehension		X	
Grammar	X	X	
Oral/Speech Presentations	X	X	X
Essay Writing	X		X
Short Answer Questions	X	X	
Reflection Assignments	X		X
Math			X
Word problems		X	X

Religion		X	X
Science		X	X
Second Language	X	X	
Art	X	X	X
Drama	X	X	X
Music	X	X	X
Note taking	X	X	
Phys Ed	X	X	X
Computer	X	X	

Handwriting

The ability to press keys and have letters and numbers show up on a screen has increased the speed of recording ideas, paragraphs and stories. In the process, though, we are weakening the connection between our procedural memory and fine motor skills. Handwriting relies on the integration of a number of cognitive and motor functions, whereas typing is limited to its motor and benefits as soon as the typing skill becomes intrinsic. Handwriting involves procedural memory - remembering the steps it takes to create shapes and strokes; working memory - maintaining the flow of our ideas from sentence to sentence; and in note-taking, a fine-motor skills which includes the precision of the shoulder, arm, hand and fingers to manipulate an object to create recognizable shapes and strokes.

An Indiana University study which measured neural activity in the brains of children using a fMRI (functional Magnetic Resonance Imaging machine) before and after receiving different letter-learning instruction showed that children who wrote out the letters by hand had "adult-like", and far more enhanced neural activity than children who were just shown the letters.

Research replicated in many psychology classes shows that taking notes does not necessarily mean more information will be recalled(the note-takers and the non note-takers remembered about 40% of the lecture,) but the information remembered by the note-takers included more key facts than the non-note-takers. This and other research suggests that during the writing phase there is an internal evaluation and ordering process which helps to anchor down ideas allowing for more efficient memory recall in the future.

The physical act of writing:

1) Helps with visual identification of graphic shapes;

2) Stimulates a particular part of the brain called the Reticular Activating System, which filters out less relevant information giving more attention to relevant points;

3) Improves memorization by tricking the brain into thinking it's performing the activity, instead of just recording it; and

4) Improves memory recall as a result of the writer being

engaged in an evaluation and ordering process.

Cursive Fundamentals: *fluidity, procedural memory, style, fast communication, autonomy.*

The importance of practising the fundamentals in the acquisition of any new physical skill, like a tennis backhand, and in keeping the skill sharp is imperative. The same is true for handwriting. Each letter has its own order or step, style, shape, and feel. In the same way that the parts of a complex movement requires proficiency in each individual movement, cursive writing (and activities including like note taking and essay writing) can only be fluent if the fundamentals are automatic.

Proficiency in this area allows us to create our own style (or, even, multiple styles) to use at different times or to express different emotions. Good handwriting also helps students create strong connections; filter out relevant material; and anchor down key facts.
Tricking the brain into thinking it's performing a real act - much like visualizing a performance – is possible through the mere rehearsal that occurs when recording an event manually, because the time required for a handwritten description allows for a more thorough mental image than a typed one of the same.

To improve cursive fundamentals:
- Practice or change paper position for right- and left-handed individuals
- Pull downstrokes/slant strokes, using dots to create straight lines on the page
- Practice Understrokes
- Practice Undercurves
- Practice Downcurves
- Practice Overcurves
- Practice Descenders

⚔ Practice Checkstrokes
⚔ Practice Slants

*To make these tasks more difficult, ask students to turn their heads left and right, or use only their right or left eye when writing; or distract them.

Self evaluate on the properties of:
⚔ Spacing
⚔ Smoothness
⚔ Size
⚔ Shape

Cursive Writing Practice

Name: _____ Date: _____

The vestibular

system takes in

information from

our other senses:

taste, smell, touch,

sight, and

Cursive Writing Practice

Name: _____ Date: _____

hearing. The

vestibular system

compares this data

to the position of

the body in space

to create a picture

Examples of Visual Practise

racking inside objects– around chalk boards, door frames, in straight lines, from toes to the ceiling, in x-shapes or circles, far away, and then close practise, tracing outlines of letters, books, desks, posters, weights, tracking left to right, jumping over words, doubling back, peripheral items, pursuits while moving...these can all be implemented as part of a comprehensive visual practice session. For best results, include a lot of variety. The following are several examples of drills you can create to improve visual evaluation:

Track a square 10 times alternating directions (Left and right)	From tip of nose track each object between you and the end of the room and back. 10 times.	Track as far left and as far right as you can without turning your head. Look at each object between the right and left. 10 times	Track an X from the top right corner to the bottom left corner of the room. Track from the top left corner to the bottom right corner and each object in those lines 10 times	Track up, down and around shapes of objects in the room Adjust table c to right. 10 times

Track around a circular object 10 times, alternating directions.	Track from left to right using only the bottom of your vision. 20 times Track left to right using only the top of your vision. 20 times	Track up and down using the far right peripheral. 10 times. Track up and down using the far left peripheral 10 times	Track letters on a page backwards for 3 minutes	Track words on a page and skip over every second word. Then double back and read right to left the words you skipped over.

Tracking outside– tree lines, distance to tip of nose, trace buildings, objects, watch a moving object try and catch license plates at high speeds, track a bird, a squirrel, etc, left to right...

Track the horizon from side to side going up, down and around the shapes. 10 times	From the tip of your nose to as far as you can see, track every object between you and the horizon	Search for squares and track around each square. (windows, buildings, etc.)	Track as much of the branches and leaves on a tree in 3 minutes	Track side to side a power line without turning your head. 10 times alternating directions
Try and read the license plates of the passing cars.	Track a bird's flight for as long as possible.	Track the shapes of clouds.	Outline the shape of every (colour) object you see	Track around every round object you can see.

Tracking inside the classroom or home:

Circle the picture that is exactly the same as the picture on top. Use a comparing picture activity	Using something in the classroom that everyone has, construct an image have the class make the same thing. Building blocks	Show the students a picture for 5 seconds then take it away. Try and recall as much of the image as possible.	Word search of the day for time	Incomplete pictures and have the students fill in the rest for time, or as many as possible.
Circle the picture that is different. (Use a comparing picture activity.)	Take the object and identify what it's mirror image would be. What an opened cube looks like, etc.	Using a facial expression page, identify what emotion is being portrayed. For time	Match the letters of each font with its block letter for time.	Using these shapes decide what the picture is (puzzle) for time.

These are some examples of the practise that *Ignite!* Academy students will use through for handwriting. The *Ignite!* Academy is the private facility in which most NeuroMotive Coaches and Therapists practice, be it their gym, their practice office, or another location. *Ignite!* Strongly encourages NeuroMotive Therapists and Coaches, teachers, and parents to consider opening their own *Ignite!* Academy. Details on licensure and affiliation are available at **www.ignitegym.com.**

Conclusions

For Students and Teachers

Whether they realize it or not, students are already using strategies to help them focus during a lesson: tapping their feet, balancing on two legs of their chair, clicking their pens, sitting backward in their chair, chewing gum, wiggling in the chair, getting out their seat, putting their arms in the air..... Unfortunately, while these strategies increase focus, the focus may not be on the lesson that the teacher is attempting to impart. Sometimes, students are embarrassed to say they're "just stretching," because no one else seems to need a stretch.

Putting their head down on their desk, or supporting an arm in the air with another resting on the desk when raising their hand, is a sign that the student may have weaknesses that are not limited to – but may be created by – physical strength, and not a cognitive impairment.

When do most of these behaviours occur? During lecture time when everyone is supposed be quiet, sitting still and paying attention.

To a teacher, these apparently impulsive movements are a result of immature behaviour, disruptive behaviour, lack of respect for the class; or they're just a bad kid, who will eventually have difficulty in the real world, in the teacher's judgement.

Teachers: did you go through to 4 years of school, plus student teaching, plus numerous AQ courses to teach children how to behave? Notice the correlation between Classroom management workshops or Differientated-learning strategy topics during Professional-Development Days and meetings. Compare the rise of disruption in the classroom with the decreased amount of physical activity in the student's school day. Remember how it feels to teach a class where a majority of the students were actually interested in what you were talking about? They found personal relevance in the message, and not because you said it was on the test. They were genuinely interested.

The interest may not have even been about your subject area; you could have been shooting from the hip about life, and the kids were fully engaged. "Oh man, this is surprising, they're actually participating in conversation, listening when I'm talking, asking questions!? I love teaching!" Have you ever had a few of those days in a row?

Now, imagine a class where you give the students the ability to feel that way all the time: "Mr. Belanger really cares about the way we grow up, and is showing me relevance between this subject and life." It's not an everyday occurrence that we can put together a lesson plan that answers the question, "*Why do we have to know this?*," but you now have the knowledge to say, "It's practise for your reading, writing, listening, critical thinking... etc. If you can perform this skill with information that you don't feel is relevant, imagine how much you'll succeed with information you DO find relevant."

Good: giving kids an opportunity to succeed through an education.

Better: teaching to students' needs, multiple intelligences, and making modifications to help learning happen.

Best: teaching students *how* to create their own circumstances for successful learning. At the same time, stretching the students' perceived limits of physical and cognitive function through frequent interventions. The best-case scenario is really teaching people about the growth mindset. The best *method* is to praise effort and hard work.

For Adults Trying To Improve Their Life

Everyone is great at something. As a result of their circumstances and practice, anyone can be efficient and adept at a task. Whether as a cashier, adding money as an automatic cognitive function; or as a procrastinator who practices the avoidance of initiating tasks, they're good because they've logged the hours. Where *Ignite!*

can help is through the appreciation that they're not as bad at everything as they may believe. *Ignite!* helps people unearth their best; starts them on the path; and helps them stay in the middle of the road.

Ignite! NeuroMotive Coaches are not experts in everything. However, they do understand how to foster improvement that will help in any situation. Investing the time and effort is up to the individual; no formula will provide immediate life-altering changes. Teaching people to expect small, frequent podium finishes – teaching people how to *win* – is extremely powerful. Perhaps the biggest question most should ask themselves: "If my day was successful, how would I *know it*?"

Ignite! Director of Education Tyler Belanger writes,

One of the greatest lessons I've ever learned as a Coach was, "There is no such thing as a totally hopeless case." Projecting that belief onto someone can motivate on a very primitive level.

Some people call me an optimist or Mr. Positive, because I rarely get upset with situations and tend to roll with the punches well. But even optimistic people can experience deflated spirits after a number of failures. I prefer to be real about the events that life has in store and attack them with 'guns blazing' and a thousand hours of practise in the chamber, instead of closing my eyes and hoping for the best. Sometimes, it comes across as if I don't care. What I do care about is my mental health and physical health. While things that are upsetting, like forgetting to lock the door behind me at home; forgetting to book a client or making a mistake at work; failing at a lift or workout; eating something I shouldn't; losing at a game, etc. can ruin my day, I know that way I choose to respond to the situation develops into behaviours. The behaviours I use most often are the behaviours I'm hardwiring into my brain. Do I want anxiousness, nervousness, and frustration to be a part of my life; or do I want joy, interest, contentment and love? It's a choice.

"It's better to burn out than to fade away" is a famous line in a song by Neil Young. Burning out is a result of doing work; taking action; multitasking; saying 'yes,' rather than 'no.' Fading away, however doesn't take any work at all.

We've shown how connected the mind and body really are, and when one part begins to fade, so does the other. Muscular atrophy and cognitive decline together or thrive together.

Good - being active, eating healthy, doing your job

Better – exercising 3 days a week, consistent healthy eating, being productive at your job

Best - Being awesome.
Giving someone hope vs. letting them wish for something are two very different things. One is a growth mindset and one is not.

Since discovering that circumstances can define a person and that we actually have some control over our circumstances, I have always conducted myself in this manner.

When you are in control of a situation, how do you feel? How do you conduct yourself? Why are you unable to feel that way all the time?

> *"In our African idiom they say, "A person is a person, through other persons." - Desmond Tutu*
>
> As NeuroMotive Coaches, it is our responsibility to set the example of positive, hard-working people. What does every person have to deal with? Things they don't like. Avoidance of these tasks will only teach you how to avoid in the future. Take a look at what you're building.
>
> When I was young, I often thought about being a professional at *something*. But I based my model of professional athletes around things I couldn't control, like genetics. I have to be 6'2 to play pro baseball, or from the States. I never made the connection to the circumstances of the players and the amount of hours they put in to become great players.
>
> In starting to research and build the *Ignite!* method, what I envisioned was a program that created the best possible circumstance for children to succeed in whatever they want to do. There's no way a subject, a sport, or any experience should deflect a child from his path, or push them down and hinder their growth. Every subject has relevance, whether it be just to practise the skill of reading, writing, or memory, and a sport should be played to develop the motor functions of the human body.

Success in life is largely determined by circumstance. From birth, everyone has a different environment in which they grow up and mature; consider the circumstances that allowed you to be in any realm of success in your own life. The bully in the schoolyard who pushed you around was awful at the time, but perhaps taught you how to behave with respect around others. Being the shortest kid in the class may not have been fun, either, but it taught you how to be faster. As the saying goes, *'dance with the one who brung ya'*. Take what you've been given and run. The important part of this truth: we can create the best circumstances out of the bare minimum available.

When writing this book, the authors said to each other at least once a week, "I wish I knew this stuff when I was younger." That's true. Things would have been different. On the downside, though, things would have been different.... If you can look back and be happy with how your circumstances shaped you; and can be happy with the outcome of those circumstances, then good for you. You've led – and continue to lead – a successful life.

From Chris Cooper, founder of Catalyst Fitness:

"Coop, it's Ty. You've gotta get me out of here, man. I can't take it." This was the phone call that started *Ignite!*: a teacher disappointed by the system that paid his rent. He felt that his students were being underserved; that his hands were tied by overlapping bureaucracies; that he could do so much more.

I've always been interested in the benefits of exercise for the brain, and my approach to business, fitness, and life has usually been described as 'unconventional.' In 2006, when we realized that clients weren't doing their 'extra homework' that we were providing them in our Personal Training sessions, we demanded to know the reason. We launched a two-year study that cost nearly $40,000....but we found out. And now, as a result, if we're a bit critical of programs aimed to increase participation in exercise and sport....but don't consider the reasons most people have for quitting, maybe we can be forgiven.

When my wife and I started Catalyst Fitness in 2005, we really only had two things going for us:

1) We can outwork anyone.

2) We can learn anything, given enough time and mistakes.

Luckily, we recognized these truths, even then; this allowed us to take some large risks that would limit others. One of those risks was to give Tyler a year to build his *Ignite!* concept into a viable career.

Nine months later, Tyler's overbooked with clients seeking help. Insurance companies are referring clients to *Ignite!*. We're delivering the system online. We're preparing to deliver Certifications across the continent within the next few months. We're continuing to expand our Academy. Schools are competing for our time before the exam season. And, at 4am, we're writing this textbook.

Appendix A1 – Bright Spots worksheet

Bright Spots Worksheet

1. Copy Success. Find a Bright Spot and clone it.

What's working right now? List some things you're doing right:

example: I'm eating more fruit and vegetables.

a)

b)

c)

d)

How do you feel when you're doing those things?

*Example: I have fewer mood swings. I don't feel as tired.
I have more energy. My skin is better. My digestion is
smoother. I have less anxiety.*

a)

b)

c)

d)

2. Clone the behaviours that are working to deliver
   the same benefits. What could you do, specifically,
   that would make you feel the same way?

*Example: exercising would give me more energy and
less anxiety.*

a)

b)

c)

d)

3. Take action accordingly. How will you know when the process is starting to work? How will you feel? What's the FIRST SIGN you'll have?

Example: I'll know that my plan is working because I'll wake up more easily in the morning. I'll know that it's working when I'm less stressed at work.

a)

b)

c)

d)

Congratulations! You've identified some Bright Spots. Those are your first goals; your first milestones on the journey toward long-lasting change!

APPENDIX A-2: The Change Checklist

The Change Checklist

What's something that's working already? What are your initial Bright Spots?

1.

2.

3.

4.

How can we clone the behaviours that are already successful?

1.

2.

3.

4.

What are the first Bright Spots that we can identify in the future? What's the first indication we'll have that you're being successful?

1.

2.

3.

4.

Appendix C – Sample Interventions, By Subject

Static Postural Balance Interventions

All Static Postural Balance workouts will include:

1) Locomotor movement: walking lunge, skipping, bear crawl, running,

2) Complex movement: mountain climber, dots, side hops, skipping ropes,

3) Static hold: plank, squat, overhead, arms out, handstand

All Static Looking and Reaching workouts will include:

1) Locomotor movement: walking lunge, skipping, bear crawl, running,

2) Complex movement: mountain climber, dots, side hops, skipping ropes,

3) Static hold: plank, squat, overhead, arms out, handstand **PLUS** looking R/L and reaching with L/R hands in multiple directions. Cue instructions using time domains.

All Static Follow a line workouts will include:

1) Locomotor movement: walking lunge, skipping, bear crawl, running,

2) Complex movement: mountain climber, dots, side hops, skipping ropes,

3) Static hold: plank, squat, overhead, arms out, handstand **PLUS** having to stay on a square, line with hands and feet, 1 or both.

All Static External Force workouts will include:

1) Locomotor movement: walking lunge, skipping, bear crawl, running,

2) Complex movement: mountain climber, dots, side hops, skipping ropes,

3) Static hold: plank, squat, overhead, arms out, handstand **PLUS** having a partner challenge their balance with light resistance.

Postural Reach and look   Follow a line External Force

10 mountain climbers	15 m bear crawl	15 m sideways bear crawl	10 skips
20sec plank	10 rolling situps	10 right foot hops on a line	10 push ups
10 mountain climbers	10 squats looking, and reaching to the left with right arm.	10 left foot hops on a line	30 sec push up hold with a right side push.
20 second plank R			Alternate right and left side pushes. 3 rounds
10 mountain climbers	10 squats looking and reaching to the right with left arm	20 skips	
		20 walking	
			10 walking

20 second plank L	3 rounds	lunges on a line	lunges
		10 squat shuffles on a line right	5 forward rolls
1:00 Jump rope 5 Handstand holds, wall walks 20 squats	10 walking lunges	10 squat shuffles on a line left	10 sec squat hold with partner pushing on front, back, and shoulders
3 rounds	5 stink bugs	3 rounds	
	Hold plank for 1 minute, every 10 seconds reach out alternation right and left hand.		3 rounds
10 burpees		10 high knee run	
10 side to side hops	5 rounds	10 jump to supports	15 m bear crawl
10 squat holds		10 m tight rope walking on a line	10 situps
3 rounds		3 rounds	10 sec situp hold with partner pushing down on hands or shoulders.
	30 seconds of burpees		
	30 second hollow rock		
5 Handstand attempts	30 second superman alternating looking and reaching to the right and left.		
Bear crawl 15 M			
10 squats			
15 M high knee			

skip			
200 M Basic dot drill x 10 30 second plank hold (each side) 3 rounds			
15 m High knee skipping 15 m Bear crawl			
15 sec overhead squat hold			
30 seconds of burpees			
30 second hollow rock			
30 second superman			

Dynamic Postural Balance Interventions

All Dynamic Postural Balance Workouts will include:

1) Locomotor movement

2) Complex movement

3) Jumping and change of direction/hold component

All Dynamic Looking and Reaching Workouts will include:

1) Locomotor movement

2) Complex movement

3) Jumping and change of direction/hold component **PLUS** looking R/L and reaching with L/R hands in multiple directions. Cue instructions using time domains.

All Dynamic Follow a line workouts will include

1) Locomotor movement

2) Complex movement

3) Jumping and change of direction/hold component **PLUS** all while staying on a line, or square

All Dynamic External Force workouts will include:

1) Locomotor movement

2) Complex movement

3) Jumping and change of direction/hold component **PLUS** having a partner add resistance - bands

Postural Looking Reaching   Follow a line   External Force

Looking Reaching	Follow a line	External Force	
10m bear crawl (5m forward+5m	10 mountain climbers	10m run	10 walking lunges

backwards)	5 box jump looking and reaching right	10m two footed hops	while partner is putting pressure on right shoulder.
15 lateral hops			
5 squats	5 box jump looking and reaching left	10m two footed hops on a line	
5 rounds		5rounds	Then left shoulder
	5 squats		
			5 deadlifts
	2 rounds		
100m run (10m shuttle)		20seconds high knee running on the spot	5 rounds
5 burpees			
5 situps	20m high knee running	5 walking lunge	
4 minute AMRAP	5 pushups	5 walking lunge following a line	5 broad jumps
	30 second plank hold looking and reaching to the right	4 rounds	10 push ups
25 jumping jacks		10m bear crawl x 2	15 m resisted side shuffle.
10 squat jumps	30 second plank hold looking and reaching to the left	10 lateral hops	5 rounds
5 kick to handstand attempts	3 rounds	5 pushups	
3 rounds		5 rounds	10metre shuttle run (x4)
	10m shuttle x 2		
	5 broad jumps	10 metre Run	2 man on fire burpees
50 metre Run	10 pushups (alternate	5 pushups	

10 pushups	looking and reaching with left hand and right hand at the top of each pushup)	5 one leg broad jump	10 hop overs and have your partner check your balance with a shoulder push.
5 one leg broad jump		5 rounds	
4 rounds	3 rounds		
20 seconds:running on the spot	10 skips	jumping lunges on a line	5 minute AMRAP
20 seconds:of mountain climbers	5 burpees	5,4,3,2,1 of	
20 seconds: jumping lunge	5 situps reaching and looking to the left	10m bear crawl on a line	
20 seconds: rest	5 situps reaching and looking to the right	burpees	10 jumping squats 100m(10x 10m shuttle)
3 rounds		push up hold with hands and feet on a line. Lengthwise	10 Push ups 100m 10 jumping squats 100m 10 Push up
20 skips	3 rounds		
10 pushups	20 jumping jacks	5 stinkbugs	
5 squat jump to motorcycle landing1310	5 squats	7 jumping squats landing on the line	Partner resistance during change of direction.
	3 jump half turn looking and reaching right	9 mountain climbers	
3 bear crawl U-patterns	3 jump half turn looking and		

5 single leg line hops (each leg) 7 burpees 3 rounds	reaching left 4 rounds 10m bear crawl x 3 5 lunges 10 squat jumps (alternate looking and reaching left and right in the air) 2 rounds	5 Rounds 5 pushups 10 metre bear crawl trying to keep hands and feet on the line. More like a cat on a fence crawl. 5 Rounds	
21-15-9 Jumping jack lateral hops situp			
5,4,3,2,1 of 10m shuttle run side to side hops over a small barrier squats	10 mountain climbers 4 burpees (alternate looking and reaching left and right in the air) 5 rounds		
20 jumping jacks 10 walking lunge 5 burpee box	10m shuttle run x 3 5 squats		

jump	10 Lateral hops (alternate looking and reaching left to right each jump)
3 rounds	
	4 Rounds
20 mountain climbers	
10 broad jumps	
10 lateral hops	15 Side to side jumps over a small barrier
3 rounds	10m Bear crawl 10m Bear crawl backward alternating looking over your left and right shoulder
3 burpee broad jump	15 Squats
10m jump rope running	3 rounds
5 single leg hops	
3 rounds	Run 10 m
	Run 10 m backward looking over left shoulder
5 squats	
10 jumping lunge	Run 10 m
10m shuttle run x 4	Run 10 m backward looking over right shoulder

3 rounds	4 Rounds		
10 walking lunge			
10 metre inch worm			
10 situps			
3 rounds			
25 Side to side hops over small barrier 20 Sit ups 15 Squats 10 Push ups			
2 rounds			

Laterality Interventions

Laterality

R hand,eye	L hand, eye	R foot-eye	L foot-eye

R hand- L eye	L hand- R eye	R foot- L eye	L foot – R eye

All laterality workouts will include:

1) Locomotor movement

2) Perform the locomotor movement laterally

3) bi lateral complex movements and agility drills

Hand – Eye   Foot-Eye

Hand – Eye	Foot-Eye
30 second forward bear crawl	10m shuttle run
30 second bear crawl to the left	10m cross over left
30 second bear crawl to the right	10m cross over right
30 second rest	5 rounds
3 Rounds	
	10m sprint
10 walking lunge	10m shuffle left
2 Lateral pushup hops right	10m shuffle right
2 Lateral pushup hops left	5 basic dot drill
4 Lateral pushup hops (left-right)	3 rounds
5Rounds	

	5 Broad Jump
10 skips moving forward	5 Lateral hops right
5 pushups	5 Lateral hops left
10 skips moving backwards	10 Lateral hops (left-right)
5 pushups	5 Rounds
10 skips moving left	
5 pushups	2 burpees
5 rounds	2 man on fire burpees to the left
	2 man on fire burpees to the right
10m forward plank walk	
10m backward plank walk	4 man on fire burpees (alternate left and right)
10m plank walk left	2 rounds
10m plank walk right	
3 rounds	21-15-9
	Squats
	side to side hops
	straight squat jumps

10 two foot hops forward

5 two foot hops left

5 two foot hops right

10 hops alternating left to right

3 rounds

10 squats

10m bear crawl left

10 squats

10m bear crawl right

3 rounds

1 burpee box jump

1 lateral burpee box jump left

1 lateral burpee box jump right

2 lateral burpee box jumps
(alternated left and right)

3 rounds

10 seconds High knee running on the spot

10 seconds Burpee Lateral hops left

10 seconds rest

10 seconds High knee running on the spot

10 seconds Burpee Lateral hops right

10 seconds rest

4 Rounds

10 skips moving right

5 pushups

2 Rounds

5 pushups

2 log rolls right

5 pushups

2 log rolls left

5 situps

2 log rolls right

5 situps

2 log rolls left

1minute, 30 second break

3 Rounds

3 bear crawl U-patterns

5 line hops (left to right)

7 burpees

3 rounds

2 box jumps

2 lateral box jumps left

2 lateral box jumps right

4 lateral box jumps (alternated left and right)

3 rounds

Math-Specific Interventions

Body Awareness and Coordination

Comparing	Goal Setting	Comparing	Problem solving
lower body	upper body	midline	
			complex

All Comparing BA/Coordination workouts include:

1) Locomotor movement

2) 3 variations of a complex movement eg. (Squat – narrow stance, wide stance, toes out)

3) the complex movement (squats)

All Goal Setting BA/Coordination workouts include:

4) Locomotor movement

5) Coordination skill (skipping, precision)

6) Pose a goal setting question using the coordination skill. Provide a challenge to activate the problem solving parts of the brain "how many x can you do in x seconds"?

Comparing Setting	Goal
10 jumping jacks	10m shuttle run
5 tuck jumps	20 skips
5 star jumps	Challenge: How many shuttle runs can you complete in 30 seconds
5 straight jumps	
	3 rounds
10m Bear Crawl	
2 narrow stance squat	10 mountain climbers
2 wide stance squat	5 basic agility drill
2 toes out squats	Challenge: How many rounds can you complete in 2 minute?
2 natural stance squat	
3 rounds	30 seconds High knee running on the spot
20 skips	5 Precision jumps (jumping to a target from a distance)
20 staggered stance skips (left foot forward)	3 rounds
20 staggered stance skips (right foot forward)	Challenge: What is the greatest distance you can cover on a precision jump?
4 Rounds	

	20 high knee skips
10m of high knee skipping	5 lengths of a basic pattern on the agility ladder
1 burpee straddle jump	
	2 rounds
1 burpee tuck jump	
	Challenge: How many times can you complete the basic pattern in 45 seconds?
1 burpee straight jump	
7 Rounds	
	3 burpees
10m agility run	4 pushups
2 raised leg pushups (left leg raised)	5situps
2 raised leg pushups (right leg raised)	3 rounds
2 wide leg pushups	Challenge: How many pushups can you do in 30 seconds? Repeat challenge 3 times.
2 regular pushups	
	1 burpee
20 seconds of mountain climbers	5 squats
20 second plank with left leg raised	5 dot drills
20 second plank with right leg raised	Challenge: How many continuous dot drills can you complete

20 second plank with wide foot	5 rounds
20 second plank	
	6 lunges
15 skips	5 pushups
15 wide stance skips	4 squats
15 narrow stance skips	3 mountain climbers
15 skips	Challenge: How many rounds can you complete in 2 minutes?
30 second rest	
5 rounds	
	5 pushups
	5 situps
	5 dot drills
	Challenge: How many basic dot drills can you complete in 1 minute?
	3 rounds
	20 skips
	10 situps

20 skips

10 pushups

Challenge: How many unbroken skips can you complete?

3 rounds

3 box jumps

5 skips

3 box jumps

10 skips

3 box jumps

15 skips

3 box jump

20 skips

continue by adding 5 more skips after each round of box jumps

Challenge: How many skips can you complete in 3 minutes

21-15-9 then challenge

skips

two footed hops forward

situps

Challenge: How many
continuous side to side hops
can you complete?

1 kick to handstand

2 wall walks

4 pushups

8 situps

Challenge: How many kick to
handstands can you complete
in 20 seconds?

5-7-9

squats

situps

2 foot lateral hops

Challenge: How many single foot lateral hops can you complete in one minute (30 seconds for left foot, 30 seconds for right foot)

20 skips

1 kick to handstand

20 skips

2 kick to handstand

20 skips

3 kick to handstand

.... continue up the ladder as high as you can

Challenge: How far up the ladder will you get in 3 minutes

Visual Interventions

Tracking inside – around chalk boards, door frames, straight lines from from toes to the ceiling, x's, circles, far then close practise, tracing outlines of letters, books, desks, posters, weights, left to right, jumping over words, doubling back. Peripheral, pursuits while moving

Track a square 10 times alternating directions. Left and right	Track from tip of nose each object between you and the end of the room and back. 10 times.	Track as far left and as far right as you can without turning your head. Look at each object between the right and left. 10 times	Track an X from the top right corner to the bottom left corner of the room. Track from the top left corner to the bottom right corner and each object in those lines 10 times	Track up, down and around shapes of objects in the room from left to right. 10 times
Track around a circular object 10 times alternating directions.	Track from left to right using only the bottom of your vision. 20 times. Track left to right using only the top of your vision. 20 times	Track up and down using the far right peripheral 10 times. Track up and down using the far left peripheral 10 times	Track letters on a page backwards for 3 minutes	Track words on a page and skip over every second word. Then double back and read right to left the words you skipped over.

Tracking outside – tree lines, distance to tip of nose, trace buildings, objects, watch a moving object try and catch license plates at high speeds, track a bird, a squirrel, etc, left to right

Track the horizon from side to side going up, down and around the shapes. 10 times	From the tip of your nose to as far as you can see, track every object between you and the horizon	Search for squares and track around each square. le windows, buildings, etc	Track as much of the branches and leaves on a tree in 3 minutes	Track side to side a power line without turning your head. 10 times alternating directions
Try and read the license plates of the passing cars.	Track a bird's flight for as long as possible.	Track a fly/bee's flight for as long as possible	Outline the shape of every (colour) object you see	Track around every round object you can see.

Perception- understanding, analyzing and interpreting what we see:

Finding patterns, making assumptions with facial expressions, incomplete pictures, adding to pictures,

Discrimination – seeing the differences between objects that are similar.

Example 1. Using a set of building blocks in front of the class, have the students construct the same shape, time trials etc. Earn blocks by doing exercises or wods.

Word puzzles, word searches, picture comparisons, matching

visual memory, visual closure, ability to turn and rotate objects in our minds and picture what they would look like.

Circle the picture that is exactly the same as the picture on top. (more difficult pictures): Circle the picture that is exactly the same as the picture on top	Using something in the classroom that everyone has, construct an image have the class make the same thing. Building blocks	Show the students a picture for 5 seconds then take it away. Try and recall as much of the image as possible.	Word search of the day for time	Incomple te pictures and have the students fill in the rest for time, or as many
Circle the picture that is different. (more difficult pictures): Circle the picture that is different	Take the object and identify what it's mirror image would be. What an opened cube looks like etc	Using the facial expression page, identify what emotion is being portrayed. For time	Match the letters of each font with its block letter for time.	Using these shapes decide what the picture is (puzzle) for time.

Focusing – starring to make things clearer and avoid distractions around the object.

Figure ground – picking out details without getting confused by the background or surrounding images.

Focus while you are moving. Catching things with someone passing in front of you. Deflection drill.

Someone running in front of you while trying to catch a ball.

Which one was the 6th pencil to be dropped in the pile for time	Catching a ground ball between the legs of the classmates	Where's waldo, eye spy for time	Reading while things are being moved around the object for 1 minute	Eye crossing focus drills

Single Eye – performing these tasks with just one eye, then the other.

Read for 3 minutes with your left eye, right eye	Track as far side to side as possible 10 times with each eye.	Track up and down with your left eye only	Perform a word search with one eye.	Complet e a math assignm ent with one eye.

Appendix D: Daily Enrichment Challenges Incorporating Cognitive Skills and Exercise

"Shuzzle"

Using a shuttle run format, set up a chair at 10m, 20m, or 30m (distances may vary according to the age of the students participating.)

Break up a puzzle, or two puzzles (if two students are participating at a time.)

Place 1/3 of the puzzle pieces on each chair.

On 3-2-1 Go!, students race to the first chair and collect their first puzzle piece. They return it to the start area, and then race to the second chair and collect the second. They continue, building the puzzle as they go, and always running to the chairs in order (first, second, third; first, second, third) until the puzzle is built.

Students may choose to build the puzzle as they go (one piece at a time,) or save the pieces until the end and compile the puzzle then.

Students may race the clock or each other; the winner (or end time) is determined when the puzzle is complete.

Variations:

- length of shuttle

⅄ puzzle pieces involved

⅄ movement (hop to the first chair, backpedal to the second, do twist jumps to the third, etc.)

⅄ movement while doing the puzzle (squats, paused squats, plank position, 3 burpees per round, etc.)

Record time and number of puzzles pieces for each student.

"Math Bear"

Set a deck of cards at one end of the classroom; push the tables and chairs toward the centre to create a clear 'lap' of 3-4 feet around the perimeter.

Bear crawl one full lap. Draw 2 cards; multiply the two numbers together (J = 11, Q = 12, K = 13, A=1.) Bear crawl two full laps. Draw 2 cards; multiply the two numbers together. Bear crawl three full laps; multiply the two numbers together. Bear crawl two full laps; multiply the two new cards together. Continue in a bear crawl lap pattern of : 1-2-3-2-1-2-3-2-1-2-3...etc. until all the cards are gone.

Rules: if the student draws two face cards and successfully multiplies them together, they may immediately draw another two cards without doing any laps of bear crawl.

If the student answers the multiplication question incorrectly, they must wait 10 full seconds before attempting another answer (maximum three attempts per round before the teacher gives them the correct answer.)

Winner: the student to accumulate the most cards in 10 minutes.

"The Ol' Grocery-Getter"

As a simple exercise for working memory, write 12 common grocery items (eggs, cheese, milk...) on a hidden piece of paper.

Set up a 4-station circuit. For example, squats; jumping jacks; pushups; and tuck jumps.

On the first round, a student is given the name of the first grocery item on the list; she then proceeds through each of the exercise stations, doing 1 rep of each, and repeats the grocery item to the teacher at the end of the circuit.

On the second round, a second grocery item is added, along with a second repetition of each exercise. At the end of the round (2 reps at each station,) the student repeats both grocery items to the teacher.

On the third round, a third grocery item is added, and the student performs 3 reps of each exercise at each station. The game continues until the student can't recall, in order, all the grocery items assigned.

To increase difficulty, add a time cap to achieve all 12 items, or add more items to the list.

A key component of being a good public presenter is the ability to make connections between points "off the cuff." Repeating a memorized message; relying on cue cards; reading a PowerPoint presentation...these are the hallmarks of the speaker who isn't confident in his message.

Every good presentation carries an element of salesmanship: at the most basic level, if the speaker isn't confident in her message, the audience will not perceive value, and lose interest quickly. Fear of social isolation wreaks havoc among those speakers who must present only rarely; it is our belief that frequent exposure to and practice with public speaking is critical for student development.

To overcome the differing levels of anxiety in a typical classroom, we deliver our Oral challenges with twists to level the playing field. In this, Descriptive Intervals, we leave gaps at regular intervals to allow the student to make connections between one point and another mentally, and then deliver on them verbally.

From a large selection of nouns, the teacher/coach draws one at random. The student must speak about that noun, using descriptions or stories, for 30 seconds straight; at the 30-second mark, they must be silent for 10 seconds before resuming, whether at the end of a thought or in mid-sentence. The teacher determines the number of intervals, or the challenge could be to fill a given number.

For example: speak for :30, pause for :10 on "Snow."

The student speaks for 30 seconds about snow: it's white, it's cold, it's fluffy. The teacher says, "Pause!" precisely on the 30-second mark, and the student must fall silent immediately and think about their next point. After 10 seconds, the teacher says, "Go!" and the student resumes talking. They need not pick up where they left off, but can start anywhere.

To change levels of difficulty:

1) change the number of intervals from 2 or 3 up to 10

2) allow or disallow repetition of facts/data/stories

3) Set a minimum number of facts to be achieved per round (ie the student must deliver 2 unique facts in each 30-second interval)

4) allow or disallow audience help (collaboration)

5) add bonuses like, "Phone a friend"

6) change topics every few rounds

7) lengthen or shorten the interval length.

The point of the exercise is to provide breaks for the student to regroup, reorganize, and consider their next point. Some students won't need the breaks; some will. Keep the atmosphere light and fun.

Speech Practice: Improv

Improvisational comedy is an excellent example of confident off-the-cuff speech. If the speaker isn't comfortable with failure, or in front of an audience, their failure will be quick (though temporary.)

There are few rules in improvisational comedy. Unwritten, though, is the law that you never leave your partner with a dead-end. For that reason, each person must start their portion of the story with an agreement: "Yes, and...."

Challenge: in teams of two or three students, standing in front of a class. Teacher gives the "3,2,1..." and follows with the topic (a noun or verb.) The first student gives a sentence or short story relating to that verb; the second student must immediately follow with, "Yes, and...." and then add a sentence or two of their own. The Improv continues until the team is stymied (ie they stop for a full three seconds.) They must stick with the pattern of 1-2-1-2 or 1-2-3-1-2-3 (in the case of larger 'teams,' the team can't be carried by one or two members, but must equally rotate among all participants.) The goal is to continue as long as possible.

Example:

Teacher: "3, 2, 1....running."

Student #1: "I love running. I joined the athletics club last year so that I could run more."

Student #2: "Yes, and you did a race last year, I think...right?"

Student #1: "Yes, and I finished second in my age category. Do you like running?"

Student #2: "Yes, and...." etc.

Example: 3-person team

Teacher: "3,2,1...house."

Student #1: "I live in a white house, over by the ballpark."

Student #2: "Yes, and I have been to your house. It's really big, and I like the porch."

Student #3: "Yes, and I think your little dog is really funny."

Student #1: "Yes, and he loves it when people come over to play with him."

Student #2: "Yes, and he has so many toys to play with. The squeaky bone is his favourite, I think." Etc.

Note: it's not necessary for the 'discussion' to stay on the original topic; that's the beauty of Improv!

To increase or decrease the challenge:

Set sentence minimums. For example, you must say three sentences before passing the story on.

Question: each student must end their speaking portion with a question.

Movement: each student must perform squats or lunges while speaking.

Speech Practice: Auctioneer

A fun way to practice enunciation, volume, and projection is by varying the pitch, diction, or speed of speaking. Kids love to try talking faster, but invariably wind up slurring all the words together out of haste.

In teams of two, one student assumes the role of auctioneer, and one of buyer. Much like the card-memorization event at the World Memory Championships, the player must work through a list of items as quickly as possible...and be checked at the end. However, in this game, memory is not an issue.

The auctioneer is given a list of nouns to 'sell.' They must read them (or recite them) as quickly as possible to the 'buyer.' As soon as they've finished, the buyer must repeat the nouns back in the correct order.

In the first round, the auctioneer has only one item. In the second round, she has two items; in the third, three; etc. The game continues until the buyer can no longer recall all of the items in the correct order; the auctioneer tries again with the same items.

After they've completed all of the items on the list, the players switch positions and start with one item again. The team score is the total amount of time required for the two players to finish the lists given to them by the teacher.

Example: the shopping list of Garlic, Cream Cheese, Fish, Socks, and Orange Juice.

Auctioneer: "Garlic."

Buyer: "Garlic."

Auctioneer: "Garlic, cream cheese."

Buyer: "Garlic, cream cheese."

Auctioneer: "Garlic, cream cheese, fish."

Buyer: "Garlic, cream cheese, ...uh...."

Auctioneer: "Garlic, cream cheese, fish."

Buyer: "Garlic, cream cheese, fish."

Auctioneer: "Garlic, cream cheese, fish, socks."

etc. When they've reached the end of the grocery list successfully (the buyer has repeated the items back in the correct order,) the team reverses roles and begins with a new list.

New Auctioneer: "Grapes."

New Buyer: "Grapes." Etc.

To increase or decrease the difficulty:

Increase or decrease the number of items on the list

Allow or disallow players to write down the words (requires more time, but carries far less risk of mistakes)

Allow younger children to have multiple 'buyers' to help recall the items

Speech Practice: Tall Tales

Children are often discouraged from verbal creativism because many parents fear that they'll be encouraging the child to develop their lying skills. In reality, the ability to think quickly, expand on a topic, support a case, or create a story is vital for communication.

Many cultures rely on storytelling for the long-term transcription of their history. In surveys done among tribal cultures who still rely heavily on storytelling, it's interesting to note that they all share a few things in common:

- stories are not memorized by rote, but by major points and 'morals'

- though the stories may change slightly from teller to teller, the main points stay rigidly the same, and usuallly carry great detail, such as exact dates

- most storytellers will say that they all tell the story precisely the same, word for word, as the others telling the same story. This isn't true, but their idea of "precisely" is different than the researcher's in most cases.

This is a very simple challenge: given a fantastic topic (ie mermaids, knights, kings) the student has one minute to prepare a 'tall tale.' They must then deliver the story for as long as possible in front of the class.

The short preparation time is to place students on an equal footing and alleviate anxiety.

The best thing about this challenge is the multitude of possible reasons to 'reward' students. Teachers can give out praise or awards for the longest tale; the most believable; the funniest; the biggest stretch of the imagination, the most exciting....

Oral presentations in schools are stressful for students for the same reason they're stressful for adults: exposure to risk and social isolation. Fear or ego damage from "screwing up." Fear of going blank. Fear of laughing or crying...

The idea that a shorter speaking duration decreases anxiety in students is flawed, because the same anxieties persist before the initiation of the speech, whether thirty seconds or five minutes. Frequent exposure, though, in a non-judgmental environment where everyone has an equal playing field, will put students into the Growth Mindset required for long-term oral success.

Daily challenge: "Reaping The Benefit"

In teams of two, students earn pennies by completing the following:

1 burpee OR three squats OR five situps

Teams collect as many pennies as possible in 5:00. Only one partner may move at a time, though students may mix the exercises any way they like.

1 minute rest

Students must accumulate as many box jumps as possible, alternating partners, in 1:00. However, for every penny earned, they may 'buy' 5 seconds to be added to the clock.

The winning team is the one who scores most box jumps.

Daily Challenge: Math Shuttle - "Daniel"

Start with a stack of 6 plates (45-35-25-10-5-2.5lbs for adults, or smaller for kids,) and three circles set 10' apart.

You must move the entire stack, in order, into another circle. Rules:

- ⚖ You may only move one plate at a time;

- ⚖ You may not set a heavier plate on top of a lighter plate.

Example:

Move the 2.5lbs plate to the first circle, and then retrieve the 5lbs plate. Move it to the second empty circle. Return to the 2.5lbs plate, and place it atop the 5lbs plate....have fun!

"Rabbit, Rabbit"

When a body is placed under duress, the brain activity required for memory is depressed. Higher anxiety levels dictate a lower capacity for memory. For instance, consider that most people have little recollection of the last few seconds before a car crash, when they see it coming; most victims of crime by an unknown perpetrator struggle to correctly describe their oppressor.

Immediately after the stress is removed, though, their capacity for memory vastly increases. Their brain, perceiving a high degree of relevance ("I certainly don't want to go through THAT again!") recalls the event in great detail.

In the classroom, students are sometimes placed in circumstances where their anxiety levels are very high. Hormonally, their brains are more concerned with more basic instincts (fight/flight/social isolation) than with higher cognitive processes, like data recall and processing. When a final exam is worth 40% of their final grade, a student can face a lot of 'test anxiety,' which stacks the chemical deck against him.

Conversely, if a student faces absolutely NO stress, their brains are free to become distracted by irrelevant stimuli. Placed into a seated position (or another position of absolute rest, where the body isn't challenged at all,) their brains will seek stimulation from other sources.

The challenge: memorization of a simple rhyme or childrens' poem. In this case, "Mr. Brown The Circus Clown:"

Mr. Brown, the circus clown

puts his clothes on upside down.

He wears his hat upon his toes

and socks and shoes upon his nose.

He ties his ties around his thighs

and wraps his belt around his eyes.

He hangs his earrings from his hips

and stockings from his fingertips.

He puts his glasses on his feet

and shirt and coat around his seat.

And when he's dressed, at last he stands

and walks around upon his hands.

--Kenn Nesbitt

The student must maintain a challenging physical pose (a paused squat; hanging from a bar with their knees up; in 'guard' position on a heavy bag; in a 'plank' position on the floor) and attempt to memorize as much of a poem as possible. As soon as they can no longer maintain the physical challenge, they must recite the poem as far as possible with complete accuracy.

When we tested 'Rabbit, Rabbit' on combative MMA fighters, they swung from a heavy bag in 'Guard' position (legs and arms wrapped around the bag, ankles locked) and tried to memorize a simple poem called, "Mr. Brown The Circus Clown." Though they could hold on for a long time, they were clearly struggling to stay on the bag. On average, the MMA fighters recalled about two lines of the poem.

We tried the same challenge on a young athlete in three different ways. In the first, Karl recalled the first verse of the poem easily while in a basic squat position. The squat is an exercise Karl's intrinsically learned but that still provides adequate challenge for the body; his brain is engaged in the poem while his body does the work. He's focused by the exercise, which requires enough cognitive processing room to block out distractions, but not enough to require all of his attention.

In the second, Karl attempts to memorize the second verse of the poem while hanging in Guard position - a very tough physical challenge. This type of physical duress is similar to the anxiety levels created by tests in high-stress situations. He can't recall the first two lines.

In the third, Karl attempts to memorize another verse of the poem, in a seated position. Karl is completely relaxed, requiring no attention to body position. At first, it appears that he's recalled far more of the poem...until his coach later reveals that he was incorrect with many of the words.

What do you think is best for learning and memory - some physical engagement; a lot of physical engagement; or none at all?

To make the challenge harder: use more difficult physical holds that require more attention. Easier: decrease the difficulty of the poem or the physical portion.

Example for younger students: 'Rabbit, Rabbit'

Rabbit, Rabbit, 1,2,3

Won't you come and play with me?

Camel, camel, 4,5,6

Why do you have a hump like this?

Monkey, monkey, 7,8,9

How do you swing on that vine?

When the elephant reaches 10

Then I start to count again.

Thanks, Karl, for being the model...you did best of anyone!

The ability to recall facts and data is rarely challenged in an uncomplicated way. While most research revolves around students' or subjects' ability to recall strings of numbers over time, it's rare that their recall is measured outside the research vacuum.

In real life, though, it's now normal for a worker to memorize facts and data and be required to use them while being distracted.

In Working Memory Word Search, a coach keeps a list of words at one end of the gym (or classroom, or basement, or park...) and a word search puzzle containing the words at the other end of the gym, out of sight of the participants. Between the list and the puzzle are a variety of exercises that require conscious effort to complete (these may vary by the user, depending on skill level.)

Example: the coach dictates three words: Athlete - Practice - Memory.

Students perform 20 "man on fire" burpees, 20 box jumps, and 20 wall ball, and then race to the word search puzzle and attempt to find the words Athlete, Practice and Memory first. They circle the words, and then race back to the coach for the next three words.

The students are required to remember the words on their own. If they can't recall a word, they must return to the coach to hear the words again...and complete the exercises again before attempting to find the words in the puzzle.

Scaling options: add more words to the list to be memorized at one time;

use words that are more relevant (or less relevant) to the student;

use exercises that require more conscious attention (or less)

use more or fewer total words in the puzzle.

Sample puzzle:

```
C U P N H I R V J I N N
I P I E J L L L N N I A
H A C H U T U R L T J N
P T G L N I H V I E H A
O U N D L L C E P R G R
R N N P R H A P I V A L
T E H E A D A C H E P I
O R C N I A E H N N U P
R U E A J I U J I T S U
U P U L L U P E C I H A
E G N E L L A H C O U L
N L U T N H A J I N P E
```

CHALLENGE   INTERVENTION   NEUROTROPHIC
RECALL   JIUJITSU   PULLUP
PUSHUP   PAIN   HEADACHE

Memory-Enhancing Tools

A refresher:

Short-term memory acts as a kind of "*scratch-pad*" for temporary recall of the information which is being processed at any point in time, and has been referred to as "the brain's Post-it note". It can be thought of as the ability to remember and process information at the same time. It holds a small amount of information (typically around 7 items or even less) in mind in an active, readily-available state for a short period of time (typically from 10 to 15 seconds, or sometimes up to a minute).

The term *working memory* is often used interchangeably with short-term memory, although technically working memory refers more to the whole theoretical framework of structures and processes used for the temporary storage and manipulation of information, of which short-term memory is just one component.

Mnemonic devices are tricks used to translate data into pictures or other sensory data to help the learner recall them. They can be simple, as you'll see, or extremely complex – to the point where humans have become capable of recalling over 84,000 digits of Pi. Listed below are the most common, but there ARE more (like 'pegging,' which is a complicated way of remembering lists of up to 10 items.) These are most efficient, depending on the number of items to be recalled:

The Link and Story Methods

As reiterated several times through this text, the greatest way to form a long-lasting memory is through the use of context: adding colours, sensations, smells.....building a story around the data.

The simplest style of creating 'sticky' memories is the 'story' style. In this method, the learner simply creates a story linking the items in a list together.

Example: A grocery list includes oranges, butter, bread and milk.

Story method: Sally was an orange-picker. One day, she was eating her lunch of bread and butter in a tree, and she slipped! She fell onto a cow, and milk squirted right out!

Link method: items in the list are formed into images which interact with each other, but without a 'storyline.'

Visualize spilling milk on the floor, and squishing an orange into it; the milk curdles into butter, and the whole mess is sopped up with bread.

Memory Palaces

I know Joshua Foer's grocery list by heart.

The author of *Moonwalking With Einstein* uses it as an example of memorization using a mnemonic device in his new book. *Moonwalking With Einstein* is the story of Foer's quest to compete in the World Memory Championships with only one year of training.

Foer uses a mnemonic device - his house - to help him remember simple things. Essentially, he places each thing on his list into a graphic scene with which he has an emotional connection. This new context helps him retain the information with 100% accuracy; since our brains are contextual, they don't behave in a linear way. This means that simply READING information is the poorest way of ensuring that it's permanently stored, but having a STORY or PICTURE of the information locks it into your brain permanently.

Example: Foer's grocery list (which I can still name by heart, five days after hearing it only once) : a clove of garlic, a tub of cottage cheese, smoked salmon, six bottles of wine, and new tube socks. How can I possibly remember his list, when I can't remember what I packed for lunch today? I can picture his Memory Palace.

Memory Palaces were used long before the written word. It was essential to remember facts, dates, names, and places, because there was no way to transcribe them. And while the stories DID change as they were passed from mouth to ear to mouth, the essential bits of data - the core knowledge - was usually maintained.

Think of your Memory Palace as a vault with many rooms. Every room is different (like a house,) and you'll place one item on your list in each. We'll use YOUR house in this example, to keep things easy,but don't worry: you can have thousands of Memory Palaces without ever running out of space.

And so, here we go:

At the foot of your driveway, I'd like you to imagine a giant, stinky clove of garlic. Too big to drive your car around. Your neighbour is leaning on the fence, complaining about the smell. It's sizzling on the hot sidewalk (use as many sensory cues as possible, and include emotions like the cranky neighbour.)Make your way around the garlic, and up to your doorstep. On your welcome mat is a giant tub of watery cottage cheese. There's a beautiful woman taking a bath in it.

Imagine her face. Since both erotic AND disgusting images imprint themselves into your memory more efficiently, it doesn't matter what your reaction is to this image, as long as it's a strong one. Smell the cheese on her!

Now, step in your front door, and smell something smoking: like salmon on an outdoor grill. Follow your nose into a room on the left (in Foer's house, this room contained a piano, and the salmon was grilling on the piano wires beneath the top.) Lift the top. Feel the smoke on your face. Smell the delicious salmon; hear it sizzle. Yum.

Walk into the next room: there, on the couch, is something you never thought you'd see: wine bottles. They're having a heated argument. "I'm better," says the Claret, " because I come from better soil!" Imagine them having different accents, especially French. One of the other wines (be specific - maybe a Sauvignon?) loudly disagrees: "The air and sunlight make all the difference! That's why I'M better!" One falls off and breaks, spilling red wine all over your carpet....

In the last room, the light seems a bit dim. That's when you see them: athletic socks draped over a lamp. They're warm from the bulb, and soft. Feel them against your cheek. What colour are they? How soft are they?

Now walk back out of your house. Anytime you need Joshua Foer's grocery list, you've got it. Your only task: find more Memory Palaces! Walk through museums, friends' houses, grocery stores...but use big, obvious, stinky cues!

Note: this method is also used as the "Journey" method, in which a learner attaches items in her list to obvious places along her trip to work, or through a shopping mall.

Long-String Memory: The PAO Method

Get out your deck of cards! The PAO method is how competitive mental athletes remember long strings of numbers (or, in this case, objects like cards.) While cards are used for training and competition, you can use the technique to remember virtually any longer series of objects.

Each card is assigned a Person, Action, and Object. The HARD part is remembering the pictures you mentally paint for each card, but this step is much easier if you can choose images with personal relevance.

For example, in '*Moonwalking With Einstein*,' Joshua Foer chose Michael Jackson(person) singing (action) into a microphone (object) for the King of Hearts. I'm going to choose Lady Gaga (person) wearing (action) a yellow hat (object) as the Queen of Clubs, because I think a lot of clubs probably play her music. And I'm going to choose an African Child-Miner (person) swinging(action) a pick (object) for the Ace of Diamonds. The last image is particularly poignant and 'sticky' because I tried to avoid buying 'blood diamonds' when I purchased my wife's engagement ring.

Now, to remember the order of three cards, you take the Person from the first; the Action from the second; and the Object from the third to create a NEW mnemonic picture. In this case: Queen of Clubs, King of Hearts, and Ace of Diamonds becomes a picture of Lady Gaga singing into a miner's pick. If the cards were in a different order, we'd get an African Child-miner wearing a microphone. Can you guess the order of the last example?

A person (Michael Jordan)
An action (slam dunks)
An object (basketball) This could mean something to

somebody with a PAO system.

A person (Chris Hardwick)
An action (solves)
An object (rubiks cube)

This breaks a deck of cards down into 17 single pictures, with 1 card left over.

You memorize in this order.

P->A->O->P->A->O->P->A->O

Try it with 9 cards first, then 12....

The Major System For Memorizing Numbers

Your natural limit for remembering a series of numbers is about 7 digits. That's why phone numbers are seven digits long, and that's why they're broken into two parts with a hyphen. This is generally called, "The Rule of Seven," and it's true (plus or minus two digits) for about 98% of the population.

When you're trying to remember slightly longer numbers, though - your credit card number, your SIN, someone's birthday - you'll need a mnemonic device. Earlier, you read about Memory Palaces - another mnemonic device, useful for remembering short lists or specific details.

Now: the Major Method, which was originally touted as the best way to remember LONG strings of numbers...until the context of 'long' changed. The world record for the most digits of Pi (3.1416...etc.) recited without a single error is over 83,000 digits. For very long strings, we'll need something different. But for everyday use, the Major Method is terrific:

The Major Method works by converting numbers into consonant sounds, and then into words by adding vowels. Since images can be remembered more easily than numbers, exchanging a three-digit number for an obscure picture makes it simple to store medium strings in your brain for easy access.

Copied from *Wikipedia*:

Numeral	Associated Consonants	Mnemonic
0	s, z, soft c	"z" is the first letter of zero. The other letters have a similar sound.
1	d, t	d & t have one downstroke and sound similar (some variant systems include "th")
2	n	n has two downstrokes
3	m	M has three downstrokes and looks like a "3" on its side
4	r	last letter of

		four, also 4 and R are almost mirror images of each other
5	l	L is the Roman Numeral for 50
6	j, sh, soft "ch" , dg, zh, soft "g"	a script j has a lower loop / g is almost a 6 flipped over
7	k, hard c, hard g, hard "ch", q, qu	capital K "contains" two sevens
8	f, v	script f resembles a figure-8. V sounds

		similar. (some variant systems include th)
9	b, p	p is a mirror-image 9. b sounds similar and resembles a 9 rolled around
Un as sig ne d	Vow el sou nds, w,h, y	These can be used anywhere without changing a word's number value

Each numeral maps to a set of similar sounds with similar mouth and tongue positions. The link is phonetic, that is to say, it is the consonant sounds that matter, not the spelling. Therefore a word like *action* would encode the number 762 (k-ch-n), not 712 (k-t-n); and *ghost* would be 701 (g-z-t), while, because the *gh* in *enough* is pronounced like an *f*, the word *enough* encodes the number 28 (n-f). Similarly, double letters are disregarded. The word *missile* is mapped to 305 (m-z-l), not 3005 (m-z-z-l). To encode 3005 one would use something like *mossy sail*. Often the mapping is compact. Hindquarters, for example, translates unambiguously to 2174140 (n-d-qu-r-t-r-z), which amounts to 7 digits encoded by 8 letters, and can be easily visualized.

For most people familiar with this system, it would be easier to remember 3.1415927 (the number known as pi as:

MeTeoR (314)
TaiL (15) PiNK
(927)

Short-term visual memory of imagined scenes allows large numbers of digits to be memorized with ease, though usually only for a short time.

Whilst this is unwieldy at first, with practice it can become a very effective technique. Longer-term memory may require the formulation of more object-related mnemonics with greater logical connection, perhaps forming grammatical sentences that apply to the matter rather than just strings of images.

The system can be employed with phone numbers. One would typically make up multiple words, preferably a sentence, or an ordered sequence of images featuring the owner of the number.

Remembering Names: The Repetition Method

While rote repetition is less effective at storing long-term memories, it can work when combined with other of the methods above.

When attempting to anchor a face to a name, it's common to try one of two techniques:

1. Repetition – While speaking to the person, you may try to repeat their name three or more times, and hope that it 'sticks.' This is very common among salespeople who haven't studied more advanced mnemonic devices.

2. Association – choosing an unusual feature about the new friend's face, and attempting to rhyme their name with the feature. Be forewarned: associating your nephew's girlfriend, "Molly," with the dark mole on her cheek to recall her name can have disastrous consequences around the Christmas tree.

Appendix E – Sample Exercise Progressions

CLEAN	POWER CLEAN	FRONT SQUAT	CLEAN PULL	DEADLIFT

From a squatting position, the athlete accelerates the bar to above the knee (first pull.) "scoops" his hips forward to brush the bar (the scoop) and drops below to catch the bar at his collarbone (second pull.) The athlete lands in a squat, and then rises with the bar on his collarbone, hands in "rack" position.	From a squatting position, the athlete accelerates the bar from the floor into a high-pull, elbows above the bar, feet plantarflexed. Then athlete drops into a shallow squat and "catches" the bar in rack position, elbows in front.	Holding the bar in 'rack' position (bar on collarbone, elbows in front of the bar, head high, chest big) the athlete squats with even pressure on the foot (no rolling onto toes or heels.) The athlete's knee angle goes below 90 degrees, and then the athlete returns to standing without dipping her elbows on the ascent.	From a squatting position, the athlete pulls the bar rapidly from the floor to a position just above the knee with a hook or clean grip.	From a position with the hips as far horizontally from the bar as possible, and shins touching the bar, the athlete pushes his hips forward until standing, holding the bar just below the waist. Emphasis should be on keeping the torso rigid (though not vertical until the finish) and maintaining a safe lower-back arch.
	10 in a row without losing balance or posture, using a loaded barbell.	10 in a row without losing balance or posture, using a loaded barbell.	10 in a row without losing balance or posture, using a loaded barbell.	20 without losing posture, using a loaded barbell.

HANDSTAND PUSHUP	HANDSTAND HOLD	WALK UP WALL	KNEES ELEVATED	STINKBUG

From full lockout (toes on wall, elbows fully extended) athlete lowers themself by bending the elbows until the crown of their head touches the floor, and then presses back to full extension without driving force from the legs.	Athlete achieves a handstand (with wall support) with four points of contact: feet and hands. Athlete holds position at full lockout for as long as possible.	With hands braced on floor facing away from wall, athlete plants one toe on the wall and walks backward, up the wall, until legs reach full extension. Then they walk their hands backward, closer to the wall, until a vertical position is reached (knees not touching the wall.)	With hands braced on floor, facing away from an elevated surface (box or bench,) athlete places both knees on elevated surface and presses with torso as level and presses with torso as close to vertical as possible.	Athlete places both hands on the floor, palms flat. Bending at the waist, they walk the feet toward his hands until the knees can no longer remain locked out. Pivoting on the ball of his foot, they lower their body with the arms ONLY until the top of the head touches the floor, and presses back up to full elbow extension without flexing the knees.
1:00 three rep up	Up and hold for 30	10 three rep	10 straight.	

TOES TO BAR	KNEES TO ELBOWS	KIPPING	HANGING KNEE RAISE	REVERSE CRUNCH

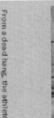

TOES TO BAR

From a dead hang, athlete generates a kip and brings their toes to touch the bar between their hands with knees straight (bent at the waist.)

KNEES TO ELBOWS

Start from full hang; athlete creates a 'C' position from head to heel; the athlete lifts the knees to touch the elbows as she drops her head back behind her shoulders and looks up. The athlete keeps her torso under the bar as she returns to the 'C' position. Forward momentum of the knee does not create swing of the torso; knees strikes elbows while athlete is looking up.

KIPPING

From a dead hang, the athlete swings their legs forward while pushing their hips back to counter the swing of their torso. Then the procedure is reversed: the legs swing back while the athlete arches their torso forward, creating a 'C' shape.

HANGING KNEE RAISE

From a dead hang, the athlete raises their knees until their knees and hips are at 90 degrees (or smaller) and then lowers back to the vertical start position.

REVERSE CRUNCH

Balanced on their tailbone, the athlete places their hands on the ground behind them and lengthens their legs in front of them (heels off the floor). Then they draw their knees up to their chest and repeat.

10 metre row. 20 metre row. 10 metre row.

THRUSTER	WALL BALL	FRONT SQUAT	PUSH PRESS	SQUAT

From a 'rack' position (bar on collarbone, elbows in front of the bar) the athlete will descend into a low front squat, and then rapidly ascend and transfer smoothly into a push press. The bar returns to start at the chest.

Holding a ball beneath the chin, the athlete descends into a front squat position (elbows high) and then ascends rapidly, pushing the ball overhead to reach a set height (usually 10') Catching the ball, the athlete rapidly descends back into a front squat.

Holding the bar in 'rack' position (bar on collarbone, elbows in front of the bar, head high, chest big) the athlete squats with even pressure on the foot (no rolling onto toes or heels.) The athlete's knee angle goes below 90 degrees, and then the athlete returns to standing without dipping her elbows on the ascent.

Using a slight dip in the knees to assist with overhead 'drive,' the athlete presses the bar from chest to overhead, finishing with the bar over his centre of gravity (upper arms behind the ears.)

With even pressure on the foot, the athlete sits back into a position of hips behind the heels. Hands may be in front for counterbalance. Pressure should be on the heel instead of the forefoot. Athlete rises smoothly, activating their hips first, with a rigid torso and slight forward lean.

20 m at low without a miss.

10 m at low with a golbs bar.

10 m at low with golbs bar.

20 nonstop.

PUSHUP

Starting from a position in the air with arms extended, athlete lowers until chest and thighs brush the ground (elbow angle smaller than 90 degrees) and presses back to full extension.

ROCKING PUSHUP

Starting from the floor, an athlete pushes up to the knees, quickly lifting the hips to pull the knees off the ground. Then the athlete lowers the knees back to the ground first, and lowers the chest to the ground. The toes never leave the ground.

10 in a row.

KNEE PUSHUP - DEEP

With feet in the air, athlete touches the chest to the ground with elbows reaching a smaller angle than 90 degrees. Knees remain on the ground.

10 in a row.

NEE PUSHUP - SHALLOW

With feet in the air, athlete lowers themself toward the ground. Elbow angle approaches 90 degrees; torso stays in a straight horizontal line with the hips.

10 in a row.

WALL PUSHUPS

Balancing on the balls of their feet, athlete maintains a rigid vertical posture (no flexion of knees, hips) and bends their elbows (shoulder height) such that his torso approaches the wall. Then they press back to vertical again.

30 straight, without stop

RING DIP	RING SUPPORT	RING DIP - HEELS UP	RING DIP - HEELS	DIP - KNEES LOCKED	DIP - KNEES BENT

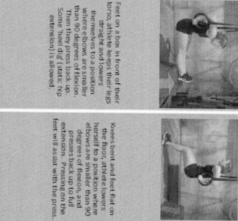

RING DIP

Athlete starts from fully extended elbows, feet off the ground, and lowers herself until her thumbs are at armpit level (elbows smaller than 90-degree angle). She presses up to return to full extension (suspended).

RING SUPPORT

From the ground, with hands in rings and elbows smaller than 90 degrees, the athlete presses herself to full extension, suspended off the ground, and holds for 3 seconds.

RING DIP - HEELS UP

Feet on a box in front of their torso, athlete keeps their legs straight and lowers themselves to a position where elbows are smaller than 90 degrees of flexion. Then they press back up. Some "heel dig" (static hip extension) is allowed.

RING DIP - HEELS

Knees bent and feet flat on the floor, athlete lowers herself to a position where elbows are smaller than 90 degrees of flexion, and presses back up to full extension. Pressing on the feet will assist with the press.

DIP - KNEES LOCKED

With hands on a stable surface behind them, fingers pointed forward, the athlete lowers herself using her arms. Flexion comes from the elbow; torso stays within 1 inch of the stable object, instead of travelling far out from the object. Maximal elbow flexion is the goal. Legs remain straight with heels on the ground or an elevated surface in front of the athlete.

DIP - KNEES BENT

In a chair position, the athlete places her hands on a stable surface with fingers pointed forward. She lowers herself using primarily arm strength until elbow angle is smaller than 90 degrees. Torso stays close to the dip station.

| 10 in a row. | 10 in a row. | 20 in a row. | 15 uninterrupted | 15 uninterrupted |

PULLUP	KIPPING PULLUP	KNEES TO ELBOWS	NEGATIVE PULLUP	BODY ROW - STRAIGHT	BODY ROW - BENT

Double-overhand grip; chin clears bar; start at full hang; no kip	Start from full hang; athlete creates a 'c' position from head to heel; the athlete lifts her knees to touch the elbows as she drops her head back behind her shoulders and looks up. The athlete keeps her torso under the bar as she returns to the 'c' position. Forward momentum of knee does not create swing of torso; knees strike elbows while athlete is looking up.	Start from full hang; athlete creates a 'c' position from head to heel; the athlete lifts her knees to touch the elbows as she drops her head back behind her shoulders and looks up. The athlete keeps her torso under the bar as she returns to the 'c' position. Forward momentum of knee does not create swing of torso; knees strike elbows while athlete is looking up.	Starting from a position of full elbow flexion, athlete descends as slowly as possible to full hang, then returns to the start position with assistance	Starting from a prone position on the ground, the athlete places her hands on the rings with arms at full extension. At the apex of the movement, the athlete's ribs are at her wrists, and only her heels are touching the floor (legs straight.)	Starting from a prone position on the ground, the athlete places her hands on the rings with arms at full extension. At the apex of the movement, the athlete's ribs are at her wrists, and only her heels are touching the floor (legs bent, hip drive allowed.)
3 linked	10 without breaking the kip.	5 in a row lasting longer than 5s each	20 straight - chin past wrists - without stop.	10 full - chin past wrists - nonstop.	

OVERHEAD SQUAT	FRONT SQUAT	FRANKENSTEIN SQUAT	WALL BALL	RACK POSITION	SQUAT
With the bar over the hips (behind the head,) the athlete descends to a below-parallel position and rises. Weight must be kept on the heels to prevent the bar from drifting forward.	Holding the bar in 'rack' position (bar on collarbone, elbows in front of the bar, head high, chest big) the athlete squats with even pressure on the foot (no rolling onto toes or heels.) The athlete's knee angle goes below 90 degrees, and then the athlete returns to standing without dipping her elbows on the ascent.	With the bar in rack position, resting on the collarbone, the athlete extends their arms in front of the body and squats, balancing the bar on their shoulders.	Holding a ball beneath the chin, the athlete descends into a front squat position (elbows high) and then ascends rapidly, pushing the ball overhead to reach a set height (usually 10'.) Catching the ball, the athlete rapidly descends back into a front squat.	With a bar resting on their collarbone, the athlete raises their elbows until they 'point' forward. Wrists should be extended; bar rests in fingertips.	With even pressure on the foot, the athlete sits back into a position of hips behind the heels. Hands may be in front for counterbalance. Pressure should be on the heel instead of the forefoot. Athlete rises smoothly, activating their hips first, with a rigid torso and slight forward lean.
20 with a weighted barbell	10 without pause.	20 nonstop.		Enter and exit 'rack position' on demand. Elbows must be in front of the bar with bar resting on collarbone.	20 nonstop.

MUSCLE-UP	RING DIP	PULLTHROUGHS	KIPPING PULLUP	RING SUPPORT

From a full hang, athlete pulls themselves up to the rings with a kip, quickly passes their torso forward through the rings, and presses up to a fully-locked-out elbow position and remains suspended for a full second.	Athlete starts from fully-extended elbows, feet off the ground, and lowers herself until her thumbs are at armpit level (elbows smaller than 90-degree angle.) She presses up to return to full extension (suspended.)	With feet on the ground, balls of the feet directly under the bar suspending the rings, the athlete explosively pulls themselves onto the ball of their feet, and then presses up into a position of full elbow extension, and remains suspended for 1 full second.	Start from full hang; legs generate upward force; chin clear bar at the top of each rep; should be able to generate 3 linked	From the ground, with hands in rings and elbows smaller than 90 degrees, the athlete presses herself to full extension, suspended off of the ground, and holds for 3 seconds.
10 in a row - suspended	10 in a row.	10 in a row.	10 in a row.	10 straight.

Appendix F - References

1. Brown, J., Cooper-Kuhn, C. M., Kempermann, G., van Praag, H., Winkler, J., Gage, F. H., & Kuhn, H. G. (2003). Enriched environment and physical activity stimulate hippocampal but not olfactory bulb neurogenesis. *European Journal of Neuroscience*, 17, 2042–2046.

2. Kempermann, G., Kuhn, H.G., Gage, F.H. (1997). More hippocampal neurons in adult mice living in an enriched environment. *Nature*, 3;386(6624):493-5.

3. van Praag, H. (2008) Neurogenesis and exercise: past and future directions. *Neuromolecular Med.*, 10, 128–140.

4. Kee, N., Teixeira, C.M., Wang, A.H. & Frankland, P.W. (2007) Preferential incorporation of adult-generated granule cells into spatial memory networks in the dentate gyrus. *Nat. Neurosci.*, 10, 355–362.

5. Imayoshi, I. et al. (2008) Roles of continuous neurogenesis in the structural and functional integrity of the adult forebrain. *Nat. Neurosci.*, 11, 1153–1161.

6. Molteni, R. et al. (2002) Differential effects of acute and chronic exercise on plasticity-related genes in the rat hippocampus revealed by microarray. *Eur. J. Neurosci.* 16, 1107–1116.

7. Liu, Y.F. et al. (2008) Upregulation of hippocampal TrkB and synaptotagmin is involved in treadmill exercise-enhanced aversive memory in mice. *Neurobiol. Learn. Mem.*, 90, 81–89 .

8. O'Callaghan, R.M. et al. (2007) The effects of forced exercise on hippocampal plasticity in the rat: A comparison of LTP, spatial- and non-spatial learning. *Behav. Brain Res.*, 176, 362–366.

9. Farmer, J., Zhao, X., van Praag, H., Wodtke, K., Gage,

F.H. & Christie, B.R. (2004). Effects of voluntary exercise on synaptic plasticity and gene expression in the dentate gyrus of adult male Sprague-Dawley rats in vivo. *Neuroscience*, 124(1): 71-79.

10. Eisch, A. J., Barrot, M., Schad, C. A., Self D.W., & Nestler, E. J. (2000). Opiates inhibit neurogenesis in the adult rat hippocam- pus. *Proceedings of the National Academy of Sciences of the United States of America*, 97, 7579–7584.

11. Harburg, G. C., Hall, F. S., Harrist, A. V., Sora, I., Uhl, G. R., & Eisch, A. J. (2007). Knockout of the mu opioid receptor enhances the survival of adult-generated hippocampal granule cell neurons. *Neuroscience*, 144, 77–87.

12. van Praag, H., Christie, B.R., Sejnowski, T.J. & Gage, F.H. (1999). Running enhances neurogenesis, learning, and long-term potentiation in mice. *Proceedings of the National Academy of Sciences of the United States of America*, Nov 9;96(23):13427-31.

13. Bland, B.H. & Oddie, S.D. (2001). Theta band oscillation and synchrony in the hippocampal formation and associated structures: the case for its role in sensorimotor integration. *Behav Brain Res*, 127:119–136.

14. Orr, G., Rao, G., Houston, F.P., McNaughton, B.L. & Barnes, C.A. (2001). Hippocampal synaptic plasticity is modulated by theta rhythm in the fascia dentata of adult and aged freely behaving rats. *Hippocampus*, 11:647–654.

15. van Praag, H. (2009). Exercise and the brain: something to chew on. *Trends Neurosci.*, May;32(5):283-90.

16. Cotman, C.W. et al. (2007). Exercise builds brain health: key roles of growth factor cascades and inflammation. *Trends Neurosci.*, 30, 464– 472.

17. Sweatt, J.D. (2001). The neuronal MAP kinase cascade: a biochemical signal integration system subserving synaptic plasticity and memory. *J. Neurochem.*, UT, 1±10.

18. Soderling, T.R. (2000). CaM-kinases: modulators of synaptic plasticity. *Curr. Opin. Neurobiol.*, IH, 375±380.

19. Ge, S. et al. (2007). A critical period for enhanced synaptic plasticity in newly generated neurons of the adult brain. *Neuron*, 54, 559–566.

20. Russo-Neustadt, A., Beard, R.C., Huang, Y.M. & Cotman, C.W. (2001). Physical activity and antidepressant treatment potentiate the expression of specific brain-derived neurotrophic factor transcripts in the rat hippocampus. *J. Neuroscience*, 101:305–312.

21. Gobeske, K.T., Das, S., Bonaguidi, M.A., Weiss, C., Radulovic, J., Disterhoft, J.F., Kessler, J.A. (2009). BMP signaling mediates effects of exercise on hippocampal neurogenesis and cognition in mice. *PLoS One*, Oct 20;4(10):e7506.

22. van Praag, H., Kempermann, G. & Gage, F.H. (1999). Running increases cell proliferation and neurogenesis in the adult mouse dentate gyrus. *Nature Neuroscience*, 2(3): 266-70.

23. Kitamura, T. et al. (2003). Enhancement of neurogenesis by running wheel exercises is suppressed in mice lacking NMDA receptor e1 subunit. *Neurosci. Res.*, 47, 55–63.

24. Iso, H., Simoda, S. & Matsuyama, T. (2007). Environmental change during postnatal development alters behaviour, cognitions and neurogenesis of mice. ***Behav Brain Res.,*** Apr 16;179(1):90-8.

Other Research Supporting the *Ignite!* Approach

Adlard, P.A., Cotman, C.W. Voluntary exercise protects against stress-induced decreases in brain-derived neurotrophic factor protein expression. Neuroscience 124 (2004) 985–992

Adlard, P.A., Perreau, V.M., & Cotman, C.W. (2005). The exercise-induced expression of BDNF within the hippocampus varies across life-span. Neurobiology of Aging, 26, 511-520.

Akito A. Mochizuki and Eiji Kirino (2008). Effects of Coordination Exercises on Brain Activation: A Functional MRI Study . International Journal of Sport and Health Science, 6: 98-104 .

Atlantis E, Chow CM, Kirby A, Singh MF. An effective exercise-based intervention for improving mental health and quality of life measures: a randomized controlled trial. Prev Med. 2004 Aug;39(2):424-3

Berchtold NC, Chinn G, Chou M, Kesslak JP, Cotman CW. Exercise primes a molecular memory for brain-derived neurotrophic factor protein induction in the rat hippocampus. Neuroscience. 2005;133(3):853-61.

Bernaards C., van den Heuvel S., Ihendriksen I.., Houtman I., Bongers P. Can strenuous leisure time physical activity prevent - psychological complaints in a working population? Occup Environ Med. 2006:63:10-16

Basile VC, Motta RW, Allison DB. Antecedent exercise as a treatment for disruptive behavior: testing hypothesized mechanisms of action. Behavioral Interventions 1995;10:119–40.

Booth FW, Chakravarthy MV, Spangenburg EE. Exercise and gene expression: physiological regulation of the human genome through physical activity. J Physiol. 2002 Sep 1;543(Pt 2):399-411. Review.

Brisswalter J, Collardeau M, Rene A. Effects of acute physical exercise characteristics on cognitive performance. Sports Med. 2002;32(9):555-66.

Brown SW, Welsh MC, Labbe EE, Vitulli WF, Kulkarni P. Aerobic exercise in the psychological treatment of adolescents. Percept Mot Skills 1982;74:555–60.

Burdette HL, Whitaker RC. Resurrecting free play in young children: looking beyond fitness and fatness to attention, affiliation, and affect. Arch Pediatr Adolesc Med. 2005 Jan;159(1):46-50.

CAREY, J.R., E. BHATT, and A. NAGPAL. Neuroplasticity promoted by task complexity. Exerc. Sport Sci. Rev., Vol. 33, No. 1, pp. 24–31, 2005.

Carrasco G., Van de Kar L., Neuroendocrine pharmacology of stress. European Journal of Pharmacology 463 (2003) 235– 272

Castelli DM, Hillman CH, Buck SM, Erwin HE. Physical fitness and academic achievement in third- and fifth-grade students. J Sport Exerc Psychol. 2007 Apr;29(2):239-52.

Coe DP, Pivarnik JM, Womack CJ, Reeves MJ, Malina RM. Effect of physical education and activity levels on academic achievement in children. Med Sci Sports Exerc. 2006 Aug;38(8):1515-9.

Colcombe SJ, Erickson KI, Scalf PE, Kim JS, Prakash R, McAuley E, Elavsky S, Marquez DX, Hu L, Kramer AF.Aerobic exercise training increases brain volume in aging humans. J Gerontol A Biol Sci Med Sci. 2006 Nov;61(11):1166-70.

Colcombe, S. & Kramer, A. F. (2003). Fitness effects on the cognitive function of older adults: A meta-analytic study. Psychological Science, 14, 125-130.

Colcombe, S., Kramer, AF, Erickson, KI, et al. (2004). Cardiovascular fitness training and changes in brain volume as measured by voxel-based morphometry. Meeting Soc Psychophysio Res., New Mexico.

Colcombe, S., Kramer, AF, et al (2003). "Aerobic fitness reduces brain tissue loss in aging humans." Journal of Gerontology (A Biol Sci Med Sci) 58: 176-180.

Colcombe, S., Kramer, AF, et al. (2005). Cardiovascular fitness training improves cortical recruitment and working memory in older adults: evidence from a longitudinal fMRI study. Proceedings of the Annual Meeting of Cognitive Neuroscience, New York.

Cotman, C. W. & Berchtold, N. C. (2002). Exercise: a behavioral intervention to enhance brain health and plasticity. Trends in Neuroscience, 25, 295-301.

Covassin T, Weiss L, Powell J, Womack C. Effects of a maximal exercise test on neurocognitive function.Br J Sports Med. 2007 Jun;41(6):370-4;

DALEY, A. J., and J. RYAN. Academic performance and participation in physical activity by secondary school adolescents. Percept. Mot. Skills 91:531–534, 2000.

DATAR, A., STURM R., MAGNABOSCO J.. Childhood overweight and academic performance: national study of kindergartners and first-graders. Obes Res. 2004;12:58

Dawbarn, D. & Allen, S.J. (2003) Neurotrophins and neurodegeneration. Neuropathology and Applied Neurobiology 29: 211-230.

DeVries, H. A., Wiswell, R. A., Bulbulian, R., & Moritani, T. (1981). Tranquilizer effect of exercise: Acute effects of moderate aerobic exercise on spinal reflex activation level. American Journal of Physical Medicine, 60, 57–66

Dik, M., Deeg, DJH, et al. (2003). "Early life physical activity and cognition at older age." J Clin Exp Neuropsychol 25: 643-53.

Dishman, R.K., Berthoud, H.R., Boot, F.W., Cotman, C.W., Edgerton, V.R., Fleshner, M.R., Gandevia, S.C., Gomez-Pinilla, F., Greenwood, B.N., Hillman, C.H., Kramer, A.F., Levin, B.E., Toran, T.H., Russo-Neustadt, A.A., Salamone, J.D., Van Hoomissen, J.D., Wade, C.E., York, D.A. & Zigmound, M.J. (2006). The neurobiology of exercise. Obesity Research, 14(3), 345-356.

Dishman, R., Renner, KJ, et al. (2000). "Treadmill exercise training augments brain NE response to familiar and novel stress." Brain Research Bulletin 52(5): 337-342.

Dwyer, T., Coonan, W. E., Leitch, D. R., Hetzel, B. S. and Baghurst, R. A. (1983). "An Investigation of the Effects of Daily Physical Activity on the Health of Primary School Students in South Australia." Int. J. Epidemiol. 12(3): 308-313.

DWYER, T., J. F. SALLIS, L. BLIZZARD, R. LAZARUS, and K. DEAN.Relationship of academic performance to physical activity and fitness in children. Pediatric Exercise Science 13:225–237, 2001.

Education, C. D. o. (2005). California Physical Fitness Test: A Study of the Relationship Between Physical Fitness and Academic Achievement in California Using 2004 Test Results. Sacramento, CA.

Etnier, J.L., Caselli, R.J., Reiman, E.M., Alexander, G.E., Sibley, B.A., Tessier, D. & McLemore, E.C. (2007). Cognitive performance in older women relative to ApoE-e4 genotype and aerobic fitness. Medicine & Science in Sports & Exercise, 39, 199-207. Tyler WJ, Alonso M, Bramham CR, Pozzo-Miller LD (2002) From acquisitionto consolidation: on the role of brain-derived neurotrophic factorsignaling in hippocampal-dependent learning. Learn Mem 9:224–237.

Etnier, J.L., Nowell, P.M., Landers, D.M. & Sibley, B.A. (2006). A meta-regression to examine the relationship between aerobic fitness and cognitive performance. Brain Research Reviews. 52, 119-130.

Fabel, K., Fabel, K. & Palmer, T.D. VEGF is necessary for exercise-induced neurogenesis. Eur. J. Neurosci. 18, 2803–2812 (2003)

Field T, Diego M, Sanders CE. Exercise is positively related to adolescents' relationships and academics. Adolescence 2001;36:105–10.

Ferris LT, Williams JS, Shen CL. The effect of acute exercise on serum brain-derived neurotrophic factor levels and cognitive function. Med Sci Sports Exerc. 2007 Apr;39(4):728-34.

Nature Neuroscience 5, 1177 - 1184 (2002)
Published online: 30 September 2002 |
doi:10.1038/nn927

BDNF release from single cells elicits local dendritic growth in nearby neurons

Hadley Wilson Horch[1,2] & Lawrence C. Katz[1]

Hannaford, Carla, PH.D. Smart Moves, Why learning is not all in your head. 1995 Fig.8.1 p147

Hariri AR, Goldberg TE, Mattay VS, Kolachana BS, Callicott JH, Egan MF, Weinberger DR. Brain-derived neurotrophic factor val66met polymorphism affects human memory-related hippocampal activity and predicts memory performance. J Neurosci. 2003 Jul 30;23(17):6690-4.

Hillman CH, Castelli DM, Buck SM. Aerobic fitness and neurocognitive function in healthy preadolescent children. Med Sci Sports Exerc. 2005 Nov;37(11):1967-74.

Hillman CH, Motl RW, Pontifex MB, Posthuma D, Stubbe JH, Boomsma DI, de Geus EJ. Physical activity and cognitive function in a cross-section of younger and older community-dwelling individuals. Health Psychol. 2006 Nov;25(6):678-87.

Jenson, Eric. Brain-Based Learning (1995) fig. 12.2 p.163

Academic and Motor Skills. The 5 stages of learning. p. 31.

Kelder SH, Perry CL, Klepp KI. Community-wide youth exercisepromotion: Long-term outcomes of the Minnesota Heart Health Program and the Class of 1989 Study. J School Health 1993;63:218–23.

Lambourne K. The relationship between working memory capacity and physical activity rates in young adults. Journal of Sports Science and Medicine (2006) 5, 149-153

Lopez-Lopez, C., LeRoith, D., Torres-Aleman, I. (2004). Insulin-like growth factor I is required for vessel remodeling in the adult brain. Proceedings of the National Academy of Science USA, 101 (26), 9833-9838.

Molteni, R, Barnard, RJ, Ying, Z, Roberts, CK, Gomez-Pinilla, F. (2002). A high-fat, refined sugar diet reduces hippocampal brain-derived neurotrophic factor, neuronal plasticity, and learning. Neuroscience, 112: 803-814.

Molteni, R, Wu, A, Vaynman, S, Ying, Z, Barnard, RJ, Gomez-Pinilla, F. (2004). Exercise reverses the harmful effects of consumption of a high-fat diet on synaptic and behavioral plasticity associated to the action of brain-derived neurotrophic factor. Neuroscience, 123(2): 429-40.

Neeper SA, Gómez-Pinilla F, Choi J, Cotman CW. Physical activity increases mRNA for brain-derived neurotrophic factor and nerve growth factor in rat brain. Brain Res. 1996 Jul 8;726(1-2):49-56.

Netz Y, Tomer R, Axelrad S, Argov E, Inbar O. The effect of a single aerobic training session on cognitive flexibility in late middle-aged adults. Int J Sports Med. 2007 Jan;28(1):82-7

Page RM, Tucker LA. Psychosocial discomfort and exercise frequency: An epidemiological study of adolescents. Adolescence 1994;29:183–91.

Palmer, T.D. (2003). VEGF is necessary for exercise-induced adult hippocampal neurogenesis. European Journal of Neuroscience, 18, 2803-2812.

Pate RR, Heath GW, Dowda M, Trost SG. Associations between physical activity and other health behaviors in a representative sample of US adolescents. Am J Public Health 1996;86:1577–81

Reynolds D, Nicolson RI.Follow-up of an exercise-based treatment for children with reading difficulties. Dyslexia. 2007 May;13(2):78-96.

Rosenzweig, M. R. & Bennett, E. L. (1996). Psychobiology of plasticity: effects of training and experience on brain and behavior. Behavioral Brain Research, 78, 57-65.

Russo-Neustadt, A., Ryan, C.B. & Cotman, C.W. (1999). Exercise, antidepressant medications, and enhanced brain derived neurotrophic factor expression. Neuropsychopharmacology, 21, 679-682.

Sanders CE, Field TM, Diego M, Kaplan M. Moderate involvement in sports is related to lower depression levels among adolescents. Adolescence 2000;35:793–7

Sallis, J., et al. (1999). "Effects of health related PE on academic achievement: Project SPARK." Research Quarterly for Exercise and Sport 70(2): 127-134

Sallis JF, Prochaska JJ, Taylor WC. A review of correlates of physical activity of children and adolescents. Med Sci Sports Exerc 2000;32: 963–75.

SHEPHARD, R. J. Habitual physical activity and academic performance. Nutr. Rev. 54:S32–S36, 1996.

SHEPHARD, R. J., and H. LAVALLEE. Academic skills and required physical education: the Trois Rivieres experience. CAHPER J. Res. Suppl. 1:1–12, 1994.

SIBLEY, B., and J. ETNIER. The relationship between

physical activity and cognition in children: a meta-analysis. Pediatric Exercise Science 15:243–253, 2003

Swain, R.A., Harris, A.B., Wiener, E.C., Dutka, M.V., Morris, H.D., Theien, B.E., Konda, S., Engberg, K., Lauterbur, P.C. and Greenough, W.T. (2003). Prolonged exercise induces angiogenesis and increases cerebral blood volume in primary motor cortex of the rat. Neuroscience, 117, 1037-1046.

Tillerson JL, Caudle WM, Reverón ME, Miller GW. Exercise induces behavioral recovery and attenuates neurochemical deficits in rodent models of Parkinson's disease. Neuroscience. 2003;119(3):899-911

Trejo, J.L. Carro, E. & Torres-Aleman, I. (2001). Circulating insulin-like growth factor mediates exercise-induced increases in the number of new neurons in the adult hippocampus. The Journal of Neuroscience, 21, 1628-1634.

TREMBLAY, M. S., J. W. INMAN, and J. D. WILLMS. The relationshipbetween physical activity, self-esteem, and academic achievement in 12-year-old children. Pediatric Exercise Science 12:312–323, 2000

TOMPOROWSKI, P. Cognitive and behavioral responses to acute exercise in youths: a review. Pediatric Exercise Science 15:348–359, 2003.

Uysal N, Tugyan K, Kayatekin BM, Acikgoz O, Bagriyanik HA, Gonenc S, Ozdemir D, Aksu I, Topcu A, Semin I. The effects of regular aerobic exercise in adolescent period on hippocampal neuron density, apoptosis and spatial memory. Neurosci Lett. 2005 Aug 5;383(3):241-5.

Van Gelder, B.M., Tijuius, M.A.R., Kalmijn, S., Giampaoli, S., Nissinen, A. & Kromhout, D. (2004). Physical activity in relation to cognitive decline in elderly men: The FINE study. Neurology, 63, 2316-2321.

Vaynman, S. & Gomez-Pinilla, F. (2006). Revenge of the "sit": How lifestyle impacts neuronal and cognitive health though molecular systems that interface energy metabolism with neuronal plasticity. Journal of Neuroscience Research, 84, 699-715.

Vaynman, S., Ying, Z., & Gomez-Pinilla, F. (2004). Hippocampal BDNF mediates the efficacy of exercise on synaptic plasticity and cognition. European Journal of Neuroscience, 20, 1030-1034

Other Resources

CrossFit Kids – a whole-body approach to exercise for children. Uses a combination of weightlifting-style movements, gymnastics, calisthenics, running, and acrobatics to teach positional awareness, self-control, and mind/body connection. www.crossfitkids.com

BrainGym.Org – a frontrunner in the field of cognitive exercise therapy,

John J. Ratey – author of *"Spark: The Revolutionary New Science of Exercise and the Brain"*, Ratey continues to follow research and build the case for linking exercise with academia. Ratey coined the phrase, "Miracle-Gro for the brain."

CrossFit – novel exercise combinations incorporating Olympic Lifting, calisthenics, running, gymnastics, powerlifting, and other sports. www.crossfit.com

About The Authors

Chris Cooper is the President of Catalyst Fitness Inc., and Founder of *Ignite!*. Addicted to education, Chris was lucky enough to be involved with Enrichment classes in elementary school. He was introduced to CrossFit  while researching exercise adherence in 2006, and has been an advocate for strength training, calisthenics, and functional movement since 1996. Chris is a former competitive powerlifter and cyclist, and maintains 12 separate blogs relating to exercise, learning, writing, and the business of fitness. He owns Catalyst Gym and the *Ignite!* Academy, where he spends 12-14 hours daily. Chris lives in Sylvan Valley with his extremely patient wife and two extremely amazing kids.

Tyler Belanger is the Director of Education and Research for *Ignite!*. Tyler is a former collegiate athlete, and achieved his Teaching credentials while on a baseball scholarship. His incredible gift for coaching  and well-practised charisma have made him an incomparable Coach, and he practises his skills daily for hours on end. Tyler interacts with physiotherapists, occupational therapists, speech language pathologists, teachers, parents, coaches and clients on a regular basis, and is constantly testing new methods to further refine the *Ignite!* Curriculum. His research warrants a new book every few months.... Tyler lives in Sault Ste.

Marie, Ontario, with his girlfriend, Dawn.

Also available from IgniteGym.com:

The *Ignite!* Student Handbook: track student progress in your classroom, the Ignite! Academy, or in your home with handy daily and weekly charts. Progress begins with measurement: track your improvements, identify Bright Spots, and be accountable!

Ignite

HOMEWORK TRACKING WORKSHEET

	MON	TUES	WED	THURS	FRI	DATE:
SUBJECT:

ASSIGNMENT TYPE: _____ **DUE DATE:**

INSTRUCTION METHOD: _____ NUTRITION — Good — Better — Best
SLEEP 1 2 3 4 5 6 7 8 9 10
FOCUS DRILL: _____ STRESS 1 2 3 4 5 6 7 8 9 10
MOBILITY 1 2 3 4 5 6 7 8 9 10
NOTES: PRIOR KNOWLEDGE 1 2 3 4 5 6 7 8 9 10

TIME STARTED:
TIME COMPLETED:

BRIGHT SPOTS:
GROWTH MINDSET: _____

HOMEWORK TRACKING WORKSHEET

	MON	TUES	WED	THURS	FRI	DATE:
SUBJECT:

ASSIGNMENT TYPE: _____ **DUE DATE:**

INSTRUCTION METHOD: _____ NUTRITION — Good — Better — Best
SLEEP 1 2 3 4 5 6 7 8 9 10
FOCUS DRILL: _____ STRESS 1 2 3 4 5 6 7 8 9 10
MOBILITY 1 2 3 4 5 6 7 8 9 10
NOTES: PRIOR KNOWLEDGE 1 2 3 4 5 6 7 8 9 10

TIME STARTED:
TIME COMPLETED:

BRIGHT SPOTS:
GROWTH MINDSET: _____

The *Ignite!* Student Handbook contains valuable tracking charts for nutritional intake, homework, daily workouts (interventions,) weekly challenges, and goals & action plans worksheets. Great for parents, great for students, and great for teachers to help with the *Ignite!* curriculum!

Want to become a NeuroMotive Coach, or start an *Ignite!* Academy in your city?

Weekend Certification seminars and Affiliation schedules and information are available at

www.ignitegym.com!

Made in the USA
Lexington, KY
15 May 2012